James Connolly and the Irish Left

James Connolly
and the Irish Left

W. K. ANDERSON

IRISH ACADEMIC PRESS

IN ASSOCIATION WITH
NATIONAL CENTRE FOR AUSTRALIAN STUDIES,
MONASH UNIVERSITY

This book was set
in 10.5 on 12pt Times
by Seton Music Graphics, Bantry, for
IRISH ACADEMIC PRESS LTD
Kill Lane, Blackrock, Co. Dublin
and in the United States of America by
IRISH ACADEMIC PRESS
c/o International Specialized Book Services
5804 NE Hassalo St, Portland, OR 97213
and in Australia by
National Centre for Australian Studies,
Monash University,
Clayton, Melbourne, 3168 Australia.

A catalogue record for this title
is available from the British Library.

ISBN 0-7165-2522-4

Printed in Great Britain
by Redwood Books, Trowbridge, Wiltshire

For my parents John and Agnes (Nessie) Anderson,
and for my wife Esther—'Till a' the seas gang dry'.

Contents

PREFACE   9

ABBREVIATIONS   11

INTRODUCTION   13

Part One: Connolly's Theory and Practice

1   The Women's Movement   16
2   Religion   25
3   Syndicalism   32
4   Socialism and Nationalism   41
5   The Revolutionary Party   49
6   Political Violence and Insurrection   58
7   Revolution   67

Part Two

8   Easter 1916—'A Terrible Beauty'   72

Part Three: Connolly's Legacy and Legatees

9   The Women's Movement   76
10   Religion   86
11   Syndicalism   97
12   Socialism and Nationalism   107
13   The Revolutionary Party   123
14   Political Violence and Insurrection   137
15   Revolution—Conclusions   149

APPENDIX: Summary of Political and Labour Organisations 158

NOTES   159

BIBLIOGRAPHY   179

INDEX   195

Preface

I HAVE RECEIVED a great deal of help and encouragement whilst researching and writing this book. I would like to acknowledge and express my gratitude to the following individuals, organisations and institutions in Ireland and Australia.

Ireland: Dr David Fitzpatrick, Trinity College (Dublin); Peadar O'Donnell; Michael O'Riordan: Manus O'Riordan; Ann Neary, archivist, Dublin Castle; Irish Transport and General Workers Union; Communist Party of Ireland; National Library of Ireland (Dublin); Public Records and State Papers Office (Dublin); Public Records Office of Northern Ireland (Belfast); University College Archives Department (Dublin) and the Royal Irish Academy (Dublin).

Australia: Dr Roy Hay, Professor Bill Rubinstein and Dr Ray Duplain of Deakin University; State Library (Melbourne); University of Melbourne Library, Professor Peter Spearritt and John Arnold of the National Centre for Australian Studies at Monash University, Melbourne (who by agreeing that the National Centre act as Australian distributors of the book helped to ensure its publication) and my friends Dr Val Noone and Stewart Fyfe.

Scotland: My brothers Ian (John) and Thomas, my cousin Paul Reddiex and my friends Irene Fyfe, David Gibson and Tony O'Boyle provided inspiration encouragement and support.

Professor Stuart Macintyre of the University of Melbourne provided untiring support, encouragement, guidance and friendship when he supervised the academic thesis on which this book is based.

Finally I would like to acknowledge the unstinting help and support which I received from my wife Esther and the patience and good humour with which she and our children Kirsty, John and Patrick accepted the dislocations and separations which researching and writing this book involved.

Abbreviations

Comintern	Third (Communist) International
CPGB	Communist Party of Great Britain
CPI	Communist Party of Ireland (1921–23; 1933–41)
ECCI	Executive Committee of the Communist International
H	*The Harp*
IC	*Irish Citizen*
ICA	Irish Citizen Army
ICO	*Irish Communist*
ILP	Independent Labour Party
ILPTUC	Irish Labour Party and Trade Union Congress (1918–30)
IOVL	*Irish Opinion: Voice of Labour*
IRA	Irish Republican Army
ISF	Irish Socialist Federation
ISRP	Irish Socialist Republican Party (1896–1903)
ITGWU	Irish Transport and General Workers Union
ITUC	Irish Trade Union Congress (1894–1912; 1930–59)
ITUCLP	Irish Trade Union Congress and Labour Party (1912–18)
IW	*Irish Worker*
IWFL	Irish Womens' Franchise League
IWL	Irish Workers League (1923–32)
IWW	Industrial Workers of the World
IWWU	Irish Women Worker's Union
O'Brien	William O'Brien Papers (National Library of Ireland, Dublin)
OBU	One Big Union
PCWRP	Preparatory Committee for the formation of a Workers Revolutionary Party (1930)
RC	*Republican Congress*
RWGs	Revolutionary Workers' Groups (1930–33)
SDF	Social Democratic Federation
SDP	Social Democratic Party
SLP	Socialist Labor Party
SPA	Socialist Party of America
SSF	Scottish Socialist Federation
SPI	Socialist Party of Ireland (1908–21)
UIL	United Irish League

VL	*Voice of Labour*
W	*The Worker*
WL	*Watchword of Labour*
WPI	Workers' Party of Ireland
WR	*Workers' Republic*
WRP	Workers' Revolutionary Party (1930)
WUI	Workers' Union of Ireland
WVL	*Watchword and Voice of Labour*

Introduction

Of all the men whom I have ever known or could ever read of in a
tome of history, there is not one who brought a cleaner soul, a more
disinterested enthusiasm or a courage more undaunted to the service of
the working people than did James Connolly.

John Leslie, Justice, 18 May 1916.

THIS BOOK EXAMINES the political legacy (in terms of both political theory
and personal example) of James Connolly (1868–1916), Scots-born Irish revolutionary socialist and labour leader. It also addresses the question of the extent to
which Connolly's legacy provided real guidance and inspiration to the Irish Left
from 1916 to 1940. One of the major problems encountered in examining Connolly's legacy has its roots in Connolly's status as a much honoured and greatly
revered national hero. During the years 1916–40, Connolly was widely praised in
Ireland, and many individuals and organisations proclaimed adherence to his
beliefs and objectives. In the absence of more substantial evidence of the clai-
mants' understanding of and commitment to Connolly's revolutionary marxist
teachings, such claims have to be treated with great caution. Fitzpatrick has noted
that 'the Republic like the Nation Once Again, was a vessel into which each man
could pour his own dream'[1]—in many respects Connolly and his political legacy
was another such 'vessel'. After his execution, Connolly's name and memory were
embraced by a large number of his countrymen but the embrace was more often
than not an embrace which stifled and smothered rather than one which supported
and empowered the causes and objectives to which he had devoted his life.

A substantial literature has grown up around Connolly's life and work. Ryan[2]
wrote the only study of any real worth published during the period encompassed
by this study. Subsequently Fox,[3] Greaves,[4] Levenson,[5] Ransom,[6] O'Riordan,[7]
Reeves,[8] Morgan[9] and Allan[10] have all made valuable contributions to Connolly
scholarship. Two of Connolly's daughter's, Nora[11] and Ina[12] published reminiscences of their father which have, to some degree, helped to broaden our picture of
Connolly's private life. While not exhaustive, this list embraces the most
significant and substantial studies. My own approach differs in ways which are
made clear in the body of the text. The first section of the book has been based on
an exhaustive study of Connolly's writings (which are both copious and scattered)
and other contemporary sources. By far the most important and rewarding of these

13

is the magnificent collection of records relating to Connolly contained in the William O'Brien Papers held by the National Library of Ireland in Dublin. For the second section of the book, which deals with the post-rising period, there are the substantive studies of Mitchell[13] and Milotte.[14] Both were informative and stimulating but my own interpretations are based on primary source materials, notably the myriad left-wing newspapers which appeared during the period.

The concept of a 'Connolly Legacy' is well established. During his lifetime Connolly was not particularly well known outside labour circles in Ireland and Scotland. His public reputation, such as it was, owed more to conservative detractors than to the efforts of militant or radical groups—labour, republican and feminist—which recognised his personal and intellectual qualities. However, after his 'martyr's death' and subsequent elevation to the pantheon of national heroes, Connolly's name and supposed political legacy were frequently and very loosely cited in Irish political debate. Indeed in Ireland during the period under examination, individuals and organisations which tended towards the left of the political spectrum almost invariably described themselves, often quite subjectively and inaccurately, as 'Connolly Socialists'. This book will attempt to show that Connolly's name was frequently cited in an almost apolitical, talismanic fashion which reveals little of the real depth and importance of his political legacy.

The book is in two sections with a short interlinking chapter. Part One is an interpretation of Connolly's political thoughts and practice and comprises seven chapters under the headings 'The Women's Movement', 'Religion', 'Syndicalism', 'Socialism and Nationalism', 'The Revolutionary Party', 'Violence' and 'Revolution'. Following an interlude dealing with the Easter Rising, Part Three contains an examination (under the same seven headings) of the Irish Left's understanding of and reaction to Connolly's political legacy.

No attempt is made in this study to offer a biography of Connolly; nor, given its particular focus, does it make any claim to be a general political study of the period. The specific problems of working-class organisations in Ireland's six North-Eastern counties are of such complexity that it would have required a separate and lengthy study to make any worthwhile contribution. The book thus deals only with the twenty-six counties which today constitute the Republic of Ireland.

James Connolly's significance does not rely solely on his role as a founding father of the Irish Republic, nor even on the undoubted heroism, class loyalty and spirit of self sacrifice which ennobled his life. Connolly had powers of intellect to match his strength of character. A man of action but no mere adventurer, Connolly's actions—however wild and dangerous they may have appeared— were premeditated, the outcome of deep study and reflection. Connolly was in many ways an unorthodox revolutionary socialist, his political positions were sometimes opportunistic and he was not afraid to compromise in the short term if he perceived a long term advantage to the cause. Driven as he was by an intense and unrelenting hatred of capitalism and an absolute commitment to establishing a workers' Republic, Connolly's political thought had a particularly sharp edge.

Undeviating in his objectives, he was nonetheless a flexible and imaginative political theorist and one for whom political theory and political action were integrated to a remarkable degree. That such a man should produce an impact on the Irish left is hardly surprising. In the following pages an attempt is made to assess both the nature and the extent of this impact.

CHAPTER 1

The Women's Movement

Ireland has today within her bosom two things that must make the blood run with riotous exaltation in the veins of every lover of the Irish race—a disenchanted working class, and the nucleus of a rebellious womanhood. I cannot separate these two things in my mind, to me they are parts of one great whole; different regiments of one great army of progress.

[1]James Connolly, Dublin, 1912.

CONNOLLY'S ASSERTION THAT in his own mind the working class struggle and the women's movement were inseparable parts of the one great forward movement, may, at first glance appear somewhat startling—particularly given the time and place of its publication. Very few of Connolly's contemporaries would have recognised such an identity of interests between the two movements and the Irish as a whole were hardly noted for their feminist sensibilities. Clearly if Connolly was, as I take him to have been, making a serious political point in his comment, rather than merely indulging in colourful rhetoric, any analysis of his political legacy will of necessity involve a close investigation of his views on women and the women's movement.

The first evidence we have of Connolly's views on women's suffrage is found in the manifesto which he drafted for the Irish Socialist Republican Party (ISRP) in 1896. In this document Connolly calls for the creation of an Irish Socialist Republic. Pending the realisation of this goal he cites a number of immediate objectives for 'palliating the evils of our present social system'; one of these objectives was 'Universal Suffrage'; another called for—'free maintenance of all children'.[2] We cannot of course read too much into this early support for 'Universal Suffrage' but it is worth noting that even amongst socialists this was no automatic objective—many who considered themselves socialists were at best unenthusiastic in regards to extending the vote to women.

The ISRP, the first political party in which Connolly was the leading force, did not devote its energies to an active campaign in favour of women's rights—the party in fact did not have a single woman member.[3] To balance this, it must be said that the party had very few male members either and membership was open to any women who cared to join. It is perhaps more to the point to note that the question of women's suffrage and women's rights in general were not prominent social or political issues during the period of the ISRP's brief existence (1896–1903). At this period in his political development Connolly had not yet recognised the full importance and ramifications of the oppression of women, nor understood how this oppression related to the destruction of capitalism and the subsequent construction of a socialist society.

After the break up of the ISRP and his emigration to America Connolly spent a stormy few years in the American Socialist Labour Party (SLP). One of the many arguments which Connolly had with the SLP leader Daniel De Leon centred upon his refusal to accept De Leon's view that it was 'reformist to struggle for the special needs of women workers'. De Leon's stance that campaigns for women's suffrage, wage equality and legislative protection for women workers were valueless, indeed counter productive (the socialist revolution being 'the one viable demand for the working class')[4] was unacceptable to Connolly and he made his views known to all who would listen. It would appear that during his first few years in America Connolly began to move from a somewhat passive commitment to women's emancipation towards a more active one.

A qualitative change in Connolly's perception of the struggle for women's rights can be traced to his becoming aware of the militancy which had grown up within the women's movement in Ireland. Militancy—the willingness and ability to fight—was a quality upon which Connolly throughout his life placed the very highest value. In 1908 he received a copy of a new Irish Journal *Bean na hÉireann* (Woman of Ireland). On behalf of the Irish Socialist Federation (ISF) Connolly welcomed the new journal, proclaimed the ISF's belief in 'the absolute social and political equality of the sexes' and expressed satisfaction with this 'proof' that 'the women of Ireland are not in any mood to go begging for rights when they are able to take them'. The 'way to establish political rights' urged Connolly is to 'assume them, not beg for them'.[5]

A few months later Connolly again took up the issue of militancy within the women's movement. Commenting on the acid statement by a 'contemporary socialist' that the United Irish League (UIL) convention in Dublin had 'recognised the rights of a dead language and denied the rights of living women', Connolly somewhat tongue in cheek, castigated the man who made the statement for his failure to understand the real reasons behind the success of the language movement in gaining the support of an anti-progressive organisation such as the UIL. This success he suggested lay in the fact that 'the language had a well organised movement of the best male and female fighters in Ireland behind it; the women were only represented by an idea, a principle'. What politician, he asked 'ever allowed a great principle to weigh so much with him as the fear of losing cash and votes?' The lesson which he drew from the language movement's success and its significance for the women's movement was short and to the point; 'the Irish politicians will respect the women's movement when it is strong enough to kick them, not before.'[6]

When Connolly and his family returned to Ireland in 1910 he was quick to commit his support to the militant arm of the women's suffrage movement.[7]

His daughter Ina recalled in her reminiscences that soon after their arrival back in Ireland Connolly, accompanied by his two eldest daughters, visited the offices of the Irish Women's Franchise League (IWFL) to offer their services.[8] The selection of the IWFL as the body to which Connolly and his daughters offered their services was no random choice. There were many suffrage organisations in Ireland at this time. The IWFL, strongly influenced by the Pankhurst's Women's Social and Political Union, was the most militant and also the most receptive to radical social thought—one can hardly imagine Connolly offering his services to Conservative and Unionist Women's Franchise Association.

Whilst working as Northern organiser for the Irish Transport and General Workers Union (ITGWU) Connolly became involved in the Belfast Mill girls strike in 1911. His daughter Ina, herself working in a textile mill, recalled that the girls were forced to work under intolerable conditions 'to keep the girls on their toes (and pit them against each other) they were forbidden to talk or sing or arrange their hair during working hours and were promised the sack if they did'.[9] The girls asked Connolly to organise a strike for them. Connolly brought the girls into the ITGWU as a textile branch and, at their request, called a strike. The strike was unseasonable and existing financial support inadequate, and Connolly was forced to recommend a return to work. However, the strike was far from being a total defeat for the girls. Before their return to work Connolly suggested tactics to them through which they could improve their conditions:

> If a girl is checked for singing, let the whole room start singing at once, if you are checked for laughing, let the whole room laugh at once, and if anyone is dismissed, all put on your shawls and come out in a body. And when you are returning, do not return as you usually do, but gather in a body outside the gate and march in shouting and cheering.[10]

The girls used these tactics and are reported to have achieved a marked improvement in their conditions of work. Fox, for example, cites one 'exasperated manager who sent a girl home for singing [and] had to send for her again, work was resumed only when she returned and she was welcomed with a song'.[11]

In a message of support to English suffragettes in 1913, Connolly was unequivocal in his support 'when the trimmers and compromisers disavow you, a poor slum bred politician, I raise my hat in thanksgiving that I lived to see this insurgence of women.'[12] Connolly's support was by this stage of his career not merely semantic, he was actively supporting the struggles of organised women. Louie Bennett, a middle class suffragette and pacifist who later became a labour leader (secretary of the Irish Women Workers Union, IWWU) after witnessing the injustices inflicted upon the ITGWU members during the 1913 lock-out, said of Connolly that he was 'one of the best suffrage speakers I have ever heard and a thorough feminist in every respect' and claimed that he 'taught the transport union of Dublin to support women workers' struggle for industrial and political rights.'[13] In a similar vein, Francis Sheehy-Skeffington, militant socialist, feminist and pacifist, described Connolly as 'the soundest and most thorough-going feminist among all the Irish labour men'.[14] Sheehy-Skeffington's wife Hanna, who was herself a radical and extremely active feminist, noted in her *Reminiscences* that Connolly's support for women's suffrage marked the beginning of a close relationship between the suffrage movement and the labour movement and the gradual realisation that the movement or at least the militant part of it—was pursuing votes for 'women' and not just votes for ladies.[15]

The importance which Connolly placed on women's issues and the respect in which he held the militant suffragettes is clearly evident in a letter he wrote in 1913 to his friend J. Carstairs Matheson:

> I am unfeignedly glad to hear that you are on the right side in this women business. The attitude of most socialists, including the chief Socialist Press in that matter is just beneath contempt. All glory to the women, say I. Their hearty rebellion is worth more than a thousand speeches of the doctrinaires with which the socialist movement . . . is infected. I am with the militants all the way.[16]

It is also attested by the fact that he was willing to present the suffragettes' case to meetings of organised labour, one example of this being the Irish Trade Union Congress (ITUC) held in Cork in 1913, when he took the opportunity to speak from the floor and denounce the liberal Government's use of coercion against suffragettes.[17]

Connolly's support for the suffragettes was not based on a minimalist 'votes for women' position; he believed that the militancy and dynamism of the suffrage struggle should be expanded into the struggle for a radical reconstruction of society. In a speech to a suffrage meeting in Belfast in 1914, Connolly took as his subject 'A labourer's advice to suffragettes'. A report of this speech in the *Irish Worker* (probably written by Connolly himself) reported that Connolly, after first putting the proposition that 'force is the root of all power', went on to suggest 'that the women's movement should have recourse to the use of economic force to gain not only the vote but all the rights of man and womanhood'. Women, he argued, should 'interest themselves in the organisation of the working women and girls, not for suffragette purposes alone, but for the material benefits of the workers as well'. To this end Connolly felt that the women's movement should seek to emulate (he refers to 'similar development') the labour movement. Ending on a positive note, Connolly told the meeting that he 'admitted the fertility of resource the women had shown and had only one objection to militancy—that it was not militant enough'.[18]

In December 1915 Connolly published *The Re-Conquest of Ireland*, which was to be his last major work. This book is important in any attempt to understand Connolly's mature views on the oppression of women and the women's movement. One chapter is devoted to an analysis of women in capitalist society. Entitled simply 'Woman', it contains his most completely developed exposition of his thoughts on women's oppression. The main premise underlying his analysis was that:

> the spread of industrialism makes for the awakening of a social consciousness, awakes in women a feeling of self-pity as the greatest sufferers under social and political injustice, the divine wrath aroused when that self-pity is met with a sneer, and justice is denied, leads women to revolt, and revolt places women in comradeship and equality with all the finer souls whose life is given to warfare against established iniquities.[19]

Connolly amplifies his statement that women were the 'greatest sufferers' in capitalist society when he goes on to say that 'the worker is the slave of capitalist society, the female worker is the slave of that slave'. After giving graphic descriptions of the remorseless and debilitating life of toil experienced by women on the land and women in mills, shops and factories, he asserts that 'In Ireland the female worker has hitherto exhibited in her martyrdom, an almost damnable patience.'[20]

The main object of the chapter on women is not descriptive, still less is it an attempt to provide a profound theoretical or historical analysis of women's oppression. Connolly is attempting to establish and cement an identity of interests, a revolutionary solidarity integrating militant feminism and the labour movement. To this end we find him writing that 'In Ireland the women cause is felt by all labour men and women as their cause; the labour cause has no more earnest and whole hearted supporters than the militant women.' It is instructive to recall that Connolly later echoed these words in one of his most famous and oft-quoted statements 'The cause of labour is the cause of Ireland, the cause of Ireland is the cause of labour. They cannot be dissevered'. The similarity of wording and intent is not coincidental for although Connolly is addressing different audiences, feminists and nationalists, (those who were feminists and nationalist are doubly wooed) his rationale and objective is the same and is based on his concept of revolutionary strategy:

> A real socialist movement can only be born of struggle, of uncompromising affirmation of the faith that is in us. Such a movement infallibly gathers to it every element of rebellion and progress, and in the midst of the storm and stress of struggle solidifies into a real revolutionary force.[23]

To say this is not to doubt the honesty or legitimacy of Connolly's feminist stance, it is simply to note that his admittedly somewhat limited analytical perception of and active propagation of feminist issues is inextricably linked to his concept of socialist revolution. The nature of Connolly's attitude to the women's movement is clearly stated in the final paragraphs of his 'Woman' chapter where we find him arguing that there are:

> none so fitted to break the chains as they who wear them, none so well equipped to decide what is a fetter. In its march towards freedom, the working class of Ireland must cheer on the efforts of those women who, feeling on their souls and bodies the fetters of the ages, have arisen to strike them off, and cheer all the louder if in its hatred of thraldom and passion for freedom the women's army forges ahead of the militant army and labour.

The final one-sentence paragraph, however, destroys—and is meant to destroy—the impression that he is investing the women's movement with the central revolutionary role: 'But whosoever carries the outworks of the citadel of oppression, the working class alone can raze it to the ground.'[24] For Connolly, socialist revolution was ultimately and of necessity the task of the working class, but we can at least be certain that when he speaks of the 'working class' he refers to the whole working class and not just working-class men.

That Connolly's support for the women's movement was neither patronising nor simply politically expedient is shown by the serious attention which he devoted to studying the militant activities of the suffragettes. On at least one occasion he successfully translated and applied suffragette tactics into his own labour struggles. During the bitter and protracted 1913 lockout in Dublin, Connolly was arrested and sentenced to three months imprisonment. He went on hunger strike in gaol and was released within a week. His daughter Ina has noted that he was 'the first man in Ireland or the British Isles to adopt this method of fighting for his rights' and recalled that in explaining his use of this tactic he simply stated that 'what was good enough for the suffragettes is good enough for us'.[25] It is even possible to argue that Sylvia Pankhurst's 'Peoples Army',[26] which was inaugurated on 5 November 1913 and thus predated the establishment of the Irish Citizen Army (ICA) by a few weeks, was part of the inspiration behind Connolly's call on 13 November 1913 for 'four battalions of trained men' which led to the founding of the ICA.[27]

An examination of Connolly's writings reveals a consistent attempt to address both male and female readers. Even in his often hastily written journalistic pieces he seldom discloses a male bias. This consistent consciousness of women is highlighted in his last recorded statements. The Proclamation of the Irish Republic, a document which he not only signed but helped draft,[28] was not only addressed to 'Irishmen and Irishwomen' but also went on to state that 'The Republic guarantees equal rights and equal opportunities for all its citizens.'[29] His final statement, delivered to the court martial which sentenced him to death, shows a similar concern to recognise the contributions of both men and women, specifically drawing attention to the 'hundreds of Irish women and girls' who had supported the Republic being 'ready to affirm that truth and to attest it with their lives if need be'.[30]

That a strong feminist component was part of Connolly's political creed and revolutionary strategy is clear. It is important to note, however, that from his earliest years in the socialist movement he vehemently opposed any tendency towards sexual relations, in a physical, as opposed to economic or political sense, becoming an issue within the movement. Thus we find him arguing in 1896 that 'Socialism had no connection with speculations on family life and was nowise responsible for the opinions of individual socialists on that subject.'[31] As an experienced socialist propagandist amongst the working class, Connolly was convinced that propaganda which linked socialism with anti-marriage sentiments or sexual libertarianism was detrimental to the effort to build a mass socialist movement. An insight into his thinking on this matter is contained in an article he wrote for the Edinburgh *Socialist* in 1904 in which he notes that in his opinion the socialist movement was 'hampered by the presence in its ranks of faddists and cranks', people who he felt were not in the movement to promote socialism but as a means of 'ventilating their theories, on such questions as sex, religion, vegetarianism etc.' He wrote that 'such ideas had or ought to have no place in our programme or in our party'[32].

Connolly's concern with what he considered to be the negative effect of 'speculations on family life' and of 'questions of sex' on the advance of the socialist movement particularly among the working class—was perhaps exaggerated. He claimed, for example, in reference to Bebel's book *Woman*, that 'for every woman led to socialism by it . . . hundreds were repelled from studying socialism by judicious extracts from its pages.'[33] Whilst there is no doubt that a real problem of presentation and misrepresentation existed, it is unfortunate that he allowed this to severely limit the breadth and depth of his public analysis of the basis of women's oppression. Although Connolly was aware of the works of Marx, Engels and Bebel pointing to monogamy as having its origin in property relations, he made no attempt, despite his interest and involvement in women's issues and his own acceptance of a historical materialist analysis of society, to use his position as an influential socialist activist to explain or propagate this important analysis. This failure was explained, if not justified, by Connolly when he wrote in relation to monogamy that he believed that 'no matter what may have been the force which gave birth to any institution, its permanency will and must be tested not by its origin but by its adaptability to the . . . economic institutions of the future.'[34]

Connolly himself believed in 'monogamic marriage'[35] and was convinced that 'the tendency of civilisation is toward its perfection and completion instead of towards its destruction.'[36] Connolly has sometimes been presented as an inflexible sexual puritan and indeed it is true that all the evidence we have suggests that his own personal code of conduct was based on adherence to the very strictest definition of sexual morality. Despite his personal commitment to monogamic marriage, he was not blind to the difficulties which could arise. Indeed, he foresaw that even under a socialist system where 'no woman will be compelled to marry a man for a livelihood or for riches,' marital relationships could and would break down and 'we will have a marriage and divorce question, or a sex question, if you will, and I do not see that the fact that each is economically independent of the other will alter that fact.'[37]

Connolly did not believe in imposing his own sexual morality on others and he was prepared to publicly oppose those who attempted to do so, particularly when these attempts at external regulation were instituted by the rich to control the poor. Thus in early 1915 we find him writing in *The Worker* opposing the setting up of such a regulatory body in Dublin involving 'Women's Patrols whose function will be to look after the morals of Dublin women and girls'. Connolly described the scheme as impudent, impertinent and 'a new form of Inquisition'.[38] Although Connolly's views on marriage and external regulation of sexual conduct are perhaps somewhat less rigid than they have normally been presented, it would certainly be false to claim that he was completely free from conventional gender stereotyping—his own political career was made possible by a division of labour in which his wife Lillie stayed home caring for the children while he followed his own star as a revolutionary socialist. His commitment to socialism often led to lengthy periods of absence from the family home. During those periods Lillie struggled to care for their large family under conditions of extreme poverty and hardship. In 1920 the ITGWU conference voted to pay Lillie her deceased husband's wages as a sort of pension. Her response to this generous and well-meant offer is perhaps the only written record which has come down to us of her own view of her role in the marital relationship. She writes:

> I am glad and proud that the union decided to put on record its appreciation of his value to it, but I do not see how I can allow it to accept any responsibility for me or my family now that he is dead. When he was alive never did I ask him to consider me or the family. I felt it was his duty to pursue any line of action he particularly wished. It was sufficient to me that I helped him not hindered him. I gloried in the work he accomplished when alive. I glory in the work his death has made easy and feel that now I am sharing in the fruits of his work and death.
>
> Please tell your executive that the glory and honour of his name are sufficient for me and his family, and that we all regard it as a sacred duty that nothing we shall do will ever make that glory or honour less.
>
> To accept your bounty would in my opinion be acting contrary to his wishes and would not be acceptable to the dignity and honour of the position I occupy as his wife.[39]

Although within his own marriage the division of labour was based on conventional role models, it is worth noting that throughout his career Connolly established close and durable working relationships with many active feminists including Madame Markievicz, Hanna Sheehy-Skeffington,[40] Maud Gonne,[41] Elizabeth Gurley Flynn,[42] Helena Moloney[43] and Winifred Carney.[44] These feminist women found Connolly to be an able, loyal and non-sexist ally, and while it is fair to point out that he was almost invariably in a leadership position, this must be balanced against the fact that in organisations over which he presided women were always on an equal footing. Constance Markievicz commenting on 'Connolly's treatment of women' wrote that:

> when he began to organise the ICA he brought me along, treating me as he got to know me, as a comrade, giving me any work that I could do. This was his attitude towards women in general, we were never in his mind, classed for work as a sex, but taken individually and considered, just as every man considers men, and then allotted any work we could do.[45]

Connolly's spirited and unequivocal support for women's militancy—a militancy which many of his contemporaries considered to be unfeminine—was not his only break from gender stereotyping. The ICA under his command allowed women to bear arms and function as fighting soldiers, a non-discriminatory attitude which would still be considered radical. A good example of this attitude is contained in an article which appeared in a section of the *Workers Republic* devoted to ICA affairs. Probably written by Connolly and certainly reflecting his views the article contained advice to women which was radical in the extreme:

> Women who plainly show that they will yield to the firstcomer if the men defenders fall are not worth saving at a cost of useful lives! If you want a thing done do it yourself. Buy a revolver and shoot any man, Jew or German, Southern Irish Horse or Connaught Ranger, patriotic employer or bullying foreman, whoever he may be who attempts to injure you. Keep your last bullet for yourself, and don't whine about men protecting you. If men wanted to protect you there would be no war and no prostitution . . . Sex distinctions must go. Women must protect themselves. Sex distinctions are harmful alike to men and women.[46]

Clearly Connolly differed greatly from the conventional view of women's true place in the scheme of things, indeed his ideal of femininity often appears to take on a distinctly amazonian hue.

The objective of establishing an identity of interests and creating an alliance of forces between organised labour and the women's movement developed gradually through Connolly's career. In large part it was based on his enthusiastic response to the militancy of sections of the women's movement. In his early days he was certainly aware of the oppression of women but was not in any real sense active in their struggles—his interest and commitment appears to have been directly related to women's willingness to fight for their own rights. The mutual support and respect which Connolly helped to develop between the two movements should have provided a foundation upon which Irish labour in post-Rising Ireland could have developed a potentially very powerful alliance. Such an alliance could have addressed not only economic and suffrage issues but also less obvious but equally oppressive social pressures which curtailed human freedom. Commenting on this aspect of the struggle during a discussion of the labour and women's movements, Connolly noted that:

> To neither will it be possible to realise its ideas without first trampling underfoot, riding roughshod over all the false conventions soul-shrivelling prejudices, and subtle hypocrisies with which a tyrannical society has poisoned the souls and warped the intellect of mankind.[47]

In a later chapter we shall examine whether or not any attempt was made in the years after Connolly's death, to capitalise on the possibilities and opportunities which he had helped to create for the labour and women's movements to work together to their mutual advantage.

CHAPTER 2

Religion

Perhaps upon no point are the doctrines of Socialism so much misunderstood, and so much misrepresented, as in their relation to religion. When driven into a corner upon every other point of issue, when from the point of view of economics, of politics or of morality, he is worsted in argument, this question of Religion invariably forms the final entrenchment of the enemy of Socialism—especially in Ireland.

James Connolly, 1899.[1]

CONNOLLY CAN BE forgiven for indulging in a slight exaggeration when he wrote that socialism in Ireland was 'especially' subject to being 'misunderstood' and 'misinterpreted' as a result of what he calls 'this question of Religion'. Socialists in every country faced similar difficulties, although it is fair to say that socialists in countries such as Spain, Italy and Ireland, where the Roman Catholic rather than the Reformed Church predominated, were faced with a particularly difficult problem. Also it should be noted that Ireland, unlike such Roman Catholic countries on the Continent as France and Spain, had never developed an anti-clerical tradition. Indeed in Ireland the Roman Catholic Church was identified in a very real way with the nation and national identity.[2] For Connolly, religion was a critical factor in the development of socialism in Ireland. How could the diminutive Irish socialist movement defend itself against—let alone undermine— a popular church which exerted such a strong hold over the people and was moreover aggressively anti-socialist?[3]

Throughout his career Connolly devoted a great deal of attention to discussing the relationship between socialism and religion, particularly religion in its Roman Catholic manifestation. There is no doubt that the time and energy he expended on the 'religious question' stemmed largely from his perception that effective socialist propaganda and educational activities within the Irish context must address this issue. Two main approaches can be detected in Connolly's writings on religion. The first was a negative approach wherein he is basically on the defensive and is simply responding to attacks on socialism which were based on religious grounds—usually sermons delivered, or articles published by Roman Catholic priests. The second approach is a more constructive and interesting one through which we find Connolly attempting, with some success, to abstract positive meanings from the corpus of Christian and more particularly Roman Catholic belief which were capable of pro-socialist interpretation. Before going

25

onto explore these two elements in Connolly's response to religion, it is important
at this stage to clarify his personal religious stance. Perhaps no area of his life and
work has been subject to so much debate and controversy. The details of what
might be called his religious history are, on the surface at least, straightforward.
He was born and reared a Roman Catholic and although he married a Protestant,
the marriage was celebrated in a Roman Catholic church, his children were
brought up as practising Roman Catholics and educated in Roman Catholic
schools. Finally, and it might appear conclusively, Connolly himself received the
'Last Rites' from a Roman Catholic priest prior to his execution. In his published
writings and public speeches Connolly always referred to Roman Catholicism in a
way designed to suggest a continued belief and membership: he wrote in other
words as an insider from within the body of the church rather than as a critical
outsider.[4]

On the evidence presented above, Connolly emerges as a cradle-to-the-grave
Roman Catholic. Anyone actually reading his written works would have perhaps
been forced to qualify this impression, but would still have been able to consider
him a Roman Catholic, albeit one of independent even somewhat heretical complexion. Indeed a certain amount of doubt existed both during Connolly's lifetime
and after his death regarding the authenticity of his religious stance: Marxism
and Roman Catholicism are after all unusual if not incompatible bedfellows.
More than fifty years elapsed after Connolly's death before conclusive evidence
appeared relating to his personal, as opposed to publicly stated, religious beliefs.[5]
In the O'Brien papers there is a letter, the authenticity of which is not in doubt,
written by Connolly in 1908 to his Scottish friend Carstairs Matheson. Matheson
had directly questioned Connolly, 'Are you still in the bosom of the Church?',[6]
and Connolly in his reply stated his personal religious position with clarity:

> for myself, though I have usually posed as a Catholic I have not gone to my duty
> for 15 years, and have not the slightest tincture of faith left. I only assumed the
> Catholic pose in order to quiz the raw freethinkers whose ridiculous dogmatism
> did and does annoy me as much as the dogmatism of the Orthodox. In fact I
> respect the good Catholic more than the average freethinker.

If we accept Connolly's sincerity and chronology—that in 1908 he had been an
atheist for some fifteen years—it is clear that his atheism developed in the early
1890s, precisely the period when he first began studying socialist literature and
coming under the influence of John Leslie and other committed socialists within
the Scottish Socialist Federation (SSF). It would seem reasonable, therefore, to
conclude that Connolly's atheism resulted from his acceptance of Marx's
materialist analysis of human history and society. Indeed Connolly, although
strictly reserving comments on his personal religious stance to a private correspondence with a close and reliable friend, was willing to clearly and publicly
delineate an explicit materialist analysis of religion. In the September 1908 issue
of *The Harp* for example he wrote:

> that which the cultured man of the twentieth century would explain and understand as a natural process the mental vision of our forefathers could only see as a result of the good or ill will of some beneficient or evil spirit—some God or Devil . . . the different stages of development of the human mind in its attitude towards the furies and nature created different priesthoods to interpret them, and the mental conceptions of mankind as interpreted by those priesthoods became, when systematised, Religion . . . Religions are simply expressions of human conceptions of the natural world.[8]

Ever since the O'Brien papers entered the public domain, there has been little room for serious doubt that Connolly was throughout his active political life an atheist and a materialist. The reason why he 'posed as a Catholic' is somewhat more complex. His own explanation—that he did so to 'quiz the raw freethinkers'—is far from convincing, for as Minahane has shrewdly pointed out, 'such people may have been common in the British and American labour movements. They were not common in the Irish movement, yet it is in Ireland that he posed most elaborately.'[9] O'Riordan, another astute commentator, is surely correct when he argues that Connolly's Roman Catholic pose was 'probably motivated by the feeling that by posing as a Catholic he would be most successful in undermining some of the reactionary influence of the Church over Catholic workers'.[10]

In summary, then, Connolly was an atheist, albeit an atheist with strong cultural and ethnic feeling for the Roman Catholic Church (feelings certainly accentuated by the oppressed position of the Church and its members in the particular social settings with which Connolly was familiar)[11] and that he 'posed' as a Roman Catholic purely for propagandist purposes. Although Connolly himself stated that his purpose was to 'quiz the raw freethinkers' in the labour movement, it appears on the balance of evidence much more likely that it was an opportunist position taken to strengthen the appeal of his socialist message to the Catholic working class.[12] In regards to his acceptance of Roman Catholic sacraments in the days immediately prior to his execution, it is possible that Connolly, in the immediate aftermath of an extremely emotional and traumatic involvement in an armed uprising, suffering very great pain and physical depletion from his injuries, and facing imminent violent death by firing squad, may have genuinely been reconciled with the Church of his youth; but the most plausible explanation is that his action simply reflected a continuation, an extension of his Roman Catholic pose. Much of the confusion which has occurred over Connolly's true religious position has been directly attributable to the element of duplicity inherent in his Catholic 'pose'. In his favour it can be argued that he never (at least to my knowledge) explicitly claimed to be a practicing Roman Catholic. But there is no denying that he did intentionally assume a voice and tone which implicitly laid claim to membership of the Church. Connolly, a man of high moral standards, a man of blunt indeed often acerbic honesty, must have found the actual mechanics of his Catholic 'pose' distasteful in the extreme. That he was willing to distort and to prostitute his own beliefs in order to gain a perceived political advantage testifies in a most dramatic way to the importance which he attached to 'the question of

Religion' in Ireland and to the depth of his revolutionary commitment. The insider status which Connolly's Catholic 'pose' won for him gave a weight and legitimacy to his comments on religion and the church which would have been totally absent had his true religious position been public knowledge. Believing as he did that Catholics had been 'repelled from socialism by the blatant and rude atheism of some of its irresponsible advocates',[13] Connolly took pains to ensure that in his own writings directed as they were at a predominantly Roman Catholic audience—no atheism, whether blatant and rude or subtle and well-mannered, ever appeared.[14] A fascinating and representative example of the style and content of Connolly's writing on the issue is contained in his major extended piece of work on religion entitled *Labour, Nationality and Religion*. The subtitle of this book—*Being a discussion of the Lenten Discourses against Socialism delivered by Father Kane SJ in Gardiner Street Church, Dublin, 1910*—highlights the fact that at least in its inspiration the pamphlet was defensive, a response to an attack on Socialism. We shall see, however, in the following extract that Connolly does not limit himself to a straightforward rebuttal of Fr. Kane's anti-socialist discourse but rather with great skill and plausibility presents a well-developed theological argument from what Connolly terms the 'true teachings of catholicity' which turns the actual structure of the Church on its head:

> The recent efforts of ecclesiastics to put the socialist movement under the ban of the Catholic Church has had a good effect in compelling Catholics to examine more earnestly their position as laymen and the status of the clergy. One point of Catholic doctrine brought out as a result of such examination is the almost forgotten and sedulously expressed one, that the Catholic Church is theoretically a community in which the clergy are but officers serving the laity in a common worship and service of God, and that should the clergy at any time profess or teach doctrines not in conformity with the true teachings of Catholicity it is not only the right but the absolute duty of the laity to refuse such doctrines and to disobey such teaching. Whenever the clergy succeeded in conquering political power in any country the result has been disastrous to the interests of religion and inimical to the progress of humanity . . . he serves religion best who insists upon the clergy of the Catholic Church taking their proper position as servants of the laity and abandoning their attempt to dominate the public as they have long dominated the private life of their fellow Catholics.[15]

Although in strict Catholic terms Connolly's position is theologically shaky, he does make a serious attempt to address Roman Catholic objections to socialism and does so in a tone and manner which skilfully blends radical theological arguments, democratic reasoning and a disarming, if not altogether honest, holier-than-thou Roman Catholicism. It is clear that Connolly's main objective was to negate the anti-socialist influence of the Roman Catholic clergy. In an article published in *The Harp* in 1908 entitled simply 'Roman Catholicism and Socialism', Connolly advises the clergy that 'the cobbler must stick to his last', and goes on to argue that 'as long as the priest speaks to us as a priest upon religious matters we

will listen to him with all the reverence and attention his sacred calling deserves';
but, says Connolly, qualifying his statement somewhat threateningly, 'the moment
he steps upon the political platform or worse still, uses the altar from which to tell
us what to do with our political freedom, then in our sight he will cease to be a
priest and be simply a politician'. Socialism, argues Connolly, 'is an industrial and
political question, it is . . . not going to be settled at the altar.'[16]

Connolly can hardly be faulted for taking steps to defend socialism from
priestly censure. It was, however, perhaps unfortunate that he was unable to
resist the temptation to extend his writings beyond the purely defensive—a fact
which led to contradictory arguments and lines of thought appearing in his
works. On the one hand he very clearly, indeed vehemently, denies the right of
the priests to comment on social and political matters (thus ignoring the social
import of the Christian gospels), yet himself displays little hesitation despite
his own statements to the contrary—in attempting to provide Catholic justi-
fications for socialism and even to cloak socialism in a Catholic mantle. In
Labour, Nationality and Religion, for example, Connolly takes issue with
Father Kane's assertion that there was 'nothing in common between Social and
Christian democracy' when he writes:

> Dear, oh dear! What lunatics we must be! And yet we are in good company.
> Saints and pontiffs of the Catholic Church have gone before us on this road, and
> the wildest sayings of modern Socialist agitators are soft and conservative
> beside some of the doctrines which ere now have been put forth as sound
> Catholic teachings.[17]

Connolly then proceeds to cite St. Clement, St. Basil, St. Gregory, St. Ambrose
and St. Chrysostom to support his contention. Elsewhere Connolly, clearly enjoy-
ing a joke on his own religious name dropping, quotes the French Revolutionary
leader Saint-Just, implicitly suggesting that he was a father of the Church.

Christian socialism held no attraction for Connolly. Indeed at the very first
meeting of the ISRP in 1896, he voted against naming the party the Christian
Socialist Republican Party.[19] Many years later, writing in *The Harp*, Connolly
reflected upon the 'psychology of the Catholic mind' and noted the 'mistaken
efforts of many well-meaning comrades to convert Irish Catholics to Socialism
by means of an appeal based upon religious grounds'. He went on to argue that
whilst:

> it is perfectly right and logical for Protestants to appeal to Protestants and to
> endeavour to convert them to Socialism by interpreting Holy Scripture in ways
> other than that accepted by the teachers or clergymen of their Church . . . it is
> an entirely mistaken policy to pursue with Catholics.

In concluding this article, Connolly argued against any attempt to present a
Christian form or variant of socialism, making the point that 'every time we
approach a Catholic worker with talk about "Christian Socialism" we make this a
religious question, and on such a question his religion teaches him that the clergy

must say the final word'.[20] In truth, although Connolly rejected priests commenting on social and political matters, in practice he was only opposed to such
intrusions if they tended to be anti-socialist. Any movements within the Church,
any elements of Catholic dogma which appeared to provide support, however
indirectly, for socialism were seized upon and magnified. Thus we find Connolly
when reporting on a speech given by Fr. Lawrence to the Dublin Trades Council
stating that 'in all sincerity we could see no fundamental difference between the
views expressed by Fr. Lawrence and those views we ourselves never hesitate to
express'. Connolly went on to suggest that 'the sympathetic strike is the
affirmation of the Christian principle that we are all members of one another.'[21]

Connolly, in short, was something of an opportunist in his handling of Roman
Catholicism. His writings on this subject, when read as a whole, were somewhat
inconsistent and subject to contradictions. Indeed Connolly's Catholic 'pose' sets
him apart from the other socialist leaders who were his contemporaries. But it is
worth recalling that Lenin in 1909, militant atheist though he was, nonetheless
argued that there were circumstances where 'atheist propaganda' could be both
'unnecessary and harmful', insisting rather that the class struggle and the
conditions of modern capitalist society was 'a hundred times better calculated to
convert Christian workers to Social Democracy and to atheism than bald atheistic
preaching'. Lenin, indeed, recognized that to preach atheism was often 'playing
into the hands of the priest'.[22] Although it is hard to imagine Lenin posing as a
Roman Catholic, it is clear that he shared with Connolly some points of agreement
in regard to correct socialist tactics in dealing with the religious question.

In 1900 Connolly considered the question of the Oath of Allegiance, an issue
which was to assume critical importance in Irish politics in the 1920s. Having
both religious and political implications, the subject of the oath was a complex and
emotion-laden one. Connolly's analysis of the issue was strikingly straightforward. In his view, the oath was 'a mere formality—a declaration not regarded as
binding upon the conscience of any man to whose opinions the allegiance required
is opposed'. He argued that if a man could not 'do his duty to his constituents
except by going through the mummery of this oath, he should comply with the
required form'. Connolly could see no religious or moral problem in taking a false
oath, asserting rather that 'the crime, if crime there be, will not be his but will
attach itself to those who so outrage justice as to oppose this indecent foolery
between a people and their right to be represented'.[23] Connolly's conception of a
flexible non-binding oath is of course one which many believers and certainly the
Church would not, indeed could not, countenance.

Connolly was to a very large extent forced by circumstances into adopting his
Catholic 'pose': if his true religious position had been public knowledge his career
as a labour leader would have been very seriously hampered. He attempted to
build a socialist movement in an unresponsive, often hostile environment and
clearly he felt that on some issues the long term view justified a certain amount of
flexibility. The imperatives of revolution do not always coincide with the moral

precepts of the society which is to be overthrown. For the revolutionist truth and honesty often of necessity become relative concepts and as with Connolly and the religious question discretion and prevarication may be the better parts of valour and honesty. Finally I would suggest that in his pamphlet *Erin's Hope* Connolly offers an illuminating insight into the thought processes which underpinned his religious stance in Ireland:

> The interests of labour all over the world are identical, it is true, but it is also true that each country had better work out its own salvation on the lines most congenial to its own people.[24]

Connolly's position was fraught with difficulty for those who came after him.

CHAPTER 3

Syndicalism

> If the working-class and the employing class have nothing in
> common, and an injury to one is the concern of all, into how
> many unions ought the working class to be divided?
>
> James Connolly 1910.[1]

IN A LETTER to his fiancée written early in 1889, Connolly, expressed his
first recorded thoughts on organised labour:

> By the way, if we get married next week I shall be unable to go to Dundee as
> promised as my fellow workmen in the job are preparing to strike at the end
> of the month for a reduction in the hours of labour. As my brother and I are
> ringleaders in the matter it is necessary we should be in on the ground. If we
> are not we should be looked upon as blacklegs which the Lord forbid.[2]

A number of attitudes and personality traits can be discerned in those few sen-
tences, the most obvious being that even at this early stage he was prepared to
structure his personal life around his political activities. Connolly, aged only
twenty-one and having only recently deserted from the army, was already emerging
as a 'ringleader' assisting in the preparations for a strike. The aggressive class-
consciousness and sense of solidarity with his fellow workmen, apparent in this
letter, are characteristics that remained with Connolly throughout his career, and
will be central in our attempt to understand his response to syndicalism. Connolly's
class-consciousness and commitment to organised labour led him to join the
Scottish Socialist Federation (SSF), which was an offshoot of Hyndman's Social
Democratic Federation (SDF). The SSF owed much of its political inspiration to its
parent body and it is fair to say that during this period Connolly's political views
were shaped by SDF political analysis and objectives. In reference to this period,
Ransom has noted that Connolly accepted the view—a view seen as being self-
evident by most of the people involved with the British socialist movement—that
'trade unions were incorrigible bulwarks of capitalism and of absolutely no value
as an organisational mode for socialist mobilisation'.[3] During the early stage of his
political development, it is clear that Connolly was an orthodox adherent of the
then prevalent social democratic approach of the Second International, accepting a
political strategy involving marxist education and political propaganda, working in
tandem with gradualist reformist parliamentary parties.

In 1896 Connolly's political apprenticeship came to an end. He emigrated to Ireland to become organiser of the Dublin Socialist Club. Within a few weeks of his arrival in Dublin Connolly was instrumental in founding and drafting the platform of the Irish Socialist Republican Party (ISRP). The objectives which Connolly advanced here were very similar to those contained in Hyndman's inaugural manifesto of the SDF, *Socialism Made Plain* (1883). The ISRP manifesto called for the 'conversion of means of production, distribution and exchange into the common property of society to be held and controlled by the democratic state in the interests of the entire community'. In the ISRP political scenario this conversion was to be achieved through the 'conquest by the Social Democracy of political power' in parliament and on all political bodies in Ireland. This 'democratic conquest' of the capitalist state through its elected bodies was seen as being 'the most effective means whereby the revolutionary forces may be organised and disciplined to attain that end'[4]—the end, of course, being a Socialist Republic.

It was not until the late 1890s that Connolly's political writing began to display attitudes which, while still clearly non-syndicalist, are indicative of a move towards a syndicalist position or at least a political analysis which would have tended to create a sympathetic reaction to syndicalism. As early as August 1898, in the second issue of the *Workers Republic,* Connolly presented a quotation from the American Gronlund which made the point that 'our present trade unions will be the skeletons of our future social order'.[5] In the next issue Connolly expanded upon the future role of organised Labour when he wrote that:

> the next step in the intellectual development of the worker will be to consider . . . whether there is indeed a useful function performed by the capitalist and landlord class which the organised workers cannot perform without them. Whether the ownership of property cannot be vested in the organised community, and the conduct of industry entrusted to our trade Unions . . . We are trade unionists but we are more than trade unionist . . . the trade unionist wishes to limit the power of the master but wishes still to have 'masters', the socialist wishes to have done with masters.[6]

The reference to 'our' trade unions rather than the trade unions or simply trade unions, suggests that the trade unions he has in mind are socialist trade unions— not yet syndicalist in form but certainly moving in that direction. Commenting on Connolly's transition from an orthodox proponent of the mainstream social-democratic marxism of the SDF to a revolutionary syndicalist, Ransom has suggested that Connolly was inspired by his reading of certain sections of Volume III of Marx's *Capital*. Ransom's evidence appears to be merely circumstantial; he attempts to demonstrate a direct link between Marx's discussion of a post-capitalist economy wherein 'associated labourers' use 'the means of production for their own labour'[7] and Connolly's own views on workers' control of industry. Ransom's attempt to give Connolly's move towards a syndicalist position a Marxist basis is suspect, especially as it requires the premise that Connolly was capable of reading Marx in the original German (he gives 1894 rather than the correct date 1909 for the first English translation of Volume III), a premise which is I think extremely doubtful.[8]

If a direct influence of Marx's Volume III on Connolly's move towards syndicalism remains, at best, uncertain, the influence of Daniel De Leon is subject to no such doubts. By 1899 Connolly and his ISRP had forged close links with De Leon's Socialist Labor Party (SLP) and Connolly was clearly influenced by De Leon's promotion of 'dual unionism'. Dual unionism in essence involved the establishment of a separate union structure based on 'industry' rather than craft, these industrial unions being—in contrast to craft unions—class conscious and committed to Socialism. In De Leon's schema the Socialist Industrial Unions were to be subordinate to the revolutionary Socialist Party; thus in America De Leon's SLP controlled the Industrial Unions through a subsidiary organisation called the Socialist Trade and Labor Alliance.

In light of the stormy and acrimonious relationship which developed between Connolly and De Leon in later years, it is worth noting that De Leon's theoretical work, while undoubtedly influential on Connolly's political development, did not lead him in any fundamentally new direction. De Leon's work, which was in any case largely derivative from earlier anarcho-syndicalist sources,[9] simply helped Connolly to focus his own radical but somewhat unconnected ideas on craft unionism, workers' control of industry and the future shape of socialist society. Connolly recognised that De Leon's 'One Big Union' concept (known in America as Industrial Unionism and in a more developed and radical form in Europe as syndicalism) offered both a concrete structure and an ideology which provided a logical extension of his own, much more tentative thoughts on organised labour and revolution. Connolly was excited by De Leon's central concept, seeing it as a potentially effective new direction for the revolutionary socialist movement (there is no evidence that he was aware of French syndicalist theorists). Connolly's intellectual debt to De Leon was substantial but was not of the magnitude to inspire a master-pupil type of relationship, indeed from the outset Connolly rejected many of De Leon's ideas and never at any time displayed the slightest hesitation in expressing opposition to what he felt to be theoretical errors. This fact was in time to lead to great bitterness between the two men.

In 1902 Connolly toured America under the auspices of the American SLP. The tour was a great success. Connolly addressed many large and enthusiastic audiences and was most impressed by the size and influence of the SLP. He was also gratified to have a number of his articles published by the SLP newspaper the *Weekly People*. Despite his enthusiasm for the SLP, Connolly did have reservations. He was not very impressed by De Leon either as a socialist leader or as a man—in part this was due to De Leon's autocratic style, but in fairness to De Leon it should be said that Connolly's ingrained and aggressive class consciousness rendered him incapable of accepting middle-class leadership of socialist organisations. At another level, Connolly disagreed with some of De Leon's political views, particularly the view that labour struggles aimed at improving working conditions were inherently futile. When he returned to America as a 'permanent' resident in 1903, Connolly wasted little time before addressing himself forcibly to the task of correcting De Leon's 'mistakes'.

Connolly's return to America as an emigrant within a year of his lecture tour came about as a result of financial problems and personal antagonisms within the ISRP (some of which stemmed from his initial absence in America). The fragmentation of the party was a great blow to Connolly. In the months between his break with the ISRP and his emigration, Connolly undertook an extended lecture tour in Scotland under the auspices of the SDF. During this tour he was instrumental in founding the Scottish Socialist Labour Party (a breakaway from the SDF) and was appointed by the fledgling party as its national organiser.[11] The Scottish SLP was, as the name suggests, modelled on the American SLP. The manifesto of the new party was clearly syndicalist, excluding trade union officials and opposing all 'pure and simple'[12]—in other words non syndicalist—trade unions. This very negative view of trade unions certainly reflected Connolly's own position that trade unions attempted to 'better our lot as slaves, but never a suggestion on the point of how we might proceed to abolish OUR STATUS as slaves, and elevate ourselves instead to the dignity of free men'.[13]

On his arrival in America in 1903, Connolly immediately joined the American SLP. He was to remain a member of the Party for some four years. His years in the SLP were characterised by his championing of a number of inter-party challenges to some of the party's policies. His major criticism was directed at De Leon's theory, a theory which De Leon erroneously attributed to Marx, that workers could not improve their working conditions even temporarily by industrial action because of the existence of an 'Iron Law of wages'.[14] This economic 'law' put forward by De Leon (as well as by earlier socialists) was based on the assumption that an inevitable rise in prices followed a wage increase and always negated the positive effect of the increase. Connolly argued that De Leon's view was contrary to Marx's actual position on the matter and in fact resulted from a misinterpretation of Marx. There is no doubt that in this instance Connolly was correct. De Leon appears to have confused the German socialist Lasalle's economic views with those of Marx. De Leon's views if accepted by the labour movement would have led to extremely isolated industrial organisations—for Connolly this would have been a disaster, for while he had no time for trade unions as such, he placed the greatest importance on working class militancy. Commenting in 1900 on the subjection and robbery of the working class, Connolly noted that the working class

> perpetually rises in protest against the incidental details of the robbery, organises to reduce the stealings of the Masters and ever and anon throws down its tools and enters on a bloodless insurrection against the conditions of its servitude. These protests, these organised movements, these unarmed insurrections of labour, these strikes are the inevitable accompaniment of the capitalistic system of society—they are the salient proofs that the socialist alone knows what he is talking about when he declares that the normal condition of society is not peace, but war; That the Class War is the one, great fact in the modern world.[15]

John Lyng, who is described as a 'close friend and collaborator with Connolly in Ireland and the USA', has reported that even during his membership of the SLP Connolly would work alongside a craft union organisation if this meant that he could help the general struggle of the workers and furthermore that he was 'always ready and willing to lend a hand to any section of the working class. No matter what the intellectual level of the man—as long as he was *striking a blow against* capitalism Connolly stood with him. He was out to organise the working class, not a sect.'[16]

Connolly also challenged a number of other SLP policies notably the party's assertion that the industrial arm, the Socialist Trade and Labor Alliance, was subordinate to and less important than the political arm. Connolly argued that the industrial movement was of primary importance, believing as he did that socialists must take control of the daily fight in the work place and organise it in a revolutionary manner with a revolutionary purpose and direction.[17] Although by this stage in his career Connolly was investing primary importance to industrial rather than political organisation, he was nonetheless always careful to caution against underestimating the importance of political action.

Personal relations between Connolly and De Leon deteriorated rapidly during Connolly's determined and none too subtle onslaught on those policies of the SLP which he thought to be in error. The arguments between the two men became very bitter. Towards the end of Connolly's period in the SLP, De Leon went so far as to accuse him of being a 'Jesuit agent'.[18] The substantial political differences which separated the two men were compounded by a suspicion on De Leon's part, perhaps not altogether groundless, that Connolly was after his position as party leader, and a strong distaste on Connolly's part for middle-class leadership of socialist organisations. Connolly's bitterness towards De Leon, his sense of hurt and his class-conscious analysis of the SLP hierarchy are evident in a letter written in mid 1904:

> neither in Great Britain nor America can a working class socialist expect common fairness from his comrades if he enters into a controversy with a trusted leader from a class above them. The howl that greets every such attempt whether directed against a Hyndman in England or a De Leon in America sounds . . . wonderfully alike, and everywhere is but the accents of an army, not of revolutionary fighters but of half—emancipated slaves.[19]

In 1906 Connolly became involved with the newly formed Industrial Workers of the World (IWW). The IWW, more widely known as the Wobblies, was an organisation very much to Connolly's taste, centering as it did on the One Big Union organisational schema and operating with a superbly militant—indeed some might argue recklessly adventurous—revolutionary socialist agitational and propagandist drive. In its manifesto the IWW called for the creation of 'one great industrial union embracing all industries—providing craft autonomy locally, industrial autonomy internationally and working class unity generally'. The IWW openly declared that it was 'founded on the class struggle' and the 'recognition of the irrepressible conflict between the capitalist class and the working class'.[20] Clearly these principles were close to Connolly's heart. In the first issue of *The Harp* Connolly described the IWW as 'the only real economic organisation truly worthy of the name union' and went on to suggest that when the IWW 'launches its own political party it will put an end to all excuse for two Socialist parties and open the way for a real and effective unification of the revolutionary forces'.[21] Connolly was of course well aware of the IWW's anti-political stance and thus of their opposition to founding a political party. He believed that the nature of the struggle would eventually force the IWW to recognise the necessity of extending their organisation into the political sphere.

De Leon was very influential in the early years of the IWW. Unfortunately he attempted to use the IWW to continue his quarrel with Connolly over the 'wages' question. The end result of this continuing disagreement was that Connolly resigned from the SLP in 1907. Never a man to forgive and forget, Connolly was instrumental the following year in ensuring that the IWW convention rejected not only De Leon's economic theories but also his right to remain a member of the organisation. This convention voted to drop the IWW's contact with political parties and indeed declared itself as being opposed to all politics.[22] Connolly was pleased with the 1908 IWW convention as De Leon's débâcle was gratifying to him on both political and personal grounds. Yet the IWW's hard anti-political line, pointing as it did to a move towards anarcho-syndicalism, was one which he tried to avert and continued to oppose within the IWW after the convention. Connolly's position on 'politics versus syndicalism' was relatively straight forward. He considered that 'the fight for the conquest of the political state is not the battle, it is only the echo of the battle. The real battle is being fought out every day for the power to control industry.'[23] Nevertheless, he argued that it was 'incumbent upon organised labour to meet the capitalist class on every field where the latter can operate to our disadvantage.'[24] Connolly gave primary importance to the labour movement's industrial wing but rejected the anti-political stance propounded by many syndicalists.

During his last few years in America, Connolly was extremely active, working within both the IWW and as a National Organiser for the Socialist Party of America (which he had joined on leaving the SLP). During this period he also founded the Irish Socialist Federation (ISF) and edited its journal *The Harp*. In 1910 he transferred publication of *The Harp* to Dublin and in an article confidently entitled 'Introducing the "Harp" and a new Labour policy for Ireland' described his organisational plan as follows:

> It shall be our purpose in the 'Harp' to work for a reorganisation of the forces of organised labour in Ireland—THE ORGANISATION OF ALL WHO WORK FOR WAGES INTO ONE BODY OF NATIONAL DIMENSIONS AND SCOPE, UNDER ONE EXECUTIVE HEAD, ELECTED BY THE VOTE OF ALL THE UNIONS, AND DIRECTING THE POWER OF SUCH UNIONS IN UNITED EFFORTS IN ANY NEEDED DIRECTION.[25]

In 1910 he returned to Ireland at the invitation of the Socialist Party of Ireland (SPI). During his absence James Larkin had founded the Irish Transport and General Workers' Union (ITGWU). This union, organised along syndicalist lines and extremely militant, was greatly admired by Connolly. Writing to an Irish comrade shortly before his return to Ireland, Connolly informed him that if he were back in Ireland one of his first priorities would be the formation of an 'Irish Workers' Union', his aim being to 'combine all Irish unions gradually into one body'. He described Larkin's Union in his letter as the 'most promising sign, because it is already founded on the lines others should follow'. That Connolly was enthused and excited by this new syndicalist development in Ireland is evident in his statement that 'if things were properly handled on these lines the whole situation in Ireland might be revolutionised.'[26] Connolly never founded his proposed Irish Workers' Union but soon after his return to Ireland he did become Belfast organiser of the ITGWU and by 1914 had risen to the position of acting Secretary-General of the Union.

Connolly's adherence to a syndicalist-oriented revolutionary strategy is best understood in terms of his passionate conviction that the working class was involved in a class war. He supported the Industrial Union strategy of placing the union over and above the 'Party' because, in his own experience, revolutionary socialist parties tended to be weak and relatively insignificant, whereas labour, when organised industrially and given class conscious, revolutionary socialist leadership, seemed to be a weapon capable of waging and ultimately winning the class war.

In reading Connolly's comments on industrial unionism, one is struck by the military framework within which he understood and reacted to the 'class war'. For Connolly class war was no intellectual abstraction, it was a living reality, a reality what is more, which governed his life. Writing in the *International Socialist Review* in 1910 he argued that:

> Industrialism is more than a method of organisation—it is a science of fighting. It says to the workers: fight only at the time you select, never when the boss wants to fight. Fight at the height of the busy season, and in the slack season when the worker is one in thousands upon the sidewalk absolutely refuse to be drawn into battle. Even if the boss insults you and vilifies your union and refuses to recognise it take it lying down in the slack season but mark it up in your little notebook.[27]

A military perspective permeates Connolly's writings on what he referred to as 'the act and science of fighting the battle of labour'. Connolly counselled the working class to study the tactics and strategy of their class enemies who, he asserted, 'employ spies in war, they mass armed forces with orders to shoot to kill, they capture and imprison pickets'. Workers, he argued, should not involve themselves in strikes which would lead to mere endurance tests, battles which he termed 'simply a trial of strength between a full purse and an empty stomach'. In a similar vein he recommended that there should be no hesitation in ending a strike which was no longer winnable: 'a general in command of a. army does not consider it a point of duty to expend his last cartridge and lose his last man . . . if his experienced eye tells him that this position is untenable . . . he retires at the first opportunity . . . and rearranges his forces for another battle.'[28]

Connolly combined this pragmatism, with the attribution of an almost mystical ability on the part of Industrial Unions to transform individuals and ultimately the whole society. Writing in 1908 he asserted that:

> The power of this idea to transform the dry detail work of trade union organisation into the constructive work of revolutionary Socialism and thus make of the unimaginative trade unionist a potent factor in the launching of a new system of society, cannot be overestimated. It invests the sordid details of the daily incidents of the class struggle with a new and beautiful meaning, and presents them in their true light as skirmishes between two opposing armies of light and darkness.[29]

Writing about labour struggles in 1915, Connolly had clearly maintained his very elevated view of their importance and meaning 'all those striving for better wages and better conditions, all those squabbles over half-pennies and pennies per hour, squalid and sordid as they seem, are nevertheless in their essence beautiful and spiritual strivings of imperfect human souls for the cleansing of the environment in which they are placed.'[30]

Syndicalism is often disparaged by orthodox Marxists as an anarchist, opportunist or ultra-leftist deviation. Of course, Marx and Engels devoted a great deal of attention to combating the anarchist theories of Stirner, Proudhon and Bakunin; and syndicalism has suffered from being linked—often unfairly—with anarchist tendencies.[31] Connolly never at any stage had any sympathy for anarchism. Writing in *Justice* in 1893, he referred to anarchists as 'men whose whole philosophy of life is but an exaggerated form of that Individualism we are in revolt against'.[32] There is not a single instance in any of Connolly's writings or recorded statements which could be used to substantiate a 'charge' of anarchism. For Connolly and for many socialists of his generation, syndicalism was simply the practical application of Marxism.[33]

Lenin severely castigated syndicalism, although it is worth noting that he recognised its strength and attraction. In 1907 he wrote in support of Voinov, who had argued that Russian Social-Democrats should learn from the example of 'opportunism' and 'syndicalism'. This was, he argued, especially true in respect of 'Revolutionary work in the trade unions, shifting the emphasis from parliamentary trickery to the education of the proletariat, to rallying the purely class organisations, to the struggle outside parliament, to the ability to use (and to prepare the masses for the possibility of successfully using) the general strike, as well as the December forms of struggle in the Russian Revolution'.[34] Lenin's principal critique of syndicalism based as it was on the anarchist looseness of organisation and aversion to politics, is not—at least in Connolly's case fully justified, for while Connolly certainly did develop a 'loose' concept of the

Party, his theoretical justification was in no sense an anarchist one and in respect of the 'aversion to politics' charge Connolly was never at any time subject to such an aversion.

Connolly's syndicalism is best understood within the context of his aggressive, class-based hatred of capitalist society. He was a man of intense passions. His commitment to his class and his hatred of its oppressors was absolute. He considered himself to be a war leader and as such attempted to devise tactics and strategies best devised to fight and win the class war. Syndicalism impressed Connolly as the organisational scheme which best concentrated the offensive power of organised labour. He rejected those aspects of mainstream syndicalist theory which tended, in his opinion, to diminish the revolutionary potential of the movement. Two major examples of such rejection have been mentioned above— the anti-political bias of the IWW and the 'general strike' scenario which was so close to the heart of most syndicalists. Connolly was a committed syndicalist from the late 1890s till his death in 1916: he never wavered in his basic adherence to a syndicalist oriented revolutionary movement and indeed a future socialist society constructed around a syndicalist industrial-political base. In essence, Connolly's syndicalism was based on the straightforward premise that workers should 'take hold of the daily fight in the workshop and organise it in a revolutionary manner, with a revolutionary purpose and direction'.[36] Later in this study we will examine organised labour in Ireland, particularly the syndicalist inspired ITGWU, in the years after Connolly's death and attempt to assess the significance of his theoretical and practical influence.

CHAPTER 4

Socialism and Nationalism

Paradoxical as it may seem, I am a patriot because I am a Socialist, and a Socialist because I understand the true meaning of the word patriotism.

James Connolly 1900.[1]

An Irish Republic, the only purely political change in Ireland worth crossing the street for, will never be realized except by a revolutionary party that proceeds upon the premise that the capitalist and the landlord classes in town and country in Ireland are *particeps criminis* (criminal accomplices) with the British government, in the enslavement and subjection of the nation. Such a revolutionary party must be Socialist, and from Socialism alone can the salvation of Ireland come.

James Connolly 1909.[2]

THERE IS NO doubt that Connolly's greatest and most enduring legacy to Irish socialism lies in his recognition that the struggle for national independence was an inseparable part of the struggle for socialism, and that by combining the forces of socialism and nationalism both would be strengthened. Today, Connolly's stance on the question of socialism and nationalism seems unexceptional: the history of the twentieth century, particularly the whole process of decolonisation, is replete with examples of socialist-based national liberation struggles. But in his own day Connolly's ideas were novel and radical and as is the lot of most progressive thinkers, he was ridiculed and misunderstood by many of his contemporaries. The ISRP's agitation for Irish independence was considered by many socialists to be 'a mere chauvinism' that served only to 'perpetuate national rivalries and race hatreds'.[3] Speaking at the 1908 Conference of the Independent Labour Party, Ramsay MacDonald explained to the Conference that 'for our own organising purposes Devon and Cornwall are added to Wales and Ireland as part of Lancashire'.[4] MacDonald's words, and it should be noted that MacDonald in 1908 was still a committed Scottish nationalist, give some indication of the advanced nature of Connolly's perception of the role of national independence in the struggle for socialism in Ireland.

Nationalism was a component—an integral part—of Connolly's socialism from the beginning of his socialist agitation in Ireland. As early as 1896, within days of arriving in Ireland and prior even to the establishment of the ISRP, he published a statement which read in part:

The struggle for Irish freedom has two aspects: it is national and it is social. The national ideal can never be realised until Ireland stands forth before the world as a nation, free and independent. It is social and economic, because no matter what form the government may be, as long as one class owns as private property the land and instruments of labour from which mankind derive their substance, that class will always have it in their power to plunder and enslave the remainder of their fellow creatures.[5]

A few weeks later the manifesto of the ISRP (written by Connolly) declared that the party's principal objective was the 'establishment of an Irish Socialist Republic based upon the public ownership by the Irish people of the land and instruments of production, distribution and exchange'.[6] In an article entitled 'Nationalism and Socialism' published in *Shan Van Vocht* in January 1897, Connolly expressed his views unambiguously: 'Nationalism without Socialism without a reorganisation of society on the basis of a broader and more developed form of that common property which underlay the structure of ancient Erin—is only national recreancy.' He went on to state that 'as a Socialist' he was 'prepared to do all one man can do to achieve for our motherland her rightful heritage— independence' but warned that 'if you ask me to abate one jot or title of the claims of social justice in order to conciliate the privileged classes, then I must decline'.[7]

Thus Connolly's Nationalism was always qualified by, indeed inspired and interpreted through, his socialism. Socialism was the central dominating factor in Connolly's life. His intellectual, political and moral makeup, indeed his whole character and self-image hinged upon and revolved around his socialist faith and his commitment to revolution.

Nationalism was, therefore, primarily a facet—albeit an extremely important facet—of Connolly's socialism. Nationalism divorced from socialism held no attraction for him, indeed particularly in his early years in Ireland, he often vented his not inconsiderable powers of invective on middle-class nationalism. Thus we find him on one occasion writing that:

> The nationalism of men who desire to retain the present social system is not the fruit of a natural growth but is an ugly abortion, the abortive product of an attempt to create a rebellious movement in favour of political freedom among men contented to remain industrial slaves.It is an attempt to create a revolutionary movement towards freedom and to entrust the conduct of the movement to a class desirous of enforcing the social subjection of the men they are professing to lead . . . It professes to believe that the class grinding us down to industrial slavery can at the same moment be leading us forward to national liberty.[8]

Given the tenuous nature of the Irish socialist movement at the turn of the century, Connolly could have been forgiven if he had tried to avoid antagonising the national movement. That this was not the case speaks volumes about both his fiery temperament and his soaring political ambitions. There is a breathtaking audacity in Connolly's political objectives. In regard to nationalism and Irish patriotism, he did not seek simply to make an accommodation with the nation-alists, to find a comfortable if sterile niche for socialism on the periphery of the nationalist movement—at this time any sort of acceptance of socialism as a legitimate Irish political entity would have been a major achievement—he intended rather to make a commitment to socialism the litmus test of patriotism. Writing in the last issue of the *Workers Republic* before the break up of the ISRP, at a time when the party was in turmoil and his own political future was in grave doubt, Connolly was able to rise from the depths of his despair to advise Irish workers to 'brand as enemies to Ireland all who believe in the subjection of labour to capital—brand as traitors to this country all who live by skinning Irish labour.' 'The lesson for the working class of the world was plain: 'In every country socialism is foreign, is unpatriotic, and will continue so until the working class embracing it as their salvation make Socialism the dominant political force.' When this day of working class ascendancy arrived, 'services and devotion' to the interests of the working class would be the gauge of a man's patriotism and socialism itself would be 'patriotic and native everywhere, and the advocates of capitalistic property will be the unpatriotic ones'.[9]

Connolly's seven years in Ireland organising the ISRP were years of poverty and failure. His political work, at least in the short term, had been an exercise in futility, but he did succeed in implanting in the public mind, and more importantly in the minds of both socialists and advanced nationalists, a linkage—a basis, albeit tentative, for unity—between socialism and nationalism. The structure which Connolly proposed, the socialist republic, was non-negotiable anything less was unacceptable. Irish independence without socialist reconstruction was seen by Connolly as a recipe for disaster. Writing as early as 1897, he described (and was almost certainly the first commentator ever to do so) the process that is now known as neo-colonialism: 'If you remove the English army tomorrow and hoist the green flag over Dublin Castle, unless you set about the organisation of the Socialist Republic, your efforts will have been in vain. England will still rule you.' England would still rule, he argued, 'through her capitalists, through her landlords, through her financiers, through the whole array of commercial and individualist institutions she has planted in this country'.[10]

During his seven years in America Connolly remained true to his vision of an Irish socialist republic, his conviction that socialism was the essential prerequisite for national freedom never wavered. In 1907 he founded the Irish Socialist Federation (ISF) whose purpose was to preach socialism and revolutionary class-consciousness among the Irish working class in America and to 'spread a knowl-edge of, and help to sustain, the socialist movement in Ireland'.[11] In January 1908 Connolly published the first issue of *The Harp*, organ of the ISF. Discussing his goals as editor and principal writer, he noted that he wanted the paper to be a gathering point for the 'best intellects of the Irish race in America'. For this reason he wanted the paper to be read by 'all who love Ireland and are proud of her history and zealous of her honour'. He felt that 'high minded' people such as he described 'naturally belong to socialism', and through *The Harp* he hoped to make them 'realise that through socialism alone can the Irish race attain the fullest expression of its powers and capabilities'. Once they had made this realisation, they would, according to Connolly's scenario, 'find their greatest happiness in fighting in our ranks'.[12]

Connolly mellowed in some important respects during his years in America. Whilst retaining the fire and depth of his revolutionary commitment, he became much more willing to accept non-socialist nationalists as potential allies rather than enemies (a similar and related movement occurred in his views on the role and structure of the Socialist Party at this time (as we shall see in chapter 5). Of course he reserved the right to castigate nationalists when the occasion demanded, but a clear change in attitude can be discerned. In 1898, for example, Connolly's position on alliances was one of extreme rigidity. Thus we find him writing that:

> Socialists refuse to deny or to lose their identity in an alliance with those who only understand half the problem of liberty. They seek only the alliance and friendship of those hearts who, loving liberty for its own sake, are not afraid to follow its banner when it is uplifted by the hands of the working class who have most need of it. Their friends are those who would not hesitate to follow that standard of liberty, to consecrate their lives in its service even should it lead to the terrible arbitration of the sword.[13]

Compare this with his advice to fellow socialists published in *The Harp* almost a decade later when he suggested that they should not 'seek for something to differ upon in order to show how smart you are', but should on the contrary attempt to 'find some point of intellectual affinity' arguing that once such a point had been 'established and conceded upon both sides, then the path to agreement upon vital points will be rendered smooth and easy'.[14]

That Connolly's change of heart in regard to the possibilities of alliance with non-socialist nationalists was a purely tactical step, entailing no dilution of his revolutionary commitment or hatred of capitalism, is amply evident in his published wrltings. In 1909, for example, when he was firmly established in his more temperate bridge-building attitude toward nationalists, he was still on occasion writing and publishing deliberately provocative statements such as his comment that 'the Irish capitalist and the English government are in entire agreement upon the proposition that the Irish worker should be skinned, they only disagree as to which of them should have the biggest piece of skin'.[15]

In January 1910 *The Harp* was transferred to Dublin, the move being seen by Connolly as a sort of advance guard and hopefully a financial base for his own return to Ireland. In the first Dublin issue of, as we saw, Connolly wrote an article entitled 'Introducing *The Harp* and a new Labour Party for Ireland', which set out his future plans with some clarity, arguing from the premise that the Irish must 'tolerate each other or else be compelled to tolerate the common enemy'.[16] While taking some pains to underline the fact that his 'new labour policy' did not mean that he had 'altered or abandoned our belief in the principles for which we stood in Ireland from 1896 onward',[17] Connolly was nonetheless moving away quite dramatically from the exclusivity and intolerance which he had demanded of the ISRP during his early years in Ireland. Thus we find him writing that *The Harp* and, by implication, the whole Irish labour movement was 'willing to work and co-operate heartily with any one who will aid us in arousing the slumbering giant of labour to a knowledge of its rights and duties'. Connolly is careful to stress that he is still 'as firm as ever' in his belief that the 'only hope for Ireland, as for the rest of the world, lies in a revolutionary reconstruction of society', and that furthermore the 'working class is the only class historically fitted for that great achievement'. This expression of willingness to co-operate with non-socialist organisations—Connolly somewhat euphemistically uses the expression organisations 'far less ambitious than our own'—is clearly a major change in his thinking.

In 1914 Lenin noted in his work *The Right of Nations to Self-Determination* that in so far as the 'bourgeois nationalism of *any* oppressed nation has a general democratic content that is directed *against* oppression . . . it is this content that we unconditionally support.'[19] Connolly would certainly have supported Lenin's views on bourgeois nationalism. In the later part of his career he was quick to recognise, applaud and where necessary amplify any developments within the nationalist camp which tended, in his opinion, to show a positive or even simply a non-antagonistic attitude to a reconstruction of Irish society on more egalitarian lines.

Yet Connolly was not content to allow the labour movement to hang on the coat-tails of the nationalists on the question of Irish independence. He wanted to establish labour as the frontrunner—the group most totally and fearlessly committed to Irish independence. A good example of how he promoted labour's role in the national struggle and his own credentials as a leading 'rebel' can be seen in his reaction to the proposal to partition Ireland which was under discussion early in 1914. On this issue he was both vehement in his opposition and accurate in his prophecies. Partition, which he described as being 'the betrayal of the national democracy of industrial Ulster', would, he argued, lead to a 'carnival of reaction both North and South, would set back the wheels of progress, would destroy the oncoming unity of the Irish Labour movement and paralyse all advanced movements whilst it endured.' The depth and passion of Connolly's opposition to partition is evident when he writes that 'to it Labour should give the bitterest opposition, against it Labour in Ulster should fight even to the death if necessary, as our fathers fought before us'.[20]

In an address to the ITUC in May 1914. Connolly argued that it would be better to be 'rebel slaves in an undivided Ireland' than 'contented accomplices of English statesmen in the partition',[21] and went on to explicitly state his own perception of the relationship between nationalism and the Irish labour movement: 'there are no real nationalists in Ireland outside of the Irish labour movement. All others merely reject one part or other of the British conquest, the labour movement alone rejects it in its entirety, and sets . . . the reconquest of Ireland as its aim.'[22] For Connolly the working class was not simply a part of the Irish nation—the working class was Ireland. When he was in America in 1909 and corresponding with William O'Brien regarding his return to Ireland Connolly wrote: 'I would rather work in Ireland than anywhere else *for the cause*. Apart from the cause Ireland has no attractions for me.'[23] Connolly never faltered in his single minded devotion to 'the cause'. His devotion to and ambition for his class appeared limitless. Some months before his death, he stated his position with great candour when he wrote that 'we take our stand with our own class nakedly upon our class interests, but believing that these interests are the highest interests of the race.'[24]

At exactly the same time, indeed in the same issue of the *Workers Republic* as the above quotation appeared, Connolly was claiming that in Ireland there was a growth in that 'feeling of identity of interests between the forces of real National-ism and of Labour which we have long worked and hoped for'. According to Connolly, labour recognised that its 'real wellbeing is linked and bound up with the hope of growth of Irish resources within Ireland'. Nationalists, he confidently if rather optimistically argued, had come to recognise that the 'real progress of a nation towards freedom must be measured by the progress of itsl most subject class'.[25] The critical word in Connolly's statement is of course the descriptive and qualifying 'real' which he places in front of 'Nationalism'. Real nationalists to Connolly were those who were willing to use armed force to attain Irish inde-pendence: it was a bonus if they were also sympathetic to labour. With these 'real' nationalists Connolly was willing to make a temporary alliance of convenience. Within this alliance he attempted to exert as much influence as he could to bring about an armed proclamation of the Irish Republic—his success in achieving this objective is evident in the fact that when a rising eventually took place, he participated not only in the capacity of Commander of the ICA but also as vice-president of the Provisional Government of the Irish Republic and Commandant-General of the Dublin Division of the Army of the Irish Republic. Connolly had always recognised that Irish socialism lacked the immediate strength of the forces of non-socialist nationalism, with this in mind he extended—with both brilliance and ruthlessness—the old adage which states that 'if you can't beat them join them' to read 'if you can't beat them join them, then lead them'.

Connolly's goal was clear—he would be satisfied with no less than a socialist workers republic in Ireland. Labour co-operation with non-socialist nationalists in the struggle for national liberation was conditional. Connolly insisted for example, that the ICA would 'only co-operate in a forward movement. The moment that forward movement ceases it reserves to itself the right to step out of alignment and advance by itself if needs be, in an effort to plant the banner of freedom one reach further towards its goal'.[26] The independent socialist objectives of Connolly and the ICA were not mere wordplay. Connolly was serious, serious enough to sacrifice his life. The ICA under his leadership was dedicated not simply to an independent Republic but to a Socialist Republic. It is in this context that his statement in October 1915 that 'neither Home Rule nor the lack of Home Rule' would make the ICA 'lay down their arms'[27] should be understood. Connolly was extremely proud of the ICA and was both singleminded and ruthless in his leadership of it. Both his pride and his objectives were clearly evident when he wrote:

> The Irish Citizen Army in its constitution pledges its members to fight for a republican freedom for Ireland. Its members are, therefore, of the number who believe that at the call of duty they may have to lay down their lives for Ireland, and have so trained themselves that at the worst the laying down of their lives shall constitute the starting point of another glorious tradition—a tradition that will keep alive the soul of the nation.[28]

He was absolutely committed to an armed struggle for Irish independence and was willing to work alongside any individual or group who shared his commitment. For him, however, independence from English domination was simply the first step in an armed struggle to establish a socialist republic. He would have had no hesitation in using the ICA against the nationalists he fought alongside in 1916 if they had stood in the path of a socialist republic. This central fact must always be in the forefront of any attempt to understand the true nature of his alliance with the nationalists.

In April 1916 Connolly expressed his belief that 'the Cause of Labour is the Cause of Ireland. The Cause of Ireland is the Cause of Labour. They cannot be dissevered.'[29] These words contain the key to understanding Connolly's perception of the true relationship between socialism and nationalism and thus between socialists and nationalists. For Connolly the alliance between the labour movement and the bourgeois-led nationalist movement was simply a step—and a distasteful one at that—in the inevitable triumph of socialism in Ireland. Socialism was the true, the only true patriotism. The working class was in itself and itself alone the true embodiment of the Irish nation. When he talked about Ireland, Connolly referred not to Ireland as a geographical or cultural entity. For him Ireland was synonymous with the Irish working class.

For many socialists Connolly's nationalism appears as an aberration, a dilution, indeed a perversion of his socialism. The critique is based on the premise that an absolute dichotomy exists between nationalism and internationalism. In a series of letters published in *Forward* in 1914, Connolly debated the subject of nationalism and its relationship to internationalism with the Belfast Independent Labour Party (ILP) leader William Walker. During this exchange Connolly stated that he considered the Socialist Party of Ireland (SPI) to be the 'only International Party in Ireland, since its conception of Internationalism is that of a free federation of free peoples, whereas that of the Belfast branches of the ILP seems scarcely distinguishable from Imperialism, the merging of subjugated peoples in the political system of their conquerors'.[30] That Connolly's nationalism was not based on racial exclusivity or nationalist chauvinism is shown by his statement in the course of this at times heated exchange, that he did 'not care where you were born—(we have had Jews, Russians, Germans, Lithuanians, Scotsmen, and Englishmen in the SPI)—but I do care where you earn your living, and I hold that every class-conscious worker should work for the freedom of the country in which he lives, if he desires to hasten the political power of his class in that country'.[31] Connolly's nationalism did not denote parochialism or limited vision he was intensely interested in world affairs. The newspapers which he edited over the years bear testimony to this interest in their wide coverage of international events. The fact that between 1899 and 1903 the ISRP had exchanged articles (for the *Workers Republic*) with more than twenty foreign newspapers confirms that the nationalist component of Connolly's socialism did not lead to insularity or restrict his intellectual horizons.[32]

There is no doubt that Connolly was susceptible to the language and emotion of nationalism. He was an avid student of Irish history, a great admirer of Irish music and song (particularly 'rebel' songs); he supported, albeit somewhat half-heartedly, the Gaelic revival movement,[33] and consistently used Irish symbols and imagery (for example he named one of his newspapers *The Harp*) in his attempt to create an Irish identity for socialism—a political theory which many people in Ireland considered a foreign import. It would be wrong however to conclude from this that patriotic passion—subjective emotional nationalist fervour—played any substantive part in his political development. It is inconceivable that Connolly, a hard-headed and intellectually rigourous marxist, would have allowed his personal attachment to Irish culture and identity to distract him from his commitment to the class war and social revolution. Connolly was well in control of his 'Irishness' and in fact used his inside knowledge quite clinically in his socialist educational and propaganda work.

Connolly's legacy to Irish socialists, with respect to nationalism and republicanism, was very much a double-edged sword and there is no doubt that he was a very hard act to follow. Under his leadership, inspired by his theoretical insight, the depth of his class loyalty and the virulence of his class hatred, an alliance with the non-socialist nationalists held few real dangers. Labour, although not exactly in the driving seat, was not simply a passenger. Minority though it was, it had a coherence of vision and strength of purpose which ensured that the alliance would not dilute or corrupt its socialist commitment.

With Connolly's death, a death which was in itself an important propaganda legacy for Irish socialists, he left an extremely difficult task for his successors, how to build on his work and forge ahead to the establishment of the Socialist Republic? The task was not simply to develop an identity of interests between socialists and nationalists but to create an identification in the public mind with the concept of Ireland (and being Irish) and socialism. We shall examine in a later chapter how Irish labour rose to this challenge in post-Rising Ireland.

CHAPTER 5

The Revolutionary Party

> Of course you may say that it was not suggested to me specifically, but to our party, and then only jocularly. But that is just my peculiarity, that I am not able to draw the dividing line between myself and the party.
>
> James Connolly 1902.[1]

THROUGHOUT HIS POLITICAL career Connolly was a revolutionary socialist—in the final analysis an unsuccessful revolutionary socialist. In his own terms, therefore, his life was a failure. One can of course argue that 'objective conditions' in Ireland militated against, perhaps even precluded, the possibility of a successful socialist revolution, but this argument should not be used as a catch-all to justify ignoring those aspects of Connolly's revolutionary theory and practice which, with the benefit of hindsight, should be questioned. In this chapter I shall examine Connolly's position on the Party. This is an extremely important subject. For a revolutionary socialist operating (as Connolly did for many years) with a vanguard notion of revolutionary leadership, the Party, its role, structure and objectives are perhaps the critical questions upon which the success or failure of revolutionary socialist activity hinge.

During his early years in the socialist movement in Edinburgh, Connolly was a member of a number of political organisations including the Socialist League, the Scottish Socialist Federation and the Independent Labour Party. Through his experiences in these organisations and more particularly, perhaps, through the influence of John Leslie, Connolly developed a belief in the need for a united, tightly disciplined party structure. Leslie, who was Connolly's main political influence at this time, noted in 1893 that within the party 'unity and discipline should be enforced, or at least insisted upon.'[2] In 1893 Connolly drafted the Rules and Constitution for the Edinburgh ILP. His organisational proposal centred upon a District Council which would 'watch over and safeguard the interests of the entire party' and 'arrange for a uniform policy at elections and in all public questions'.[3] Connolly's proposals, which were accepted, were substantially less centralised than Leslie's conception of a 'definitive, unitary party authority'.[4] It is difficult to assess whether Connolly's proposals were a true reflection of his ideal party structure or whether they represented a pragmatic recognition that a watered-down version of the type of rigidly centralised party structure favoured by Leslie was the best that could be attained within the ILP at that time.

In 1896 Connolly founded the Irish Socialist Republican Party. The ISRP was extremely dependent on Connolly's drive and intellect. Despite his own denials, he was the undoubted leader of the party. From his published comments during these early years in Ireland, a clear picture emerges of his views on the role and objectives of the ISRP. Writing in September 1898, he stated that the ISRP was 'for a narrow platform, a platform so narrow that there will not be a place on it where anyone not an uncompromising enemy of tyranny can rest the soles of his feet'.[5] 'Uncompromising' is a word much favoured by Connolly at this period when commenting on 'the Party'. Reporting on a meeting of nationalists held in Wicklow in 1899, for example, Connolly noted that his attendance at the meeting had served to make him 'more and more convinced that in the uncompromising spirit, the rigid intolerance, and stern exclusiveness shown by the Socialist Republican Party are to be found the only true methods whereby an effective revolutionary movement may be built up'.[6]

Operating in a hostile environment, engaged in constant struggle just to survive, the ISRP was taught by Connolly to believe in its own importance and destiny as a party—the only party which was capable of establishing a socialist republic in Ireland. This vanguard conception of the party is clearly evident in an article which he wrote in April 1903, at a time when the Party was riven with quarrels and in fact about to break up. The Socialist Party which did not believe in itself, which did not 'cherish as its dearest belief the doctrine that it and it alone' was the party 'destined to carry the banner of Socialism to a triumphant issue', was, Connolly argued, bound sooner or later to 'die of dry-rot, or become prey to the machinations of intriguers or the doubts of weaklings'. An individual, he wrote, 'only succeeds in the degree in which he believes in himself'; the same he believed held true for a political party. The party he stated, which 'believes in itself, and whose members have the moral fibre to act up to that belief will win, and adverse storms but serve to strengthen its determination and stiffen its resolve'. In a revealing paragraph Connolly goes on to explain that these views explain his 'admiration for the bigot, the man of no compromise, the good hater, the relentless fighter whoever or whatever he may be the man who wars to the knife and the knife to the hilt'.[7]

In its actual structure the ISRP was fairly straight-forward. The fact that its membership was small and largely Dublin-based meant that it did not need to address many of the organisational problems faced by larger and more geographically dispersed political groups. In an article written in 1899 castigating The autocratic leader-centered Home Rule Nationalist organisations, Connolly gives a detailed—if somewhat rosy—description of the ISRP structure:

> The Socialist Republican Party . . . have no permanent president or chairman, thus avoiding the dangers of bossism and the perpetual intrigues for positions which disgrace every other party. They recognise no person as leader, the most prominent speaker or writer has no more sway in the organisation than the most silent worker, they allow no party manifesto or

leaflet to be signed by an individual, thus no member can obtrude his personality upon the party, they insist on a regular system of book-keeping and a weekly statement and quarterly audit of all monies received and expended, thus giving every man a full knowledge of the party's actions, and finally they transact all business at weekly meetings in which every member is invited to take part.[8]

The political and personal investment which Connolly had made in the ISRP, the hardships which he and his family had suffered through his devotion to the party, must have appeared fruitless when the party broke up in 1903. Connolly described his feelings about his resignation from the party as being like 'losing a child'[9], a simile which gives some idea of the intensity of his investment in and identification with it. His sense of loss over the disintegration of the ISRP was compounded by a sense of failure, not only in respect of the actual events which triggered the destruction of the party but also a more general failure in that the ISRP had never become the cohesive, tightly disciplined revolutionary socialist party which Connolly had hoped to build.

Although the ISRP was, in the long term, an important watershed in the historical development of Irish socialism, during the years of its existence it lacked any real influence or power. It had few links with organised labour and was largely ignored by the general public. The Party's membership was tiny in the extreme, one contemporary newspaper commenting that it had more 'more syllables than numbers, consisting mainly of a Scotto-Hibernian and a long boy'.[10] The Scotto-Hibernian' was Connolly and the 'long boy', Tom Lyng, a young man who was six foot tall. William O'Brien, who was secretary of the ISRP, recalled that the number of members that 'turned up at meetings might range from twelve to fifteen. The actual number of members on record would probably be about fifty.' O'Brien noted that at quarterly meetings which were summonsed by postcard, 'there would be a few extra . . . but if eighteen members turned up it would be looked upon almost as a mass meeting'.[11]

The problems of the ISRP were not confined to difficulty in expanding the membership, for even in qualitative terms the level of commitment of many members was suspect. Both the reliance of the ISRP on Connolly and Connolly's views on party organisation are touched upon in a letter he wrote to the party while on a speaking tour in Britain in 1901. He noted how gratifying it was that the 'many evil prophets in Dublin saying that the movement would go slump if I left Dublin' had been wrong and that this fact proved that the ISRP was 'well able to stand on its own feet, and that its growth depended upon correct principles and not upon ones personality'. The fact that he was not 'indispensable'[12] was, he argued, a tribute to his work for the Party. Two years later Connolly, once again 'knocking the life out of' himself on a speaking tour—this time in America—had occasion to write a very different type of letter back to his Party: 'You all ought to be damned well ashamed of yourselves . . . I am ashamed, heartily ashamed of the whole gang of you.' The reason for his anger was the failure of party members to publish, in his absence, the party newspaper, subscriptions to which he was busily selling in America. In his anger he questioned party members: 'If some of you do not think the cause of the Socialist Republic worth working for, why in heavens name do you not get out of the party?' The Party, he asserted, would be 'better starting again with half a dozen men as before than be cumbered by the presence of a crowd who are only socialists because it gives them a reputation for originality'. He concluded his castigation of the party members with an undisguised threat, informing them that although in the past he had always 'opposed the idea of expelling men unless for breach of principle', he was now inclined to 'believe that such leniency was 'criminal'.[13]

Connolly's intemperate letter was a desperate response to the disorganisation in the party, caused by the alcoholic intemperance of some of the party members. While he was on a speaking tour of Britain in 1902, the ISRP had taken advantage of his absence to establish a licensed bar in the party premises. Then, while he was away on his American tour, the bar proved to be very popular with the members. However, it was extremely badly run and depleted the party's meagre financial resources. Money collected by Connolly in America for subscriptions to the party's newspaper, was used to offset the bar's losses. Given the way the ISRP tended to fall apart whenever Connolly was absent for any length of time, it is small wonder that his thoughts at this time were turned towards the question of party discipline. On his return to Ireland, he was disgusted to discover the chaotic financial position which had been allowed to develop in his absence. When he attempted to reorganise the party's finances, he was obstructed and accused of 'bossism'. Party members voted to resolve the party's financial problems by the simple expedient of refusing to pay bills or honour subscriptions to the *Workers Republic*. This was too much for Connolly. Profoundly disappointed and deeply hurt, he withdrew from the party which thereafter rapidly disintegrated.

Prior to his American tour, Connolly had been influenced by the writings of Daniel De Leon, particularly in relation to his syndicalist oriented socialist schema. On meeting De Leon, Connolly was not impressed, for reasons discussed in chapter three. He was, however, very impressed both by the size (massive by the diminutive standards of the ISRP) and the tightly disciplined organisation of the Socialist Labor Party (SLP). This admiration was reflected in an article Connolly wrote for the SLP journal, the *Weekly People*. Commenting on the 'socialist' vote in the 1902 American elections, he compared the votes polled by the Social Democratic Party with those polled by the SLP. The SLP vote, he argued, was, in contra-distinction to that of the SDP, 'the vote of an army compared with the vote of a mob'. Who, he went on to ask 'would hesitate in choosing between the support of a large mob or a small army'.[14] Manus O'Riordan has argued that Connolly's comments on the American election results stand as a refutation of Desmond Greaves's statement that Connolly 'had no conception of a political party as the general staff of a class'. O'Riordan sees Connolly's position as being 'strikingly similar to Stalin's exposition of the Leninist principle of the party as the advanced detachment of the working class and the General Staff of the proletariat'.[15] O'Riordan perhaps reads a little too much into Connolly's large mob versus small army comment, but in essence it is probably true that at this time Connolly, in the light of the failure of the ISRP which was neither a large mob nor a small army, indeed if it is not a contradiction in terms, the ISRP might be best described as a small mob—was giving very serious consideration to the issue of party organisation.

On his migration to America in 1903, he immediately joined De Leon's SLP. This was of course a fairly natural move given the close contacts he had built up with this party over a number of years, but it is significant inasmuch as he chose to join a party which he knew was rigidly centralised and held extremely severe rules on party discipline. The contrast between the ISRP and the SLP is a very marked one and Connolly's decision to join the SLP must be seen as an expression of his own perception of the type of party organisation best suited to advance the socialist cause. Carl Reeves has noted in his major biography of De Leon that many of De Leon's political concepts were 'similar to those worked out by Lenin's Bolshevik Communist Party in Russia'.[16] This is certainly evident in De Leon's theories on party organisation. As early as 1896 he was expressing the view that:

> The Modern Revolutionist, i.e. the socialist, must in the first place . . . necessarily work in organisation, with all that that implies. In this you have the first characteristic that distinguishes the revolutionist from the reformer, the reformer spurns organisation . . . no principle is superior to the movement or organisation that puts it and upholds it in the field . . . The Revolutionist recognises that the organisation that is propelled by correct principles is as the boiler that must hold the steam, or the steam will amount to nothing . . . the revolutionist will not make a distinction between the organisation and the principle; He will say 'The principle and the organisation are one'.[17]

Under De Leon's leadership, the SLP laid great stress on discipline and unity. He believed that 'unity of action' was essential in 'order to accomplish results or to promote principle'. Those who did not hang together as a body were in his opinion 'bound to hang separately'. The revolutionary must 'submit to the will of the majority' and never put himself 'above the organisation'.[18] For De Leon unity and discipline within the party were no mere abstractions: he was both vigilant and ruthless in his unceasing efforts to ensure that the political purity of the party was maintained. Commenting upon the effect this had on the SLP, Reeves noted that 'the list of resignations and expulsions at the turn of the century is almost endless. De Leon's leadership of the SLP had instituted mass expulsions within its organisation in an effort to unify the membership'. The 'watchful eye' of De Leon is said to have been 'ever trained against any mistake of what he considered opportunism'.[19]

De Leon's insistence on purging the party of any member or affiliated section which deviated from party policy was not without its critics, indeed in October 1902 when Connolly was in America under the auspices of the SLP, two of the party's earliest and most respected members, Lucien Saniel and Hugo Vogt, along with 31 other party members, issued a statement opposing the 'inquisition in the SLP'. So many members departed voluntarily or involuntarily from the party that De Leon himself somewhat facetiously remarked that 'he had to look at himself in the mirror at least once a day to find out whether he had gone with the others'.[20]

When Connolly joined the SLP in 1903, he did so in full knowledge of the party's organisation. He had been reading SLP literature for a number of years and had moreover been given the opportunity during his lecture tour in 1902 to study the party at close quarters. We can assume from this (especially in the light of his recorded comments on party organisation mentioned above) that in 1903 Connolly was in broad agreement with De Leon's concept of party organisation and was in general agreement with SLP policies. Connolly's problems within the SLP arose because he assumed, wrongly as it transpired, that disciplined constructive debate was permissible, indeed essential, within the party. However, when he attempted to initiate debate on issues which he considered important and on which he felt the SLP needed to reappraise its policies, he found himself subject to a barrage of bitter, often vindictive attacks, culminating in 1907 when De Leon publicly accused him of being a spy.[21] Connolly defended himself against all such scurrilous attacks but by 1908 he felt that his position within the SLP was no longer either tenable or worthwhile and he resigned.

The subjects which Connolly wished to discuss within the SLP and the merits of his views upon them, do not come within the scope of this chapter. What we are concerned with here is the effect of the party processes, which led to his resignation, and on his concept of party organisation. We are fortunate that this is one subject on which Connolly has left a very clear record of his thoughts. Soon after his resignation, his bitterness at the treatment he had received within the SLP was evident when he wrote that the socialist movement suffered from a surfeit of 'saviours'—an obvious reference to De Leon, who, he suggested 'would rather have a party of ten men who unquestioningly accepted their dictum . . . than a party of half a million whose component parts dared to think and act for themselves'.[22]

Connolly's negative personal experiences within the SLP led him to move towards a stance on party organisation which was theoretically suspect. Greaves has argued that Connolly at this stage failed to 'trace De Leon's dogmatism to its theoretical foundation (as Marx had done with Proudhon and Lasalle). He proposed instead of theoretical clarification the 'submergence of theoretical differences'.[23] Connolly's conception of the role and organisation of the socialist party underwent a radical transformation during his membership of the SLP—his syndicalist commitment had deepened while his views on the party had become broader but shallower. Thus in July 1908 we find him arguing that the 'political party which exists for the fight at the ballot box is primarily and essentially an agitational and destructive force, the real constructive work of the social revolution must come from an economic industrial organisation'. Up to this point in his argument Connolly was merely repeating ideas which he had held for almost a decade, but as he continued his discussion, a major change in his thinking was intimated. This change was clearly evident when he wrote that since the 'political party was not to accomplish the revolution but only to lead the attack upon the political citadel of capitalism, there no longer existed the same danger of the unclearness of its membership, nor compelling necessity for insisting upon its purification'. Translating his theoretical views into concrete terms, Connolly went on to suggest that there would evolve as the 'fighting army of the workers':

> One Socialist Party embracing all shades and conceptions of political thought. One Socialist Industrial Organisation drilling the working class for the supreme mission of their class—the establishment of the Workers Republic. Between these two organisations—the advance guard and the main army of Labour—there should be no war and no endorsement.[24]

In the above extract Connolly retained a commitment to the conception of the party as the 'advance guard', but only within the context of a socialist party which he described as accepting the 'unclearness of its membership', by accepting this he would appear to be coming very close to recommending that the blind should lead the blind. In an article in *The Harp* entitled 'Political Action' Connolly discussed in detail the question of party organisation. There were, he wrote, 'two distinct and opposing ideas as to how best to build a political party to do the political work of socialism'. He went on to describe those two ideas thus:

1. That the work of the Social Revolution can only be accomplished by men and women with a clear understanding of the economics of capitalism, and therefore a clear and definite program is the first essential, and in the interest of maintaining that definite program of the party it is imperative to expel out of the said party all speakers, writers, or even members who are not in the strictest harmony with its clean cut principles, and
2. That the work of the Social Revolution depends in the last analysis upon the growth of class-consciousness amongst the working class, that therefore the chief task of a socialist political party is to educate and direct that class consciousness along correct lines, that in order to do so allowance must continually be made for the gradual nature of its development, and for the stages thereof, that therefore it must be made possible for all who have accepted the central principles of common ownership to become members of the party, irrespective of their knowledge or lack of knowledge of economics, and that the development of the political struggle of the socialist movement must be depended upon the clear minds of the members rather than any process of weeding out.

According to Connolly, the first of those ideas led to 'Dictat and despotism', whilst the second suffered from the tendency to 'compromise for the sake of getting votes'. The ideal, he states, might be a party which 'embraces both schools of thought and while not concealing their utter divergence provides in press and platform a means of discussion, as members, of the things that divide them, and insists that all must recognise the voice of the majority'.[25]

By June 1909 Connolly had moved even further away from the concept of the party as the advance guard of revolution. Writing to J. Carstairs Matheson (a leader in the Scottish SLP), and commenting on the work done by De Leon, Matheson and himself, Connolly noted that while their position had been 'absolutely sound in theory' and might have been 'sound in practice if adopted by men of large outlook', its 'practical immediate effects' had been the 'generation of a number of sectarians, narrow minded doctrinaires, who have erected socialism into a cult with formulas which one must observe or be damned'. From this Connolly concluded that their position needed 'the corrective of association with socialists of a less advanced type'. In practical terms this meant that Connolly had come to see that their 'proper position' was in the 'general socialist, or rather labour movement as friendly critics and helpers, rather than in a separate organisation as hostile critics and enemies'. Connolly had not come to these conclusions easily, indeed he described the whole process as having been 'a bitter lesson to learn'.[26]

On his return to Ireland in 1910, Connolly joined and very quickly assumed the leadership of the Socialist Party of Ireland (this party merged with four Belfast branches of the Independent Labour Party and the Belfast branch of the British Socialist Party into a new party called the Independent Labour Party of Ireland, after a short time it reverted to the title Socialist Party of Ireland). Connolly was really more committed to the Irish Transport and General Workers Union and its military arm, the Irish Citizen Army, than he was to the SPI. The ITGWU and the ICA were the primary revolutionary vehicles, the SPI was of secondary importance. Levenson has recorded an incident which highlights not only the failure of the SPI to prosper but also gives some insight into Connolly's displacement of the party as the primary revolutionary vehicle. He writes that during a visit to Cork in 1915 Connolly:

> booked a hall for a meeting of the Independent Labour Party of Ireland. The party was now a dying body, in part absorbed by the Labour Party proper; in part gone pacifist as a protest against the war. When Connolly arrived for the meeting, he found the door locked and nobody to be seen. Apparently the members had not been notified or thought the meeting not worth attending. When a member finally showed, apologising profusely for the mischance, Connolly answered quietly, 'It's all right, I'm used to that.' He was right on both counts, such rebuffs had happened hundreds of times before and he had become accustomed to them.[27]

Some political commentators have compared Connolly's views on the 'party' with those held by Lenin. Ransom and Edwards for instance detect a similarity of thought underlying what at first might appear to be very divergent modes of thought. Thus we find them writing that whilst 'Lenin's party of a new type is the vanguard of the proletariat, the guardian of revolutionary consciousness and the material creator of the new order,' for Connolly 'these tasks will be discharged by the OBU—the union of a new type . . . the OBU is thus the vehicle of revolutionary practice.[28] The comment is accurate as far as it goes; one can indeed argue that Connolly's OBU—the ITGWU with its military arm the ICA—did in fact form a vanguard of the proletariat under his leadership.

Connolly's investment of the ITGWU and ICA with the primary revolutionary roles and the consequent relegation of the SPI to an ambiguous but certainly secondary role had important implications for the Irish socialist movement. His move away from the concept of a vanguard type party—uncompromising, exclusive, rigidly intolerant—towards a belief that there was 'unity in diversity'[29] and thus in a broader but less clearly directed and disciplined party, was to have important consequences after his death. In a later chapter we shall examine the influence which Connolly's views on party organisation exerted on the Irish left in the post-Rising years and the effect this influence had on the political development of the Irish socialist movement.

CHAPTER 6

Political Violence and Insurrection

To effect its emancipation labour must re-organise society on the basis of labour. This cannot be done while the forces of government are in the hands of the rich, therefore governing power must be wrested from the hands of the rich, *peaceably if possible, forcibly if necessary*.

James Connolly, September 1898.[1]

Freedom, in its fullest and only real sense, can only come by national action. The steps to be taken here, as elsewhere are: . . . *peaceably if possible, forcibly if necessary*, to conquer the powers and material resources of national government, so that the working—class in possession of those powers may proceed to enforce its will upon society.

James Connolly, March 1908.[2]

From our earliest declaration of policy in Dublin in 1896 the editor of this paper has held to the dictum that our ends should be secured '*peacefully if possible, forcibly if necessary*'.

James Connolly, January 1916.[3]

THE FIRST AND perhaps one of the most important points which needs to be considered in discussing Connolly's attitude to political violence and insurrection is the influence which his social background exerted. Being Scots born, of Irish descent, working-class and ghetto reared, Connolly was no stranger either to violence (the Grassmarket area in which he grew up is to this day a very rough area—in Connolly's day it was very much worse) or to insurrectionary traditions. During his youth in Edinburgh Connolly was certainly influenced by the Irish nationalist sentiment within the Irish community in Edinburgh. In a rare personal comment in 1913, he recalled that 'when I was in my green and callow youth the Irish Land League was in full swing, and the literature of that revolutionary Irish organisation was the mental pabulum upon which I was nourished'.[4] It is said that Connolly was introduced to Irish nationalism by an uncle who was 'one of the old guard of the Fenian movement'.[5] The story of an early contact with the Fenian insurrectionary movement is not altogether impossible as it is known that in 1884

58

the Irish Republican Brotherhood (IRB) had a membership of some 3,000 in Scotland.[6] Whether or not Connolly had personal contact, certainly he could not fail to be aware of Fenian activities, particularly the numerous bombing attacks in Britain in the 1880s (including a number in Glasgow) and the Phoenix Park murders.[7] It is also worth noting that even outside the somewhat limited confines of the Irish community there existed nationalist—Scottish nationalist sentiments and strong if somewhat romanticaly inclined Jacobite sympathies. Although of secondary importance in Connolly's development, the rebellious Scottish nationalist, Jacobite and to a lesser extent Jacobin traditions may well have exerted an influence on his views in regards to the legitimacy of armed struggle.[8]

At the age of fourteen Connolly was forced by economic circumstances to join the army, falsifying both his name and his age in the process.[9] He was already sympathetic to Irish nationalism when he enlisted, and although he was very reticent about his army service in later years, enlistment in the British army was so common among the Irish and Irish-descended working class that it implied no apostasy of Irish nationalist sentiments.[10] Connolly served as a private in the Royal Scots Regiment for almost seven years—the impressionable and formative years of his adolescence and early manhood. He deserted from his regiment four months prior to the completion of his seven year enlistment period when he discovered that the regiment was to be shipped overseas. His years in the army left him with an extreme distaste for the brutalising aspects of military service in general and the British Army in particular, but also with a healthy respect for the power and efficiency of the Army. The effect of Connolly's army service on his intellectual development is clearly evident in his later writings, which are replete with military terminology and analogies.

After his desertion from the army in 1889, Connolly quickly involved himself in the socialist movement in Edinburgh. It is worth noting in this context that whilst the vast majority of socialists in Edinburgh, and indeed in the British socialist movement as a whole, envisaged a socialist victory through the ballot box, Edinburgh had at least one prominent socialist who was a physical force man—an insurrectionist. Leo Melliet, a leader in the Edinburgh branch of the Social Democratic Federation (SDF) was a political refugee, having been a prominent Communard in 1871.[11] Melliet, who is reported to have been an excellent and very rousing speaker, told a meeting held in Edinburgh in 1889 to commemorate the Commune, that 'without the shedding of blood there is no social salvation'.[12] Melliet's statement was echoed by Connolly in 1915 when he wrote that we 'recognise that of us as of mankind before Calvary it may truly be said: "Without the shedding of blood there is no Redemption".'[13] Greaves, one of Connolly's principal biographers, credits Melliet with being a significant influence on Connolly.[14] Certainly Connolly held the Paris Commune in extremely high regard throughout his life. Commenting in 1899 on an article in the *Daily Nation* which had described Filippino insurgents as being 'almost as degraded as the wretches who formed the provisional government for Paris during the Commune of 1871', Connolly wrote in part: 'The Commune, if it had been successful would have inaugurated the reign of real freedom the world over—it would have meant the emancipation of the working class . . . long live the Commune! If the Filippinos are akin to the members of the Commune may their shadows never grow less!'[15] Indeed, an annual celebration of the Commune was an important fixture in Connolly's socialist calendar of events.[16]

When Connolly arrived in Ireland in 1896 and founded the ISRP, he was (at least publicly) committed to the proposition that 'the conquest by the Social Democracy of political power in Parliament, and on all public bodies in Ireland is the readiest and most effective means whereby the revolutionary forces may be organised and disciplined to attain that end'—the end being of course the creation of the Irish socialist republic.[17] Less than a year later, however, he openly discussed the circumstances in which he considered socialists should resort to force. Arguing from the premise that socialist republicans 'neither exalt it into a principal nor repudiate it as something not to be thought of,' he went on to specify circumstances where the 'party of progress' had won over the majority of the people to its revolutionary conception of society and yet still had its 'way to freedom barred by the stubborn greed of the possessing class entrenched behind the barriers of law and order'. Having reached this stage and having 'exhausted all the peaceful means at its disposal', the revolutionary party was then justified in 'taking steps to assume the powers of government, and in using the weapons of force to dislodge the usurping class of government in possession'. Connolly concludes his article by suggesting that for socialists 'the question of force is of very minor importance', the question of real importance being 'the principles upon which is based the movement that may or may not need the use of force to realise its object'.[18]

It is clear that when Connolly wrote the above, he envisaged the possibility perhaps even the likelihood of a non-violent transition to a socialist society—this was always his ideal. Violence was to be used only as a last resort and subject to stringent conditions. It was only justified in circumstances wherein a clearly mandated, democratic demand for socialism by the people was thwarted by the forces of capitalism. Connolly's commitment to a peaceful democratic path to socialism, which I would suggest was never particularly deep, was shaken by the onset of the Boer War. Reflecting on this war at the start of the hostilities Connolly concluded:

> If we see a small section of the possessing class prepared to launch two nations into war, to shed oceans of blood and spend millions of treasure in order to maintain intact a small portion of their privileges, how can we expect the entire propertied class to abstain from using the same weapons and submit peacefully when called upon to yield up forever all their privileges? Let the working class democracy of Ireland note that lesson and whilst working peacefully while they may, keep constantly before their minds the truth that the capitalist class is a beast of prey and cannot be moralised, converted, or conciliated, but must be extirpated.[19]

The Boer war forced Connolly to question the possibility of a completely non-violent socialist revolution. There is in fact an account—perhaps somewhat suspect—which claims that Connolly tried to convince the Sinn Fein leader Arthur Griffith that the war was an opportunity to stage an uprising and that a number of strongpoints in Dublin should be occupied and an Irish Republic proclaimed.[20] Whilst this story is certainly lacking in hard evidence, some of Connolly's articles at this time tend to give credence to the suggestion that his mind was focussing on violent revolution. For example in November 1899 he wrote that the war was 'the beginning of the end' of the British Empire and exulted in the fact that the 'Boers had pricked the bubble of England's fighting reputation'. The weakness of the Empire, he argued, was obvious to the whole world and his advice to the enemies of Empire was straight forward: 'Have at her, then, everywhere and always and in every manner.'[21] In this aggressive frame of mind, he had no hesitation in proclaiming his pro-Boer, embryonic revolutionary—defeatist attitude to the war. He would, he stated, 'welcome the humiliation of the British arms in any of the conflicts in which it is at present engaged, or with which it has recently been menaced'.[22]

Connolly, then, even during what may be termed his democratic socialist years, always held physical force in reserve. He was never at any stage a pacifist; armed struggle always held a place in his socialist agenda.[23] What we must now examine is the process whereby armed struggle was transformed in his thinking from being an option of last resort to the primary vehicle for creating the socialist republic. This will be done by focussing on a few critical events—the 1913 Dublin Lock-out, the partition debate in 1914 and the outbreak of World War—and assessing how they affected Connolly's attitude towards armed struggle. It is, I would suggest, of central importance to bear in mind that Connolly's vision of a democratic socialist victory had shown no real signs of coming to fruition. The socialists in Ireland had made very little impact at the polls and their propaganda had met with only very limited success. Connolly was not a man noted for his patience—and accordingly he sought new avenues for socialist advancement, syndicalism, and, ultimately, armed uprising.

As a socialist agitator and labour leader, Connolly had no hesitation in placing himself at the front in any confrontation which arose in the course of the struggle. He was no stranger to political brawls,[24] police batons[25] or the prison cell.[26] Connolly's road to the 1916 rebellion was firmly established during the 1913 Dublin Lockout. This industrial struggle, and more particularly the violence which arose during its course, led to the founding of the Irish Citizen Army. The ICA, an organisation which Connolly played a major part in establishing and was soon to lead, was initially a defence force designed simply to protect the workers during the lockout; but in the wake of the ITGWU's defeat and the great bitterness which it engendered, Connolly invested the ICA with a much more constructive and aggressive role. Discussing the importance and objectives of the ICA in October 1915, Connolly noted that 'an armed organisation of the Irish working class is a phenomenon in Ireland'. In the past the Irish workers had always 'fought as part of the armies led by their masters, never as members of an army officered, trained and inspired by men of their own class'. This situation, he concluded, had changed for 'now with arms in their hands they propose to steer their own course, to carve their own future'.[27]

The ICA became for Connolly a revolutionary—perhaps *the* revolutionary—vehicle, an organisation which while working in tandem with organisations which shared some of its objectives, remained independent and unswervingly committed to its own goals. Thus although Connolly was willing to pledge that the ICA would 'co-operate in any forward movement', he took pains to warn that the 'moment that forward movement ceases, it reserves to itself the right to step out of alignment and advance by itself if needs be' in pursuit of its 'effort to plant the banner of freedom one reach further towards its goal'.[28] The Dublin Lockout and its aftermath led Connolly into assuming the role of military leader, a role which from all accounts he relished. From this time on his commitment to democratic transition to socialism was increasingly superceded by a revolutionary strategy of physical force.

Connolly was by no means alone in his move towards an acceptance of violence in post-lockout Ireland. Thomas Johnson, an important and generally rather moderate socialist, moved the following motion at the Irish Trade Union Congress and Labour Party National executive in 1914:

> That the dominant political parties in Ireland having for their own purposes raised and armed volunteer forces in their respective spheres of influence, we advise all workers in either camps to retain whatever arms they may become possessed of, and then be in a position to prevent any recurrence of such scenes as took place in industrial warfare in Belfast in 1907 and in Dublin in 1913, when the arms of the crown were used to terrorise the workers, and deprive them of their civil rights.[29]

The motion was seconded by W. O'Brien and passed by the meeting. It is worth noting that in Britain, at least, two attempts were made to organise ICA—type forces. In 1912 a 'strikers' police' of some three hundred men was organised by striking dockers at Grave and Tilbury during the National Dock strike[30] and in 1913 Sylvia Pankhurst tried to establish a 'People's Army'.[31] Connolly was well aware of these contemporary developments, both of which predated the ICA and may well have drawn inspiration and support from their example.[32]

Connolly's response to the proposal to partition Ireland gives a clear indication of his increasing commitment to physical force. Commenting on the proposal, he stated bluntly that 'to it labour should give the bitterest opposition, against it labour in Ulster should fight even to the death if necessary as our fathers fought before us'.[33] Clearly, when he wrote this in March 1914 he was in a fighting mood. It was in this frame of mind that he faced the challenge of world war, a challenge which found most of the European socialist Leaders wanting. An eminent Irish historian has written that from the moment war broke out and Connolly 'realised that all the fraternal declarations of international socialism had been powerless to stop it, [he] bent all his considerable powers of persuasion and organisation towards the Irish insurrection.[34] There is a great deal of truth in this assessment. Connolly was distraught at the failure of the European socialists to oppose the war. It is significant that one of his first actions on the outbreak of war was to ask Cathal O'Shannon to put him in touch with the IRB.[35] Connolly's stand on the war, a stand which has frequently been compared with Lenin's, was unequivocal: he opposed the war totally and with passion, taking what can be termed a revolutionary defeatist position; to the extent that he involved both himself and his daughter Nora in espionage activities in favour of Germany.[36] Connolly's anti-war writings are amongst the most passionate he ever penned. Starting from the basic premise that the war was 'the most fearful crime of the centuries',[37] he let flow a torrent of vitriolic anti-war propaganda. Writing in 1914, he argued that 'if the working class soldiers had but the moral courage to say to the diplomats that they would not march against their brothers across the frontiers . . . there would be no war'.[38] Connolly addressed his anti-war propaganda almost exclusively to a working class audience—a group who, to his dismay, were enlisting in vast numbers. Thus we find him asserting that 'as an Irish worker I owe a duty to our class counting no allegiance to the Empire', and advising his readers that if they were 'itching for a rifle, itching to fight, have a country of your own; better to fight for your own country than for the robber Empire'.[39] As the full extent of the slaughter in France became apparent, Connolly's response was unambiguous: 'no insurrection of the working class, no general uprising of the forces of labour' could, he argued, lead to a 'greater slaughter of socialists than will their participation as soldiers in the campaigns of their respective countries'.[40]

As a realist Connolly was fully aware of the unlikelihood of any immediate military success through an armed uprising. This is clearly shown when he writes:

> We cannot draw upon the future for a draft to pay our present duties. There is no moratorium to postpone the payment the socialists owe to the cause. Paid it may be in martyrdom, but a few hundred such martyrdoms would be but a small price to pay to avert the slaughter of hundreds of thousands.[41]

To him the war was both a criminal tragedy and an opportunity. Britain's weakness caused by the war was Ireland's (and, more importantly, socialism's) opportunity. From early in the war he dedicated himself to promoting and leading an armed uprising. Addressing an ITGWU meeting in 1914, he stated: 'you have been told that you are not strong, that you have no rifles'. But revolutions, he argued, 'do not start with rifles: start first and get your rifles after'. He then went on to assert that 'our curse is our belief in our weakness. We are not weak, we are strong. Make up your mind to strike before our opportunity goes.'[42]

From 1913 onwards Connolly's commitment to armed struggle had developed rapidly, changing from a defenslve to an aggressive policy in the process. An incident an October 1915 provides a good example of his attitude and tactics. During a strike involving the ITGWU and the City of Dublin Steam Packet Co., the police acted in an aggressive manner towards union pickets. Connolly solved this problem when he 'ordered out a squad of the Citizen Army men to the number of eight or ten, to march down to the quays fully equipped with rifles and bayonets, to act as an armed picket at the shipping office'. It is reported that 'the police ceased to interfere and the dispute was quickly settled.'[43]

Despite his enthusiasm for aggressive, indeed militaristic, tactics, Connolly was under no illusions as to what such a policy entailed. He refused to sanctify warfare as being in any sense enobling:

> there is no such thing as humane or civilised war! War may be forced upon a subject race or subject class to put an end to subjection of race, of class, or sex. When so waged it must be waged thoroughly and relentlessly, but with no delusions as to its elevating nature, or civilising methods.[44]

He justified his abandonment of non-violent political struggle by pointing to the violence of the times. He believed that he was 'living in an era of ruthless blood and iron' and reflected that 'in any one day of battle in the Dardanelles there are more lives lost than in all nine months of the Reign of Terror.' Those facts led him to conclude that 'should the day ever come when revolutionary leaders are prepared to sacrifice the lives of those under them as recklessly as the ruling class do in every war, there will not be a throne or despotic Government left in the world'.[45]

Connolly's participation in the Easter uprising in 1916 was the logical—one might argue the inevitable—outcome of his changed perception on the role of violence in the struggle for socialism. That violence was now an integral part of his revolutionary socialism and that the Easter Rising was in itself merely a stage in this struggle is made abundantly clear in a speech he made to the ICA a few days before the rising: 'the odds are a thousand to one against us', he told them, 'but in the event of victory, hold on to your rifles, as those with whom we are fighting may stop before our goal is reached. We are out for economic as well as political liberty. Hold on to your rifles.'[46]

Before concluding this chapter, it is worth turning to a brief examination of how Connolly's views on violence and insurrection compared with those dominant figures of revolutionary socialism—Marx, Engels and Lenin. In Marx and Engels' seminal *Manifesto of the Communist Party*, the final paragraph reads in part: 'Communists disdain to conceal their views and aims. They openly declare that their ends can be attained only by forcible overthrow of all existing social conditions.'[47] Over two decades after this was written, Marx criticised the Paris Commune for being unwilling to start a civil war in France and told the Congress of the International that:

> We must make clear to the governments, we know that you are the armed power that is directed against the proletariat; we will proceed against you by peaceful means where that is possible and arms when it is necessary.[48]

Engels has often been cited as having renounced armed struggle in favour of a 'peaceful transition to Socialism'. His last completed piece of writing, an introduction written in 1895 to a new edition of Marx's *The Class Struggles in France 1848 to 1850* has been used to support this contention. It has been established, however, that key passages of Engels' introduction were deleted by the publishers, giving the work a false complexion. In reference to armed struggle in one deleted section, Engels poses the question, 'Does that mean that in future the street fight will play no further role?' and goes on to answer:

> Certainly not. It only means that conditions since 1848 have become far more unfavourable for civil fights, far more favourable for the military. A future street fight can therefore only be victorious when this unfavourable situation is compensated by other factors.[49]

The Second International (1889–1914) debated the use of force at great length during its congresses and paid particular attention to the correct strategy for combating war. A crucial debate took place at the Stuttgart Congress in 1907. Hervé, a member of the French delegation, presented a resolution demanding that the Congress answer any declaration of war with 'the military strike and with insurrection'.[50] Hervé's motion met with little support and the motion eventually passed was a well meaning but rather vague and unspecific one put up by Bebel, with amendments by Lenin and Rosa Luxemburg. This motion concluded with the statement that it was the duty of the working class, if war should break out, to make every effort to end it, and if this failed to make use of the economic and political crisis created by the war 'to stir up the deepest strata of the people and precipitate the fall of capitalist domination'.[51] Although the International met again in 1910, 1912 and 1914, it never managed to come to any clearer or more effective agreement on the actions to be taken by socialists in the event of war. Thus at the outbreak of war in 1914 the International disintegrated.

Lenin's views on insurrection and his analysis of the correct socialist strategy in relation to World War I were in many respects similar to Connolly's. In a letter written in 1917, Lenin stated that one of the most 'vicious and probably most widespread distortions of Marxism resorted to by the dominant "socialist" parties is the opportunist lie that preparation for insurrection, and generally the treatment of insurrection as an art, is Blanquism'.[52] Given this viewpoint, it is not surprising that Lenin castigated those socialists who questioned Connolly's participation in the Easter Rising:

> to imagine that social revolution is *conceivable* without revolts, by small nations in the colonies and in Europe, without the revolutionary outbursts of a section of the petty bourgeoisie *with* all its prejudices, without a movement of politically non-conscious proletarian and semi-proletarian masses against Landlords, Church, monarchies, national and other oppression—to imagine that means *repudiating social revolution* . . . whoever expects a pure social revolution will *never* live to see it. Such a person pays lip-service to revolution without understanding what revolution really is.'[53]

That Lenin's response to World War I was very similar to Connolly's is shown by his assertion that: 'The only correct proletarian slogan is to transform the present imperialist war into a civil war . . . these are the only kind of tactics that will be truly revolutionary.'[54]

While having little taste for violence himself, Connolly was a product of violent social conditions. Moreover, he inherited a historical tradition of violent rebellion. These factors, when combined with his total commitment to socialist revolution, his intense hatred of capitalism and all its doings, and the violent and tragic nature of his times, proved an explosive mixture. Connolly was not by nature a particularly violent man, but nor was he in any way shy of violence—he was in fact a man who dedicated his life to a vision of a better world, a vision which in his own words he was willing to secure 'peacefully if possible, forcibly if necessary'. In the last few years of his life Connolly had quite simply decided that force was indeed necessary to achieve his goal.

CHAPTER 7

Revolution

The only difference that ever existed between the soulless slave and the active revolutionist was, that the first denied the opportunity when it arose, while the latter availed himself of it.

James Connolly 1898.[1]

Against the shamelessly vile methods of the politician there is but one effective weapon—the daring appeal of the Revolutionist.

James Connolly 1914.[2]

IN HIS SPEECH at Marx's graveside in 1883 Engels described Marx as being 'before all else a revolutionist'.[3] Like Marx, Connolly is best understood as being before all else a revolutionist. In 1914, at the completion of a lecture on street fighting to Irish Volunteer officers, he was asked how he had come to know so much of military and revolutionary matters. His response was short and memorable—'you forget that my business is Revolution'.[4] Connolly's business was indeed revolution. If we forget, or fail to fully appreciate this central fact, our understanding of the man and his work will be at best incomplete and at worst fallacious. It is important to note right at the outset that in relation to Connolly the term revolutionist implies no nihilism, lust for violence, or romantic indulgence— Connolly's commitment to revolution was the sober, constructive, intellectually coherent result of his Marxian socialism.

Lenin noted that 'the Marxist is the first to see the approach of a revolutionary period, and already begins to rouse the people and to sound the tocsin while the Philistines are still wrapt in slavish slumber.'[5] Connolly certainly fitted Lenin's description. Arthur MacManus, a leading Scottish socialist who had known Connolly since his early years in the Scottish Socialist Federation (SSF) described him as 'the one socialist that he had ever met who judged every public situation or political crisis with an eye upon revolutionary possibilities'.[6]

This emphasis on practicality was established early. Writing in 1900 in response to an article in the 'Capitalist Press' which praised the ITUC for being a 'practical body', Connolly noted that 'in the phraseology of the master class and its prostitute pressmen the trade unionist who is not a socialist is more practical than he who is'. When used in this way, Connolly reflected that the

67

description 'practical' was in fact a characteristic of slaves and soulless serfs. He went on to describe in some detail his own view of what was 'practical' and in the process provided us with a clear statement both of his commitment to revolution and his battle plan for bringing it about:

> Revolution is never practical—until the hour of Revolution strikes. *THEN* it alone is practical, and all the efforts of the conservatives and compromisers become the most visionary and futile of human imaginings. For that hour let us work, think and hope. For that hour let us pawn our present ease in hopes of a glorious redemption: For that hour let us prepare the hosts of labour with intelligence sufficient to laugh at the nostrums dubbed practical by our slave-lords—practical for the perpetuation of our slavery: For the supreme crisis of human history let us watch like sentinels with weapons ever at the ready.[7]

Connolly's theory of Revolution was pragmatic. Levenson quotes a conversation Connolly had with some comrades in Liverpool in 1915. The discussion revolved around the possibility of making a revolution in Ireland, asked 'But is the time ripe?', he replied, 'If you succeed, the time is ripe. If not, then it is not ripe.'[8] Connolly believed that 'dash and recklessness'[9] were essential characteristics of the true revolutionary. Writing in 1916 he noted that 'the revolutionists of the past have ever been adventurous, else they would never have been revolutionists.'[10] In a similar vein, commenting on the revolutionary possibilities of the outbreak of war in 1914, he stated that 'different occasions require different policies, you cannot legalise revolutionary actions . . . audacity alone can command success in a crisis like this.'[11]

There was a well-established division in the international socialist movement between those who emphasised the seizure of power like Blanqui, and those who insisted on patience, like Bernstein, Jaures and Millerand. Connolly clearly placed himself in the first camp. He was well aware of the debates which raged within the 1st and 2nd Internationals—only the ISRP delegates and the Bulgarians voted unanimously against Millerand at the International Socialist Congress which met in Paris in 1900—but there is no evidence to suggest that the Millerand debate or any other debate within international socialism played a formative role in the development of his revolutionary outlook. Rather, his revolutionary perspective arose from his instinctive, visceral hatred of capitalism.

As a 'practical' revolutionary socialist, Connolly's slogan was 'Less philosophising and more fighting'.[12] For him the term fighting was no euphemism. Writing in 1914, he noted: 'to my mind an agitation to attain a political or economic end must rest upon an implied willingness and ability to use force. Without that it is mere wind and attitudinising'.[13] Connolly's experience in the labour movement—the 'class war' had convinced him that 'fighting spirit is of more importance than the creation of a theoretically perfect organisation'.[14] He had no intention of dissipating his energies in doctrinal disputes or an unending series of minor defensive actions against his class enemies. Believing as he did that 'a revolutionist who surrenders the initiative to the enemy is already defeated before a blow is struck',[15] he dedicated himself to attacking his enemies with whatever force he could muster.

Connolly's acceptance of the fact that violent revolution was the only way to achieve the goal of a socialist society dates back at least as far as the Boer War. The outbreak of this war had led him to conclude that the 'master class' would never peacefully give up its class privileges and that such privileges would have to be wrested from them by force.[16] His experiences of violence directed against workers during industrial disputes confirmed his assessment. In his pamphlet *Labour, Nationality and Religion* (1910), he noted that 'when the capitalists kill us so rapidly for the sake of a few extra pence . . . it would be suicidal to expect them to hesitate to slaughter us wholesale when their very existence as parasites was at stake.'[17]

Neither the actual violence inflicted upon workers during industrial disputes— industrial warfare, in his own terminology—nor the potential, reserve violence which the capitalist class controlled through its control of the State and its armed forces (the extent of whose power Connolly, as an ex-soldier, was well aware) daunted Connolly. He believed that the working class, making up, as it did, an overwhelming majority of the population, was physically capable of overthrowing the forces of the capitalist state. Its weakness was psychological, its lack of confidence in its own strength and its aversion to violence. Writing some six months before the Easter Rising, Connolly stated the problem and bluntly expressed his solution to it when he wrote that:

> Our rulers reign by virtue of their readiness to destroy human life in order to reign: their reign will end on the day their discontented subjects care as little for the destruction of human life as they do . . . Our rulers will stop at nothing to attain their ends. They will continue to rule and rob until confronted by men who will stop at nothing to overthrow them.[18]

Connolly's favourite quotation was the French revolutionary Camille Desmoulin's aphorism 'The great appear great to us only because we are on our knees: Let us rise!'[19] He referred to Desmoulin's simple insight and injunction time and time again throughout his career—he placed the quotation at the head of the initial programme of the ISRP in 1896—and often had it emblazoned across the top of the numerous socialist papers he edited throughout the following years. Connolly was clearly attracted both emotionally and intellectually by Desmoulin's insight, recognising it as both a truism and a battle call. The certainty that victory was there for the taking, that the working class had only to recognise their own strength and in so doing expose the real weakness of their class enemies, was a central and unshakeable component of his revolutionary socialism. In his last words to his eldest daughter on the eve of his execution, Connolly echoed Desmoulin's words when he told her 'we shall rise again'.[20]

Having noted Connolly's confidence and the unquenchable optimism which underpinned his revolutionary fervour, we should also note the hardheaded realistic aspect of his revolutionism. It is not for nothing that one of Connolly's most astute biographers, Desmond Ryan, has applied to Connolly Keat's description of the true poet, 'Fire in the heart, and ice in the brain'.[21] Connolly had no illusions about insurrectionary prospects in Ireland. Some months before the uprising he referred to 'that leap in the dark which all men take who plunge into insurrection' and went on to state that it should be well understood that 'an insurrection is always doubtful, a thousand to one chance always exists in favour of the established order and against the insurgents.'[22] In his view a true revolutionist did not waste time pondering the odds, did not sit back and wait for ideal conditions to arise; his task was to seize any and every opportunity, however slim. In 1914 he expressed his position clearly when he noted that socialists could not avoid facing risks for the sake of 'the cause'.[23] It was thus the socialists' 'duty' to risk all for the cause—even if the venture appeared hopeless. For Connolly, however, despite his ability to realistically assess the military aspects of insurrection, there always existed a hope, a faith that once the initial revolutionary action had been taken, the revolutionary momentum would create new possibilities. Writing as early as 1902 on this point, he commented: 'I believe firmly that the revolutionary socialist movement will always be numerically weak until the hour of revolution arrives and then it will be as easy to get adherents by the thousands as it is now to get single individuals.'[24] In both politics and military affairs Connolly supported the old adage that 'attack is ever the best defence'. He believed that 'aggressive action will convert the waverers better than a thousand speeches, or a hundred proclamations.'[25]

The Irish labour movement was in Connolly's view qualitatively different from—in fact, superior to—the labour movements in Ulster and England. In 1914 he noted that in Ulster the labour movement's 'standpoint and intellectual bias has ever been towards the Fabian opportunism of England, while the Irish Socialists of Catholic training have been most attracted by the Revolutionary Social Democracy of the Continent of Europe'.[26] There is clearly a certain element of wishful thinking in Connolly's assessment. He wanted, and perhaps needed, to believe in the revolutionary potential of Irish labour; it was only through the inspiration of his revolutionary socialist faith that he found the reserves of strength and endurance to meet the intense demands made on him as a labour leader. The revolutionary component of Irish labour validated Connolly's work —indeed his whole life struggle. Connolly was no careerist, the life of a politician or labour organiser was not for him an end in itself; and he always insisted that if the labour and socialist movement in Ireland is not revolutionary it is nothing and of no consequence'.[27] He was able to undertake the day-to-day demands, the compromises, the deals involved in the activities of a labour organiser without dimming the fire of his revolutionary fervour only through his steadfast unshakeable belief in Irish labour's revolutionary potential.

Capitalism itself was recognised by Connolly as the real recruiting-ground of the revolution. Writing in 1910 in response to a 'flamboyant orator of Irish Capitalism' who had said that 'England has sown dragon's teeth and they have sprung up armed men,' Connolly noted that Irish socialists could with justice state that as 'Capitalism has sown poverty, disease and oppression among our Irish race so it will spring up a crop of working class revolutionists armed with a holy hatred of all its institutions'.[28] A 'holy hatred' of capitalism was certainly a quality which he himself possessed in great abundance—it is perhaps this hatred which more than any other single factor sets him apart from most of his fellow labour leaders. The intensity of Connolly's hatred of capitalism ensured that his aggressive revolutionary impetus never slackened. Thus it was that Connolly retained a clarity and urgency of revolutionary commitment that few contemporary socialists would have been capable of recognising, let alone acting upon. Connolly's appreciation of the relative merits of words and deeds, was encapsulated in his blunt assertion: 'how beggarly appear words before the defiant deed.'[29]

Socialism and socialist revolution were therefore the central and overriding concerns of Connolly's life. The depth and indeed ruthlessness—some would say fanaticism—of Connolly's revolutionary socialist was not lost on his contemporaries. Patrick Pearse (President of the Provisional Government of the Irish Republic proclaimed in 1916) who had an amicable and respectful relationship with Connolly was under no illusions as to the type of man he was dealing with. Speaking in December 1915, he commented that Connolly 'will never be satisfied until he goads us into action, and then he will think most of us too moderate, and want to guillotine the half of us. I can see him setting up a guillotine . . . For Hobson and MacNeill in particular. They are poles apart.'[30]

In conclusion I would suggest that an understanding of Connolly must centre upon the fact that he subordinated every aspect of his life—both personal and political, to his goal of socialist revolution. When this is understood, his whole career can be recognised as a calculated and undeviating drive towards one tangible, non-negotiable objective. Connolly's political and trade union activities, his attitude to nationalism, religion and the women's movement were in large part shaped by his analysis of their revolutionary—or, in the case of religion, counter-revolutionary—potential. Believing, as he did, that 'the true revolutionist should ever . . . have called into action . . . the entire sum of all the forces and factors of social and political discontent'.[31] Connolly was willing, indeed eager, to advance 'the cause' by any and every means at his disposal. He was in short a calculating political opportunist—a professional revolutionist. His political legacy to Irish socialists was apparently straightforward, centering as it did upon total commitment to socialist revolution, taking advantage of any and every facet of Irish social and political life which could be of any advantage to 'the cause' and using sheer audacity and courage—'dash and desperation'[32]—to create and seize the revolutionary movement. In practice, however, his legacy was, as we shall see in later chapters, complex and fraught with difficulties and dangers. To follow the revolutionary course of action plotted by Connolly, Irish socialists would have required great political skills and judgement backed up by revolutionary courage and fervour. They would also have to accept, and this is perhaps the most critically important point we have to constantly bear in mind, Connolly's injunction that Irish workers should 'accept help from every direction but trust only in yourselves'.[33]

CHAPTER 8

Easter 1916—'A Terrible Beauty'

We know their dream; enough
To know they dreamed and are dead,
And what if excess of love
Bewildered them till they died?
I write it out in verse—
MacDonagh and MacBride,
and Connolly and Pearse,
Now and in time to be,
Wherever green is worn,
Are changed, changed utterly:
A terrible beauty is born.

W.B.Yeats, 'Easter 1916'

Ireland is a country which teaches us that violence is never a true indication of a revolutionary state of mind.

Maurice Goldring.[1]

'A TERRIBLE BEAUTY' was indeed 'born' in the streets of Dublin during
Easter week 1916. The birth of this terrible beauty can be described and analysed
in purely military terms but such an exercise, despite its fascination, largely misses
the point. The Rising was in essence a work of art, an inspiring drama—the ultimate street theatre. In military terms, the men and women in arms against the
might of the British Empire were involved in a ridiculous, arguably insane enter-
prise. The Rising proved to be a brilliant theatrical success; the rebels who might
have been expected to produce a farce or at best a tragi-comedy instead created
an inspirational drama of epic proportions. The choice of Easter week to enact
their dramatic attempt to resurrect the nation was of course an apt one. The 1916
leaders' sensitivity to and ability to capitalise on the symbolic, emotional and
historico-political impact of their actions far outshone their actual military
achievements.

The Rising has been described as a poets' rebellion and there is much truth in
this. Poets with or without guns can be dangerous—their ability to communicate
ideas and emotions through symbolism and imagery can create revolutions within

72

the minds of their audience. In essence the Rising was sheer poetry, appearing to many as the poem of nationhood writ in blood and martyrdom. Like Abraham Lincoln's Gettysburg Address, the full impact of the Rising was in the first instance not appreciated by its audience. Time was needed to assimilate the full emotional import of the experience and still longer to construct an intellectual-political response.

A process somewhat akin to transubstantiation is evident in the concept of Republic and Republicanism in Ireland as a result of the Easter Rising. The Republic was elevated from the purely political realm to metaphysical heights. The Republic established in courage, blood and death became for many Irishmen and women a sacred, utterly irrevocable entity.

A terrible beauty had not only been born in 1916, with Connolly's death by firing squad; an equally terrible beauty can be seen to have lost its focus and direction. Connolly's execution robbed the Irish revolutionary socialist movement of a man who was incomparably better equipped to lead the movement than any of his surviving lieutenants. Connolly had, it is true, as I have attempted to show in the preceding chapters, left a substantive intellectual legacy to those who would follow him. However, by the nature of his life and work, his political writings were to a large extent contained in the files of old newspapers. Followers he certainly had, albeit followers who exhibited extremely uneven levels of understanding of his work. In a sense, the last weeks of Connolly's life were so climactic, the images of his leadership, his courage and in republican terms the glory of his martyrdom so intense, that a clear perception of the real man was clouded. The larger-than-life figure of Connolly during the Rising and its tragic aftermath cast a shadow over the life that he led, the beliefs that he held, the man that he was.

Connolly's death did not invest his beliefs with added clarity, significance and accessibility but merely enshrined and ennobled his character as an individual. That a man who was so totally and passionately committed to an absolute identification with his class and its common struggle, a man who abhorred the cult of personality, should ultimately fall victim to a cult of personal veneration rather than political inspiration is one of the ironic tragedies of the Rising. Connolly himself cannot be considered as a wholly innocent party in the posthumous reshaping of his political ideas. He was an impatient revolutionary—is there such an animal as a patient revolutionary? His years of struggle and sacrifice, of grinding organisational work, had in the final analysis achieved very little in organisational terms. Connolly's failure, despite his best efforts, to establish a coherent, effective, autonomous socialist structure is of critical importance. In the absence of such an organisation, the left was unable to fully capitalise on the revolutionary opportunities created by the national and social upheavals in post-Rising Ireland.

None of the socialist or labour organisations which Connolly left behind him had a solid revolutionary socialist basis. Directly related to this failure is the fact that of the organisations with which he was principally involved—the Irish Transport and General Workers Union, the Irish Trade Union Congress and Labour Party, the Socialist Party of Ireland and the Irish Citizen Army—

only the last named participated officially in the Rising. Thus despite the fact that the Rising can be described as 'a Workingman's Revolution'[2] due to the high percentage of working class participants, Connolly did not lead the left (such as it was), let alone the working class, into the Rising. Connolly was in some ways a difficult man to follow. He led from the front, so far in front that many of his supporters and potential supporters had great difficulty in keeping him and his goals in sight. Consequently Connolly's wild and splendid militancy, his 'dash and desperation', ultimately assisted his temporary allies—the bourgeois nationalists rather than his own class.

Apart from the ICA, Connolly had not organised any labour-based element in the struggle. There were no plans for a simultaneous general strike or even a transport strike. Connolly was the only major labour leader who was 'out' in 1916 and it is known that he ordered William O'Brien to stay out of the Rising.[3] Under no illusions about the Rising's chances of military success, Connolly appears to have tried to distance important individuals and organisations within the labour movement from the Rising. Foreseeing severe retribution and repression in the wake of the Rising, he may well have been consciously attempting to limit direct labour involvement in order to save what he could of the movement.

That the Rising had symbolic rather than military purpose was perhaps beyond Connolly's power to control. Unlike the Irish Volunteers, whose participation in the Rising was in numerical terms only a small percentage of membership, the ICA under Connolly's command had the vast majority of its members 'out'. Perhaps Connolly could have exerted some influence on the actual form of the symbolism which triumphed. The Catholic, romantically nationalist, republicanism which came to the fore during the Rising, particularly the religious crusade motif, cannot have been to his taste. Despite his long history of criticising the bourgeois nationalists, Connolly perhaps swung to the opposite extreme in order to secure and cement his temporary alliance with the non-socialist nationalists in 1916. While it would be ridiculous to suggest that he in any way renounced his socialism in favour of a purely nationalist stance, it is true that he and his cause were nonetheless very much in a minority. The separate quest for the Workers' Republic was submerged within the struggle for the broader bourgeois Catholic Republic.

One aspect of the Easter Rising impact on Ireland has never been seriously questioned. This is the fact that the Rising legitimized, indeed gave a place of national honour, to the gun. Physical force was for many years at the very centre of Irish political and cultural life. As we have seen, Connolly had always accepted violence as an element of his socialist creed, but in this he was most unusual. Many of his fellow socialists and labour activists (most notably amongst the leadership) were of a much more pacific nature. The left, as we shall see in the following chapters, had great difficulty, despite Connolly's teachings and example, in successfully coming to terms with the implicit and explicit violence which permeated the Irish political scene after the Rising.

Connolly had achieved high office in the shortlived Provisional Government of the Irish Republic; he had achieved still higher office in the pantheon of Ireland's heroes and martyrs. As a socialist he had shown high qualities of leadership in both the theoretical and the practical aspects of the struggle. It is clear, however, that only a handful of people recognised that his participation in the Easter Rising was a logical, even inevitable, result of his concept of socialist revolution. Connolly invested so much of his time, energy and talents into ensuring that the insurrection actually occurred that he failed, or at least was unable, to ensure that the ICA's role as a working class organisation with distinct and separate goals of its own was highlighted. A stricter separation between the ICA and the Irish Volunteers during Easter week, a statement, perhaps even a proclamation of some kind stating clearly the goal of a Workers' Republic, would have been of immense assistance in giving clarity and direction to the Irish labour movement and the working class in general.

In the following chapters we shall examine the use made of various aspects of Connolly's political legacy after his death.

CHAPTER 9

The Women's Movement

It is regrettable that Irishwomen should have the ability to return to the everyday task, that having won the right to share in the dangers of war, they should have relinquished their right to share in the dangers of peace. Progressive and revolutionary women have no voice in the council of the revolutionary movement. Revolutionary women are today showing once more that 'damnable patience' and are content to be the drudges of the movement. The men and women of the revolutionary movement would do well to heed the warning of James Connolly that a continuance of this policy will cause the race to lose 'its capacity to withstand the assaults from without and demoralisation from within' . . . And if some of us think the salvation of the country is to be found in the doctrines of James Connolly, then we must not exclude his doctrine on the place of women in Ireland.

Nora Connolly-O'Brien, June 1932.[1]

Capitalism we are organised to down, and down it we will. We make no apology for this. Twenty-one years after they struck the first blow we are still here, and I say it with shame. I little thought that after twenty-one years we should be in more or less the same plight. But I make this plain, and I think it should be endorsed by our whole class, that we are not going to back down on our ideals. There was nothing wrong with those ideals, contained in the Workers Republic.

Helena Moloney, May 1937.[2]

OF THE PARTICIPANTS in the Easter Rising approximately 90 were women. Two-thirds of the women involved were members of Cumann na mBan (The Irish Women's Council) and the remaining third belonged to the ICA. Of the 77 women arrested in the aftermath of the Rising, only six were imprisoned for longer than a token period. Significantly the six women whom the authorities deemed dangerous enough to warrant more extended incarceration—Constance Markievicz, Helena Moloney, Winifred Carney, Brigid Foley, Maire Perolz and Nell Ryan—were all members of Connolly's ICA. Markievicz had the singular distinction, she considered it an honour, of being the only woman sentenced to death. When her death sentence was commuted, on the grounds of her gender, to life imprisonment, she resented the discriminatory attitude which had set her apart from the male leaders of the Rising.

Women, although a relatively small percentage of the total number who were 'out' in 1916, did participate, did make an impact. This impact would have been greatly heightened and rendered more substantial if at least one woman had been a signatory of the Proclamation of the Republic. There is no evidence that this course of action was even considered by the leaders of the Rising. A woman signatory would certainly have been in keeping with the egalitarian spirit of the Proclamation and would have demonstrated that serious intent rather than lofty rhetoric underpinned the social vision of the document. With hindsight we can see that a female presence—singular or plural—among the signatories would have severely tested the 'humanitarian' reluctance of the British Government to execute women as shown in the case of Constance Markievicz. One may well doubt that this reluctance would have extended to a signatory of the Proclamation. A female signatory invested with the emotional and political mantle of the Republic would have been potentially a very formidable danger.

While it is true that Hanna Sheehy-Skeffington was chosen—almost certainly through Connolly's influence—as one of a five member Civil Provisional Government which the leaders of the uprising planned to activate if the Rising had lasted long enough to require its services,[3] it has to be said that this group was envisaged as an essentially administrative body, charged with the task of organising food and transport. In this respect the role allotted to her, secondary and supportive rather than decisive and dynamic, reflects the role ascribed to her whole sex in post-Rising Ireland. In the aftermath of the Rising, the suffrage newspaper *Irish Citizen* reflected buoyancy and confidence. One writer, after noting that 'of the dead leaders' James Connolly 'stood foremost as a friend of suffrage' and that he deserved a 'shrine in the heart of every suffragist', went on to state that 'Connolly's Provisional Government extended citizenship to Irishwomen and gave them a place on the Executive. Ireland should never permit other leaders to fall below this high standard.'[4]

With the establishment of the Free State women were immediately enfranchised, so at least to this extent the 1916 Proclamation of the republic was honoured. The long-awaited 'vote', the object of so much struggle and sacrifice, did not lead to any significant, let alone revolutionary, change to Irish political life. Here, as in other countries, the vision entertained by many feminists of a new age wherein men and women working together, under conditions of equality, would create a more just and harmonious society turned out to be chimaerical. The fruits of women's suffrage in the Irish context proved to be bitter, the crop sparse almost to the point of invisibility. The Easter Rising in particular and the struggle for independence in general were the central factors in imposing a rigid pattern on the development of Irish women's political involvement. Without exception, the women who were to achieve political recognition and advancement in post-Rising Ireland owed their position to either direct personal participation in the Rising or, more commonly, an indirect familial involvement. Of the six women in the first

Dáil, five—Pearse, Clarke, MacSwiney, O'Callaghan and English—were rela-
tives of men who had given their lives to the cause, either being executed after the
Rising or during the subsequent war of independence.[5] Constance Markievicz was
exceptional in this as in much else, since she won her seat on her own record in the
national struggle.

Once established, the pattern of women politicians being allotted a primarily
surrogate role—ambulant memorials to their dead kinsmen—proved to be
remarkably resilient. McCracken has noted that of the 518 people elected to the
Dáil between 1922 and 1948, 506 were men and only 12 were women. Women
made up a mere 2.3% of the total membership. He goes on to point out that 'Of
the twelve women who sat in the Dáil between 1912 and 1948, three were
widows and three sisters of prominent leaders in the revolutionary period and
five were widows of former members'.[6]

The post-Rising political career of Constance Markievicz is therefore an
exceptional one. Having the advantage of an outstanding '1916 record' and a high
public profile, she made rapid political advances in the turbulent years after 1916
(years in which she spent much of her time in prison). Standing on a Sinn Fein
abstentionist platform in the general election held in 1918, Markievicz was elected
to represent the St. Patrick's division of Dublin in the Westminster Parliament,
having the distinction of being the first woman to be elected to the British
Parliament.[7] This achievement was recognised and advanced upon in 1919 when
she was selected by the First Dáil to be Minister of Labour. It has been claimed
that, apart from Alexandra Kollantai in the Soviet Union, she was the first woman
to enter a popularly-based government.[8] To contemporaries, the entry of women
into political life, and indeed in Markievicz's case into the top level of government, was quite naturally seen as an opening of the floodgates. Women were
expected to pour into politics and into government. That this was not the case is
evidenced by the fact that it was to be sixty years before a woman was given the
opportunity to follow Countess Markievicz into an Irish government as a minister.[9]
Markievicz's political rise was in fact a purely personal success. In a man's world
she had played the man's part—she had borne arms, fought bravely, been a leader
of men in battle, been sentenced to death and suffered lengthy incarceration—all
as a soldier for Ireland. She had in fact won the right to be treated on the same
terms as a man, an honorary man.

Thus we have some women as surrogate men and some women, or at least one,
as a honorary man. What about the other women, the huge majority of women?
What happened to the women of ability, women with political and governmental
potential who were neither related to outstanding national heroes nor outstanding
heroic figures in their own right? Connolly had advised women that economic and
social equality would only be won when women were strong enough to take it.
Men he argued would not simply abandon their dominant position, women would
of necessity have to wrest it from them. In assessing the influence of Connolly's
political legacy for women in the decades after his death we can profitably focus
on two women's organisations, Cumann na mBan and the Irish Women Workers

Union. Cumann na mBan—the Irishwomen's Council—was founded in April 1914 (Connolly's daughter, Nora, was the principal organiser of the Belfast Branch and another daughter, Ina, was also a member). Its constitution declared it to be:

> an independent body of Irishwomen pledged to work for the establishment of an Irish Republic, by organising and training the women of Ireland to take their places by the side of those who are working and fighting for a free Ireland.[11]

In practice, however, Cumann na mBan, despite its stated goal of taking its place standing by the side of the fighting men in the struggle for national independence, found that its allotted position was not alongside the men but rather pacing along supportively, some steps behind them. Cumann na mBan was independent in name only. Its goals and objectives were laid down by the male leadership of the nationalist movement, its role was entirely secondary, operating as it did as auxiliary or appendage to the exclusively male Irish Volunteers. Hanna Sheehy-Skeffington accurately, if somewhat savagely, described Cumann na mBan as being nothing more than an 'animated collecting box'.[12]

In her study of women and Irish nationalism, Margaret Ward notes that despite the great financial and moral support the Cumann na mBan women had given the Irish Volunteers in the two years preceding the Rising, some Cumann women experienced real difficulty in having their services, even as strictly non-combatant auxiliaries, accepted during the actual fighting in 1916. When Pearse, Connolly and Clarke were informed about the women's difficulties, they took immediate steps to resolve the problem. With hindsight we can see that it was an ominous portent for the future progress of women in Ireland that the one commandant who 'steadfastly refused to have any women under his command' was 'de Valera in Boland's mill'.[13]

Although in numerical terms there were twice as many (60) Cumann na mBan women as ICA women out in 1916, the somewhat menial, low-profile nature of their involvement ensured that it was to be ICA women who established the more effective political credentials. Thus in 1917 of the four women included in the 24 member Sinn Fein executive, two—Constance Markievicz and Kathleen Lynn—had been ICA officers. The other two women had not been Cumann na mBan nor personally active during the uprising, but were widows of executed leaders. At their convention in August 1916, Cumann na mBan had already elected Markievicz as President of their organisation, an act which one suspects was at least in part a recognition of the prestige which accrued to the women ICA members, who, unlike their sisters in Cumann na mBan, had actually fought alongside the men.

The women of Cumann na mBan were extremely active in the national struggle, providing great financial and logistic support during the war of independence. Many women who had been active feminists turned their energies and talents to Cumann na mBan and the national struggle. In a long and perceptive letter to the *Irish Citizen* in November 1917,[14] Margread Ní Conaire noted that the national movement was in fact leading many women to 'stand aloof' from feminism. She went on to argue that these women had not 'justified . . . abstention from the women's struggle for liberty by becoming a force within the new movement'. The women involved in the national movement 'were but clinging to the outward fringe' of the movement and were in fact 'pale phantoms, dim reflections' of the men in the movement. Addressing Irish nationalist women, Ní Conaire stated:

> You are in revolt against a subjection imposed from without, but you are tacitly acquiescing in a position of inferiority within. Until you cast from you this spirit of slavish docility to false standards at home, your indignation directed against false standards outside is but a crackling of thorns in a pot.

She proceeded to urge her readers to:

> read James Connolly's 'Reconquest of Ireland'. There is a chapter on women, specially meant for Irish women to read and ponder over. He never visualised his countrywomen as 'ministering angels' or animated collecting boxes, filling the same old hackneyed role that women have filled for a thousand years. No! His spirits vision beheld them proudly bearing an equal part in the resurrection of Ireland.

In concluding her letter, Ní Conaire presented a scenario of future developments in Ireland if women continued on the path that they were presently taking:

> If you leave men alone to carry out the task of national creative endeavour, you will have no right to complain later that there are flaws in construction; and there will be flaws, grave and serious flaws, if the women of Ireland fail to demand and take their full woman's share in the national heritage.

This correspondent was not alone in her concern that the nationalist struggle was weakening the feminist movement; the pages of the *Irish Citizen* up until its demise in 1920 frequently voiced the same concern.

Even a very brief perusal of the position women occupied in the national movement as the country moved towards breaking its links with Britain, shows that the fears expressed in the *Irish Citizen* were wholly justified. For example, no woman was included amongst the plenipotentiaries who were sent to London to negotiate a settlement of the independence issue with the British Government.[15] Women were, however, prominent in the debates which raged around the issue of the Treaty. The Treaty was in fact rejected by all six women deputies in the Dáil.[16] Constance Markievicz and Mary MacSwiney in particular were fiercely and unequivocally opposed to the Treaty. Reflecting this hard-line opposition to the Treaty on republican grounds, Cumann na mBan was the first national organisation to officially reject the Treaty. After the Treaty had been ratified in the Dáil (by a majority of 64 votes to 57), the executive of Cumann na mBan voted by a huge majority (24 votes to 2) against the articles of Treaty and reaffirmed their allegiance to the Republic proclaimed in April 1916. At a specially called Cumann na mBan convention held in February 1922, the executive's decision was supported by 419 of the 482 delegates. This vote led to a serious split in the movement: the minority who favoured the Treaty (many of whom had strong familial links to Free State leaders), left Cumann na mBan and formed a new pro-Treaty, politically conservative organisation which they called Cumann na Saoirse (Society of Freedom).[17]

The great majority of women active in the struggle for national independence opposed the Treaty and after enduring great hardships and suffering during the civil war period, found their natural home in de Valera's Fianna Fail party. In its early years Fianna Fail to some extent reflected the high level of support and commitment that women had given to the Republican forces. Six women, including Markievicz and Hanna Sheehy-Skeffington, were on its first executive. Despite this apparent acceptance of women's role in politics, Fianna Fail under the leadership of de Valera was to prove extremely unsympathetic to women. Hanna Sheehy-Skeffington, who became rapidly disillusioned by de Valera and his party, saw the problem as being attitudinal and drew a comparison between the view of women held by Connolly and de Valera. To Connolly, she argued, 'woman was an equal, a comrade'; to de Valera, on the other hand, woman was 'a sheltered being, withdrawn to the domestic hearth, shrinking from public life'.[18]

Ward has argued persuasively in her book on women's role in Irish nationalism that the 'right of women to organise autonomously was never accepted by nationalists', women being 'conceded' only separate organisations 'within the general parameters of nationalist ideological concerns'. Within those limitations women were 'left helpless when faced with a threat to their specific interests that did not engage the concern of nationalists'. In reference to the effect of Connolly's political legacy on this area of Irish life, Ward, after making the general point that the 'writings and political practice of James Connolly have only been accepted when they have not conflicted with nationalist orthodoxy', goes on to state that 'nowhere is this more clearly evident than over the controversial issue of women; Connolly's unequivocal support for the suffrage movement has in consequence been completely obscured.'[19]

Despite Connolly's efforts to sensitize the Irish labour movement to the need for non-sexist attitudes and policies, women active on the left of politics faced the same barriers within the labour movement as women within the non-labour republican movement. The Freestaters can hardly be said to enter this equation as they made no real claims to be anything other than wholly male oriented. For example, the President of the Executive Council of the Free State, William Cosgrave, told W.B. Yeats in January 1923—the same month in which Cumann na nGaedheal was set in motion—that 'women, doctors and the clergy ought to keep out of politics, as their business is with the sick'.[20] The difficulties faced by female activists are highlighted by the development of the Irish Women Workers Union. The IWWU, when it reorganised after the disruptions of 1916, was for its size arguably the organisation most steeped in Connolly's ideas and example. The Union had very close links with the ICA (two IWWU members, Dr. Kathleen

Lynn and Constance Markievicz, had held the rank of Captain and Lieutenant respectively and were thus two of the ICA's most senior surviving officers). Of its office bearers in 1917, no less than six had been members of the ICA and these six occupied all of the Union's most important positions. However, the women did not keep up active involvement within the ICA. Frank Robbins has noted that by 1918, 'practically all the women who had taken part in the 1916 Insurrection had ceased to be members of the Citizen Army.' Robbins accounts for this withdrawal by observing that many of the '1916' women objected to the fact that some of the 'new members recruited into the women's section had a very questionable background as far as trade union loyalties were concerned'.[21] While accepting that Robbins' point has some validity, it should also be noted that the ICA was in great disarray after 1916. Without Connolly's leadership, the ICA was a shadow of its former self and it is hardly surprising that a significant number of its prominent women members decided to channel their energies and talents into developing the IWWU.

The IWWU had a close but at times distinctly uneasy relationship with the ITGWU. The Union was established by James Larkin in 1911. W. O'Brien comments that even at that time 'many people (including myself) did not see any necessity for such a union, believing that it was not desirable to organise workers on a sex basis, but Mr. Larkin had his own reasons (or prejudices) and had his way'.[22] Connolly, when working for the ITGWU in Belfast, had admitted women into membership of the union but, 'much to his astonishment and disgust', he was ordered by Larkin to cancel their membership and transfer them to the IWWU. Larkin, who acted as a one-man Executive Committee of the ITGWU, justified this decision on the ground that the word 'person' in the Union rules meant 'male person'.[23] In its early days the IWWU had Larkin as President (self-appointed) and his sister Delia as Secretary. Its relationship to the ITGWU could not have been closer for, 'though nominally an independent organisation, the IWWU was really the women's section of the ITGWU, which financed and directed it and gave it rooms free of rent in Liberty Hall'.[24]

After the uprising, with Helena Moloney imprisoned, Louie Bennett and a few others assumed the task of reorganising the union. Discussing the reorganisation with Foran and O'Brien of the ITGWU Bennett told them that she 'was of the opinion that it would not be possible to get new members to come to Liberty Hall, and that it would be better to have a room elsewhere'. It was this move, an obvious effort to achieve an independent status, that ensured the future of the IWWU, because in February 1918 O'Brien, who had always argued that men and women should be in the same union in terms of full equality, managed to get a reinterpretation of the union rules and from that point onwards the word 'person' included women. If the IWWU had still been dependent on the ITGWU, it would have ceased to exist as a separate entity at this stage. The decision of the ITGWU—by far the largest and most powerful union in Ireland—to admit women was a welcome and progressive step and one which was in line with the Connolly tradition but it was also a great blow to the potential expansion of the IWWU.

The IWWU reached a peak membership of 5,000 in 1920. By 1923 membership had fallen to 3,000, a figure which remained static until 1929 when, mainly as a result of the Irish Nurses Union severing its links, membership fell to 2,500. In less than a decade union membership had been reduced by one half.[25] Although a small union with a gradually declining membership, the IWWU did exert some influence within the trade union movement. Both Louie Bennett and Helena Moloney were elected to preside over the Irish Congress of Trade Unions, with Bennett being the first woman President of Congress in 1932. The Union also achieved some significant victories, perhaps the most important being the laundry workers' strike in 1935 which established the right of all Irish workers to holidays with pay.

Despite the great reverence which was paid to Connolly's name and deeds, not all men in the labour movement found it easy to accept that women had a place in the struggle. An underlying male supremacist position occasionally rose to the surface in the movement's newspapers. In May 1919, for example, the suffragette newspaper the *Irish Citizen* had cause to lament that a writer on the *Voice of Labour* had ignored the important economic, legal and political aspects of the case when reporting on an issue relating to women's working conditions, preferring to trivialise the women's grievance and use sexist descriptions in an insulting manner. Women, the *Citizen* argued, looked for a 'wider vision, a higher standard and greater dignity from a Labour Journal'.[26] In response to these criticisms, the women in a later edition of the *Voice* were referred to as 'Amazons', 'Wild Women' and—the ultimate trade union insult 'scabs'. This attack prompted the women on the *Citizen* to comment that they found it 'strange that a paper founded by James Connolly' should treat women in the same way as the capitalist press.[27]

The distance which the IWWU had moved from being a 'sister'—by which was meant dependant underling—of the ITGWU, is clearly evident as early as January 1920 when Louie Bennett in an article entitled 'Is an Irish Woman Workers Union needed?' wrote bluntly and combatively that 'the most live issue in the labour movement is the struggle of the trade unions outside the Irish Transport Union against the Imperialistic policy of that body.'[28]

In 1927 detailed reports appeared in both *An Behean Oibre*, (the official organ of the IWWU) and the *Voice of Labour* regarding the decisions of the IWWU Convention. In its report of the Convention, the *Voice* had stated somewhat critically that 'the feeling of the Convention showed a complete lack of confidence in the efficacy of parliamentary activities for the labour movement.'[29] These comments met an immediate response in *An Bhean Oibre*, which presented a detailed summary of the convention's debate on parliamentary involvement. It was pointed out that the feeling of the convention was that the union could not afford the possible loss of a member of staff should she be nominated on to the Labour Party's electoral panel. Further discussion had clarified the fact that the members had 'very little desire to organise support for a candidate who was not chosen by the women workers'. A high level of distrust for male candidates and politicians was reported, while on the other hand there was 'a very strong feeling in favour of

nominating a woman candidate' and the 'desire to see an IWWU representative in
the Dáil' was reiterated. Facing harsh political realities, the convention concluded
that it was 'no use to nominate a woman for the panel. She'd stay there for ever.
They won't choose a woman for any constituency whilst they have pals of their
own falling over each other trying to get the job.' One group within the Union did
hold a completely anti-parliamentary position and put the argument to the
convention that parliamentary activities were 'useless to the labour movement
whilst the capitalist system persists'.[30]

During the debate on Industrial Unionism and the One Big Union, which took
place within the labour movement in 1937, Helena Moloney, vice-chairman of the
Commission of Inquiry into trade union reorganisation,[31] presented a paper under
the title 'Reservation (A)'. She noted that while she was in favour of the general
trend of the proposed syndicalist reorganisation, she wished to draw attention to
the 'peculiar position' of the IWWU. The organisation of the IWWU, she wrote,
was not 'a deliberate pursuit of a policy of organising women on sex lines, which
would be theoretically wrong, but was, and still is, a temporary necessity,
owing to the fact that women are a separate economic class'. Referring to the
report's conclusion that there was no further necessity for the separate existence of
the IWWU, Moloney noted:

> the outlook of the Labour movement at the present time is not one that could
> be calculated to inspire confidence in women regarding their security if
> merged in a General Workers or other Unions. I feel that special safeguards
> and guarantees would need to be given to women prior to their being invited
> to give the power that separate existence gives them.[32]

It is clear from Moloney's well informed reservations that in the two decades
following Connolly's death his vision of a labour movement working in complete
solidarity and mutual trust with the forces of organised women was still a very
long way from fruition. Yet it is nevertheless true that Connolly's political legacy
and the example of his life and work were of great educational and inspirational
value to militant women struggling within the labour movement to achieve a more
just and egalitarian social order. The depth of Connolly's influence is very clearly
shown in the contributions of Helena Moloney and C. Cahalan to the *James
Connolly Souvenir May Day Celebration* pamphlet published as the *Dublin Year
Book* in 1930. In typically forthright language, Moloney began her article on
'James Connolly and Women' by stating that 'to all Irishwomen, but more particularly to Irish working women, James Connolly will ever remain an outstanding
inspiration'. Going on to describe the contemporary situation she wrote:

> fourteen years after his death, hundreds of thousands of his fellow-citizens
> give lip-service to his memory without the smallest intention of following his
> ideals. Those ideals are still too little understood by Irish workers, and the
> same elements which he spent his life in fighting have very clearly, in those
> intervening years, managed to present and interpret them in such a manner as

to make Connollyism appear as Utopian, violent, impossible, undesirable and altogether unpopular'.

Moloney argued that women 'looking out today on the sorry travesty of her 'emancipation' would do well to go back to the earliest writings of Connolly on women's movement'. She concluded by urgently asserting that 'Connolly and Connollyism must be Irish women's slogan if they wish to take their place the foremost place—in the militant army of Irish labour'.[33]

In an article entitled 'Women and the Irish Labour Movement', Cahalan concluded her own somewhat more optimistic article by asserting that the labour movement needed more women who, 'standing on the basis of independence and equality', would bring to labour a 'new spirit to inspire the movement to bolder and nobler ends and will fight desperately for that Workers Republic that James Connolly so ardently hoped for'.[34]

The view put forward by a number of feminist commentators that women in post-Rising Ireland subordinated the struggle to overcome the injustices and oppressions which they were subjected to as women, to the struggle for national independence, that women in short placed national interest before gender (and class) interests, is persuasive. I would, however, make the point that a critical factor in explaining women's failure to rise within the power structure of the nationalist movement's hierarchy was that women by virtue of their essentially non-military role in post-Rising politics—the collection can rather than the gun—slowly but surely lost ground to the men of violence. Not for nothing is the national anthem entitled 'The Soldier's Song'. In an armed struggle the weapon-less, no matter how important their logistic and other support to the fighting men, do not rise to positions of influence and power. The very nature of their role tends to relegate their influence and hence their political advancement. In *realpolitik* terms the women in the movement became an increasing irrelevance. The fact that the women who did aspire to, and did achieve, personal, as opposed to male sur-rogate status, were almost without exception women who emerged from the Connolly influenced ICA, and women, moreover, who publicly affirmed their belief in Connolly's teachings, strongly supports this contention. In the aftermath of the rising, nearly all the female ICA members drifted out of the organisation, the organisation which potentially offered more possibilities for their sex than any other organisation in Ireland. They did so because of its failure to maintain its relevance rather than because of its attitude to women.

CHAPTER 10

Religion

It is because I see how a knowledge of Connolly would resolve confusion in the awakening people that I am eager to talk of the things he did and said. Connolly's conflict with De Leon interests me only because it shows the Catholic, Connolly, taking a stand against the invasion of the essentials of the working class struggle, with ideas objectionable to Catholics. It is one of the great Connolly Traffic Lights For the Labour Movement of our day, but now that the labour leaders have corrected themselves, enemies of the people attempt to incite to confusion. The answer to every Catholic hesitation is to be found in the stand taken by Connolly.

Peadar O'Donnell 1939[1]

THE MAIN BODY of the Irish Citizen Army—the Irish Red Guard—fought in the St. Stephen's Green Command during the Easter Rising. As we have seen, Connolly invested the ICA with the role of revolutionary vanguard. It is therefore among these soldiers that one would expect to find evidence of hard-headed Socialist revolutionary ideals, to find men and women, with a sound grasp of socialist theory and socialist objectives, to match and direct their proven courage and willingness to rise in arms in the fight for freedom. In fact the members of the ICA mirrored their comrades in the Irish Volunteers in most respects, and nowhere was this more the case than in their religious stance and in the religious significance which they attached to the Easter Rising itself.

Newsinger has described the 1916 Rising as 'a Catholic revolution'[2] and indeed the Rising does appear to have taken on the aspect of a Roman Catholic Crusade. Irish nationalism and Roman Catholicism in 1916 finally, and it would appear irrevocably, after a long and at times stormy and acrimonious betrothal, united as one through the medium of the blood sacrifice of the Easter Rising. In contradistinction to previous nationalist movements in Ireland, the 1916 Rising had no Protestant amongst its leaders, and, even more significantly, some of the notable Protestants who did participate were drawn towards Roman Catholicism as a direct result of the Rising. Nationalist rebellion thus acted in the unusual role of an evangelical missionary agent for the Roman Catholic Church. Constance Markievicz was one of those converts. A lieutenant in the ICA, Markievicz had 'believed very little in religion' prior to the Rising.[3] While sharing prayers with her comrades in arms during the fighting, Markievicz, who had been brought up in the Protestant tradition, experienced 'a vision of the Unseen, which wrought such

86

a change in her that from that moment to her, too, the things that are seen became temporal and the things that are unseen eternal'.[4] The result of this experience was that Markievicz was received into the Catholic Church a fortnight after her release from prison in June 1917.

Markievicz was reacting in very much the same way that Maud Gonne—another of Connolly's friends—had done some years earlier, when she had responded to a French priest's question 'why are you not a Catholic like your Nation?' by pondering the question and converting to Catholicism. In later years Charlotte Despard, described by her biographer as 'Suffragette, Socialist and Sinn Feiner',[5] a woman very active in socialist and republican organisations and one who saw herself as a Connolly socialist, followed the tradition and proved her commitment to Ireland by converting to Catholicism.

Roger Casement, the most prominent non-Catholic amongst the leadership of the uprising, also found that his desire 'to be as close to Ireland and her heart as possible' would be assisted by conversion to Roman Catholicism and he was duly accepted into the Church prior to his execution.[6] More pertinent to our present interest is the case of Commandant Michael Mallin, the Chief of Staff of the ICA and Officer in charge of the St. Stephen's Green Command during the Rising. Mallin was second in seniority in the ICA to Connolly himself. In his last letter to his wife before his execution Mallin wrote that:

> Sentense [*sic*] of Death has been passed, and a quarter to four tomorrow the sentence will be carried out by shooting . . . God's will be done . . . With gods help I will be always near you. If you can I would like you to dedicate Una to the service of God and also Joseph, so that we may have two to rest on penance for our sins try and do this if you can pray to our Divine Lord that it may be so . . . I do not believe our Blood has been shed in vain. I believe Ireland will come out greater and grander but she must not forget she is Catholic she must keep her faith.[7]

Mallin's last instructions were carried out with interest: his daughter Una became a Loreto nun and two of his sons, John and Joseph, became Jesuit priests. Mallin's letter and the instructions contained within it are a long way from Connolly's own religious position and yet his public stance on the matter of religion—baleful imperative though it was for him—meant that he was dramatically unsuccessful in combating the deep and persuasive influence of the Church on even his closest political and military comrades. Even closer to home, Connolly's wife Lillie, who had remained a Protestant during Connolly's lifetime, converted to Catholicism after his death. Given the immense power and influence of the Catholic Church and the close identification which had grown between the Church and Irish nationalism, a certain inevitability characterises the post-1916 relationship between the Catholic Church and the Irish left, a relationship which, as we shall see, was one in which the labour movement was always on the defensive and always losing ground. The labour movement in the years after 1916 faced enmity from many quarters, not the least of which was the Roman Catholic Church. The extent of the Church's enmity and the difficulty which the labour movement, and indeed the left in general, experienced in combating what amounted to right-wing pressure couched in religious terms—pressure aimed at curbing the radicalism of the movement—emerges clearly from a reading of the labour press. The extent and effectiveness of the Church's attempt to influence the labour movement is reflected in the high priority, sometimes bordering on an almost obsessive concentration, which the labour press gave to defending the movement from religious attacks. A review of Aodh de Blacam's book *Towards the Republic*, published in the *Voice of Labour* early in 1919, is a striking example of labour's position on religion, expressed in a positive, indeed aggressive manner. The reviewer writes:

> The stock criticisms of Connolly's teaching, that it is irreligious, criminally destructive of social order, impracticable etc., are lucidly examined and thoroughly exposed. Against the current exhibitions of bigotry, reinforced personal interests of the bigots Mr. Blacam masses weight of testimony from the Catholic Doctors which does something more than prove the Workers Republic is consistent with Catholic teaching. Had Mr. Blacam stressed more heavily, as he could have done with justice, the teaching of the Canonists about usury, he would have proved that the present social order, based on interest and profit is unCatholic, despite the tolerance of usury.[8]

A less aggressive and rather more representative example of labour's response to clerical attack is contained in two articles in the *Watchword of Labour* in December 1919. On page one, reacting to the wholesale excommunication of SPI members by Fr. Finlay, The *Watchword* suggests that the SPI appeal to the Archbishop of Dublin on the grounds that 'a decision by the Archbishop would clear the air. Loyal Catholics would withdraw any word that was authoritatively condemned.' The article then goes on to argue that if SPI members were 'authoritively assured that to advocate the social production and distribution of wealth was quite open to a Catholic and that Father Finlay's slanders were condemned, they would be fortified in their loyalty and relieved of anxiety and indignation'. In the same issue the *Watchword* invites the Lord Bishop of Meath to 'end the scandal against religion caused by scurrilous attacks upon the ITGWU' by Rev. E.P. O'Reilly P.P., who had asserted in the *Midland Tribune* that the ITGWU was a 'freemason organisation'.[9]

The tendency to seek the support of the Church when under attack by the Church's own clerics, was an extremely strong, and not infrequently rather slavish, tendency in the labour press. It is perhaps exemplified by a statement in the *Voice* in December 1921 in which the writer bluntly asserts:

> In support of this argument of Labour we will quote no Labour, Socialist or Communist authority because we have no need. We fall back upon a distinguished Irish Cleric. The orthodoxy of his doctrine is guaranteed by the imprimatus of the late Catholic Archbishop of Dublin and by the ecclesiastical censorship of our old friend Rev. P. Finlay S.J.[10]

Whilst it is true that Connolly had on occasions quoted lcontemporary Churchmen when their comments could be used to support socialist arguments, he had not, and indeed would never have considered, basing his arguments on clerical support or censure. The concept that socialists would seek Church sanction for their political ideas would have been an anathema to him. In the years after his death the labour press displayed a generally subservient attitude to the Roman Catholic Church even during periods of intense labour militancy and pro-Soviet rhetoric. Connolly's 'no priests in politics' line, his commitment to a secular labour movement, and his unequivocal and spirited opposition to clerical attempts to influence and control the movement, were not forgotten and in theory the labour movement continued to support this stance. In practice, however, after 1916, the labour movement was in awe of the power and influence of the Church, which in turn was concerned about the rise of 'ungodly' political ideas and was aggressively determined to control the movement. Constantly on the defensive, the labour movement developed a pattern of accommodation. The Church was allowed to set the agenda and labour's attempt to defend its independence and integrity became increasingly premised on an acceptance of the Church's 'right' to exercise a powerful, indeed authoritative, supervisory function.

It is no coincidence that in the years following Connolly's death a number of studies appeared which were either directly aimed at establishing a specifically Catholic critique of his political theories or more generally designed to present the Church's position on socialism.[11] Indeed, in an attempt to present a more sympathetic and constructive interpretation of Connolly's position, Constance de Markievicz (who as a relatively recent convert was not noted for her interest in, or intimate knowledge of, Catholic doctrine) published a pamphlet entitled *James Connolly's Policy and Catholic Doctrine*.[12] One of the first detailed interpretations of Connolly's life and work was written by Rev. E. McKenna S.J. and published in three instalments in the *Irish Monthly* in 1919. The inspiration for Fr. McKenna's study is clearly evident in his first paragraph, when he states that while prior to the Easter Rising Connolly's 'name was not one to excite either fierce hatred or fierce enthusiasm',[13] his importance and influence had increased dramatically since his execution. McKenna notes that:

> His writings, which up to that day had not challenged much attention, were now eagerly sought after, and were found to be rich in unexpected wealth of knowledge, thought and eloquence. His teachings were vested with the authority due to the last words of a martyr. At the present time his portrait is frequent everywhere in the working class houses of Dublin; when Dublin work-folk are questioned as to their aspirations one of their commonest answers is that they hold by the ideals and the methods of James Connolly.[14]

Throughout his study Fr. McKenna is at pains to establish that he is a sympathetic critic. He writes approvingly that the 'personal integrity of James Connolly's life has never been questioned',[15] and refers to his historical works as being 'extremely valuable', 'Fresh', 'illuminating' and 'for the most part, compelling'.[16]

Not surprisingly, he notes with some relish that Connolly was a 'professing Catholic', although he admits that he does 'not know if he himself practised his religion', and that he ensured that his 'children were brought up in the Catholic Faith' and moreover was in, 'sincere Communion with the Church when he died'.[17] Fr. McKenna's objective is not mere hagiography. There is a sting in the tail of even his most fulsome praises. Referring to the 'defects of Connolly', he writes that Connolly 'for all his unselfish love of the people, his energy, his organising ability, his learning, was always a brilliant general of the army of Labour, not a statesmanlike and constructive reformer of society'.[18]

The basic critique which pervades McKenna's study is that Connolly, while in many ways a most admirable example of Catholic manhood, was intellectually incompetent. Connolly, he argues, did not in fact have 'any firm grasp on Catholic principles, or indeed to have thought, except in a very superficial way, of the relations between his socialism and his religion. He had apparently no taste of talent for such matters.'[19] McKenna extends his critique by asserting that Connolly, as a man who attached great importance to 'patriotism, religious conviction, principles of honesty, justice and purity', could only reconcile these beliefs and qualities with his commitment to Marxism through a mental process whereby he preferred to 'misrepresent his socialist authorities rather than to acknowledge openly his disagreement with them'.

The concluding paragraph of the study highlights the main purpose of McKenna's critique—to limit Connolly's influence by questioning his intellectual capacities. McKenna writes:

> It is a pity that James Connolly with his heroic spirit, his great love of the Irish people and his intimate knowledge of their history allowed himself to be obfuscated by German philosophical doctrines which he either misunderstood or interpreted in a sense different from their author's. A more intimate acquaintance with Catholic doctrine would . . . have saved him from the grating inconsistencies which mar his work, and from the errors and unpleasant things which tend to discredit it. [21]

A more substantial study appeared in the widely read and influential *Catholic Bulletin* in 1920. These articles entitled 'James Connolly's campaign against Capitalism, in the light of Catholic teaching' were written by Rev. P. Coffey Ph.D., a cleric with a reputation for being a friend of labour. Coffey's articles, written from a position which entailed a rejection of both socialism and capitalism, are in some ways very sympathetic to many of Connolly's objectives. In his introduction Coffey makes his position clear:

> There is a growing Labour movement in Ireland, and much talk of socialism. But those who understand what socialism really means are satisfied that such an economic system will never find congenial soil among Irishmen. It is, indeed, desirable to forewarn the Irish people of the evils that would follow the very unlikely event of their adopting such a system, but it is even more desirable to foster a just appreciation of the actual evils of the existing or capitalist system.[22]

In explaining his reason for studying the labour movement in general and Connolly in particular, Coffey notes that 'although the evils of capitalism are not so pronounced in Ireland as in Great Britain, the struggle of Irish labour against capitalism is already definitely knit'. This being the case, he believes that the 'origin, inspiration and tendencies of this movement call for close and sympathetic consideration' and adds that this is 'all the more so because the movement owes so much to the influence of a man whose place in Irish history cannot yet be easily determined'.[23] As a critic of capitalism, Coffey takes a more sympathetic view of Connolly than most clerical commentators, but ultimately his conclusion is rather similar in substance to McKenna's. For while Coffey at least does not accuse Connolly of having an inadequate knowledge of socialist theory, he does echo McKenna's other charge—that Connolly had not understood the actual beliefs and social positions of the Catholic Church. This is made clear when Coffey writes that Connolly 'wrongly concluded that the influence of the Catholic Church generally was really on the side of capitalism and against the workers'. This error meant that Connolly was 'betrayed into saying occasionally very bitter and disrespectful and really unjustifiable things against the Catholic authorities, and even against the great Encyclical of Leo XIII on The Condition of the Working Classes'.[24] Coffey claims that Connolly's mistake had at least three negative effects on Irish labour. First it 'tended to mislead the Catholic workers, who looked up to him into the same mistaken notion'; secondly, it made workers think that they 'could not agitate for the betterment of their conditions and remain loyal to their religion'; and thirdly, it allowed 'capitalists to misrepresent the whole labour movement as being anti-Catholic'.[25]

These articles have been discussed at some length because they reflect and indeed openly state that the Church was concerned about Connolly's influence on the Irish working class and also because they are representative of a whole series of articles and commentaries which have followed very much the same pattern of Roman Catholic criticism. The pattern combines a mixture of superficial praise of Connolly, proud assertion of his Roman Catholic allegiance, and an attempt to cast doubt upon his intellectual powers and coherence, in order to undermine his influence.

In her pamphlet *James Connolly's Policy and Catholic Doctrine*, Constance Markievicz attempts to counter clerical critiques of Connolly. In a vigorously, rather than a tightly argued case, Markievicz states that Connolly's policies were in every instance in total harmony with Catholic doctrine. Given the fact that internal evidence within the body of her argument suggests that her main source of information on what actually constitutes Catholic doctrine comes from Connolly's own writings, her conclusions were hardly surprising, and would be perhaps rather less than persuasive to Roman Catholic readers inclined to follow the Church's own interpretation of Church doctrine rather than Connolly's. A sample of her style is provided by her description of the type of schools that 'James Connolly visioned': in these schools 'all would work together for the good of all, in the spirit of Christ and not in the spirit of British Imperialism.'[26]

At about the same time that Markievicz wrote the above-mentioned pamphlet, Thomas Johnson, Chief Executive Officer of the Trade Union Congress and Labour Party and Chairman of the Labour Party in the Dail, was writing a confidential letter to the members of the National Executive of the Labour Party. Johnson, who was at the time probably the most powerful and influential figure in the labour movement, touched upon his views about the religious issue and his concerns about the movement's relationship to the Catholic faith. Johnson urges the Independent Working Class Education movement, and the Labour Party Executive to 'walk warily when entering upon an adult educational policy'. In support of his argument in favour of a policy of caution, Johnson notes that the:

> dominant ideas within the movement, as judged by the text books in commonest use, are in direct conflict with the religious faith of our people. Nothing would I dread more than to give occasion to the charge that I was even partially responsible for entering on a policy which will inevitably as I believe, mean the splitting up, on *doctrinal grounds*, of the Labour Movement in Ireland. If such a split is to come, let it rather be through the breakaway of those who accept the materialist view than that after success has come of our educational efforts, the facts are revealed to an unsuspecting people that their faith is being undermined by our agency and the break away occurs through the effects of religious teachers. [27]

A debate within the pages of the *Irish Rosary* a few years later suggests that Johnson's fear of a doctrinal—or perhaps more accurately, a sectarian-split in the labour movement was not without substance. This correspondence between labour Senator and Trade Union leader Thomas Farren and Fr. McInerney, editor of the *Irish Rosary*, centred upon an article written by a Dr Cleary in an earlier issue of the journal. In this article Cleary had argued for the creation of Catholic Trade Unions on the grounds that it was 'no longer possible for men of various religious beliefs to meet as Trade Unionists, for in some Unions the support of socialism is a test of membership'.[28] The correspondence in the *Irish Rosary* over this article consisted of Fr. McInerney arguing in a most aggressive and at times extremely condescending manner in favour of Catholic Trade Unions and Farren, very much on the defensive, noting somewhat weakly, that he had 'on many occasions from public platforms all over the country' proclaimed Labour's Charter to be Pope Leo XIII's Encyclical on the *Condition of the Working Classes*'.[29] Farren's affirmation of Catholic doctrine and its central importance to the labour movement was not enough to impress Fr. McInerney. In a later issue of the *Irish Rosary*, Fr. McInerney explicitly rejects Farren's right to quote Pope Leo and restates his demand for Catholic Trade Unions:

> If Senator Farren . . . thinks that Socialists or Communists are good enough as leaders of our Catholic working people; if he thinks that our Trade Unions, with their 95 per cent of Catholic members, ought not to be Catholic in tone and spirit then the fault is entirely his own. He is in flagrant opposition to Leo XIII, and had better abstain in future from quoting the words of that great Pontiff.[30]

In 1931 William Cosgrave, President of a Free State Government, deeply concerned by the activities and 'conspiracies' of republican and left-wing organisations, decided to enlist the hierarchy of the Catholic Church in support of the introduction of 'more effective powers to curb the activities of these organisations'.[31] In pursuit of this objective, Cosgrave addressed a letter to Cardinal MacRory, the Cardinal Primate of all Ireland, pointing out that the country was faced with new and extremely grave dangers and that doctrines were being taught and practised which had never existed in Ireland before. He went on to state that in his opinion:

> the influence of the Church alone will be able to prevail in the struggle against them . . . Only through the powerful influence of the Church will innocent youths be prevented from being led into criminal conspiracy . . . The Church alone in my view, can affect the consciences of parents and others in regard to the dangers to which our young people are exposed through communistic and subversive teachings.[32]

In support of his request Cosgrave enclosed a seventeen-page 'Memorandum Regarding the Activities of Certain Organisations'. This memorandum alleged a conspiracy to overthrow the state and claimed that the conspiracy centered upon the IRA, Cumann na mBan, Fianna Eireann and 'a number of Communistic Groups'. The memorandum gave somewhat lurid details regarding these organisations and outlined the alleged conspiracy between them.[33]

From the government's point of view, the Church's response could hardly have been more favourable. On Sunday 18 October, a joint Pastoral letter was read to every Roman Catholic congregation in Ireland warning the faithful against both the IRA and its socialist republican offshoot, Saor Eire. 'It is our duty', stated the joint pastoral, 'to tell our people plainly that the two organisations to which we have referred, whether separate or in alliance, are sinful and irreligious, and that no Catholic can lawfully be a member of them'. The pastoral, which was signed by Cardinal MacRory, three Archbishops and twenty-four Bishops concluded with a direction that priests should 'exert every effort to keep young people from secret societies, and diligently instruct them on the malice of murder, and the satanic tendencies of Communism'.[34] This pastoral, timed as it was to coincide with and support the Government's Constitution (Amendment No. 17) Act (a piece of legislation containing draconian measures to outlaw republican and socialist organisations and publications), clearly demonstrates that the Church was willing and able to work in tandem with the Government in an assault on the rights and liberties of republicans and socialists. It is clear that the fears expressed by moderate labour leaders about the dangers of antagonising the Church were far from groundless.

The Church's diatribes against socialism and communism did not cease with the passing of the Constitution Amendment Act. In March 1933 a large crowd of Catholic lay people, inspired by their Church's repeated and sometimes inflammatory denunciations, attacked and eventually burnt and looted Connolly House, the headquarters of the Revolutionary Workers Group. The crowd indulged in a spree of book-burning which included works by Sean Murray and Ralph Fox. One wonders if Connolly's status as a national hero saved his books and pamphlets from the fires— certainly naming the House in his honour had not saved it from the wrath of the crowd.[35]

Although Ireland's own fascist-inspired movement, the Blueshirts, failed to thrive—partly because of its own internal weakness and partly because of the efforts of the left to physically deny it a platform—the onset of the Spanish civil war provided the blueshirts leader, General O'Duffy, with an opportunity to revive his political career. O'Duffy's involvement with the Spanish insurgents arose out of a correspondence between Count de Camirez de Arellano, a Carlist monarchist, and Cardinal MacRory. The Count had written to Cardinal MacRory requesting assistance in the Spanish struggle against communism. In response Cardinal MacRory suggested that General O'Duffy was the man to contact for the type of assistance required. O'Duffy responded to the Spaniard's request with alacrity, and, with the blessing of the Church, he organised a body of over 700 men to accompany him on what was to turn into a singularly unsuccessful, and in many ways farcical 'Crusade to Spain'.[36] The Irish left's contribution to the defence of the Spanish Republic, while numerically much weaker than O'Duffy's contribution towards its overthrow, was, in qualitative terms, of a very different order. Their activities in Spain have been ably recorded by Michael O'Riordan in his book *Connolly Column*.[37]

At the Irish Labour Party's Annual Conference held in Dublin in October 1934, a resolution was moved regarding 'the Communist Menace'. The resolution read:

> Believing that the aim of the Irish Labour movement must continue to be the establishment of a just Social Order based on Christian Teaching, this Conference will strongly oppose any attempt to introduce anti-Christian communist doctrines into the movement.[38]

The resolution was not debated at any great length but some notable figures opposed its adoption including Cathal O'Shannon, Frank Robbins (ex ICA) and Connolly's son Roddy. One speaker named Hall opposed the resolution on the grounds that he 'did not want a sectarian movement and suggested that the mover should read James Connolly's Labour Nationalism and Religion from which he (Mr Hall) quoted'.[39] The resolution was carried.

This resolution was later quoted in a letter which William Norton, leader of the Irish Parliamentary Labour Party, sent to Cardinal Pacelli, Cardinal Secretary of State in the Vatican, in February 1937. The object of this correspondence was to take issue with an article in *Osservatore Romano* which had been reprinted in the *Irish Catholic*. This article asserted that the Irish Trade Union Congress and Irish Labour Party 'tacitly supported Communism'; Norton disputed this allegation and suggested to the Cardinal that if *Osservatore Romano* wanted to 'publish reliable information on the religious beliefs and economic viewpoint of Irish workers', it should 'in the first instance, have recourse to the distinguished Churchman who occupies the position of Rector of the Irish College in Rome, or to the other Irish ecclesiastics in that city'. Norton's letter amounted to a voluntary subjection to a form—albeit an indirect form—of clerical inquisition and supervision, and was signed 'Your Eminence's most humble servant'.[40] Indeed the letter's tone and content reflected a most subservient attitude. The labour movement was in effect petitioning the fathers of the Church as a child accused of wrongdoing protests its innocence and proclaims its obedience. Clearly by 1937 the labour movement in the Republic of Ireland had moved a great distance from Connolly's position on religion and the place of the clergy in political life, and a very long way along the road towards being, in practice, if not in theory, an organisation which took inspiration, and, to an extent, control from the Catholic Church.

If the influence of the Church on the Labour Party was still in question, the Annual Conference of the Party in April 1939 supplied an unequivocal answer. On the third day of this conference, William Norton moved a resolution, submitted by the Party's Administration Council, which moved amendments to the Constitution of the Party. The amendments in question were originally put forward by the Teachers Organisation, which had submitted them 'following a rather lengthy correspondence between that Organisation and the Irish Hierarchy'. This correspondence had led to the hierarchy 'expressing the opinion that in their ordinary everyday meaning certain principles of the Constitution appeared to be in conflict with Catholic teaching'. The Conference papers note that the Church's objections were basically twofold:

> firstly, objection was taken to the aim of the party being a Workers' Republic, and objection was taken to other sections of the principles and objects on the ground that they did not make adequate provision for the safeguarding of private property, to which the Catholic Church attached very considerable importance.[41]

In presenting the resolution, Norton referred to the fact that the amendment entailed the deletion of the words 'Workers' Republic' from the Constitution of the party and noted that 'there would be considerable feeling on the matter as some of the delegates 'would naturally associate the words with the activities of a man whose actions were revered, not merely by Irishmen and women but throughout the world'.[42] A number of delegates spoke against the resolution, most of them alluding to the fact that deleting the phrase 'Workers' Republic' was in effect a renunciation of all that Connolly had stood for. In his speech opposing the resolution, Connolly's son Roddy stated that his father had been a revolutionary socialist and that he could see no reason why this fact should be hidden or require apology.[43] When the vote was taken, 89 delegates voted in favour of the resolution and only 25 against it. The Labour Party had decided that in the final analysis a directive from the Catholic Church exerted a more powerful influence than the political and inspirational legacy of the party's founder.

The Irish left in the years 1916–40 did make some attempt, particularly in the first few years after the Rising, to follow Connolly's example and teachings in respect to its position on religion in general, and Roman Catholicism in particular.

The fact that in his own lifetime Connolly had been forced to resort to a number of half-truths and occasional outright false representations of his religious position, meant that his legacy on this issue was subject to a good deal of inconsistency and apparent confusion. His followers, faced with the same baleful imperatives which Connolly himself had been unable to surmount, were unable to establish a viable and fully independent position outside the supervision and direction of the Church. In the years after his death the labour movement came increasingly under the influence and direction of the Church, culminating, as we have seen, in an abject renunciation of Connolly's political vision at the request of the Catholic Church.

CHAPTER 11

Syndicalism

The events of Easter Week were replete with tragic suffering and cruel losses, among which the death of the author of 'Labour in Irish History' looms large, but from a political point of view, the wonderful renaissance of national sentiment which followed more than justified the prescience of the dead leaders. From the Union point of view, the immediate losses have been more than offset by the ultimate gain. Easter Week saved the Union. It cancelled out the reaction from 1913, and removed bitter prejudices which had blocked its progress. It linked up the Labour Movement with the age-long aspirations of the Irish people for the emancipation from political and social thraldom, and formed a natural moratorium under cover of which it was able to make a fresh start on better terms with increased membership.

Irish Transport and General Workers Union Annual Report for 1918.[1]

IT HAS BEEN shown how Connolly's revolutionary strategy centered upon the syndicalist oriented Irish Transport and General Workers Union and its military arm, the Irish Citizen Army. In the period immediately following the Rising for some time it appeared that his proposed revolutionary vehicles would cease to exist. Indeed, an ITGWU publication later noted that 'in the dark days that followed the Rising the Union seemed broken and bleeding'.[2] But the Union was to experience a remarkable revival in its fortunes. A combination of political and economic factors—the most important of which was the public's identification of the Union with the national struggle and in particular with the increasingly hallowed name of Connolly its martyred leader—ensured that the Union's star was on the ascendant.

At the time of the Rising the ITGWU had approximately five thousand members organised into ten branches; it had substantial debts and to its credit had exactly ninety-six pounds in its account.[3] The Rising itself led to the death and imprisonment of many members, including a large proportion of its leading lights, and to extensive destruction of the Union's headquarter's, Liberty Hall. Despite these major disruptions, the Union increased its membership to 12,000 by the Autumn of 1917 and registered a further 2,000 members by the end of the year. A Union census in mid-1918 listed almost 44,000 members, a figure which by the year's end reached just under 68,000, the Union by that time having some 210 branches.[4] This phenomenal rate of increase was not maintained, yet despite

97

fluctuating fortunes due to economic and military disruptions, the Union could still claim that when James Larkin 'returned to Ireland in April 1923 the Union had 100,000 members in 350 branches spread all over Ireland, and had a credit Balance of over 140,000 Pounds'.[5]

It is clear that Connolly's proposed revolutionary vehicle had not merely survived the difficult post-Rising years but was a thriving and expanding Union, being in fact by far the largest and most powerful union in the country. For the men who re-established the ITGWU and supervised its tremendous expansion, Connolly was not merely a revered hero-leader from the pages of the Union's history, nor simply a powerful icon to be used in attracting recruits to the Union, his syndicalist teachings remained a living force within the Union, providing it with its whole theoretical basis. The question arises, however: did the ITGWU maintain its syndicalist, and more particularly its revolutionary syndicalist, Connolly-inspired, organisation and objectives? In many countries the years following World War One saw syndicalism waning as a political and industrial movement. One reason for this decline was the fact that many erstwhile syndicalists transferred their allegiance to 'Sovietism' after the success of the Revolution in Russia.[6] In the following pages we will examine the progress of the syndicalist ideal in Ireland, a study which will, in the main, revolve around the development of the ITGWU.

In August 1916 the ITUCLP conference was held in Sligo. This Congress, the first major all-Ireland labour meeting since the Rising, was a sad and somewhat confused affair. A number of the most influential labour leaders, including W. O'Brien and T. Foran, had only recently regained their freedom after periods of internment in Britain on account of their non-military nationalist activities.[7] Despite the presence of the surviving leaders of the labour movement, the Congress failed to take a clear stand on many—indeed, one might argue, on any issues. In his chairman's address, Thomas Johnson expressed the most fulsome praises to Connolly's memory, telling Congress that having had 'intimate knowledge of him, and after careful study of his public speeches, his private conversations, and his written work, I say that never was there a man who more thoroughly saturated himself with the hopes, the aspirations, and the sufferings of the working class'.[8] Yet syndicalism is amongst the notable omissions and evasions which characterised Johnson's keynote speech, a speech considered important enough to be published in pamphlet form, 'by order of the Congress', by the National Executive of the Irish Trades Union Congress and Labour Party, under the exalted and definitive title *The Future of Labour in Ireland*. His high regard for Connolly and his teachings notwithstanding, there is little in Johnson's speech of anything which could be construed as syndicalist sentiment nor indeed of any other revolutionary strategy.[9]

Within the ITGWU, however, syndicalism was by no means dead. On 1 July 1918 the Executive Committee of the Union published a pamphlet entitled *The Lines of Progress*, the preface of which unequivocally states that the pamphlet 'accepts in advance and aims at applying to our wants the theory of THE ONE BIG UNION, the dream of James Connolly's life'. The preface then goes on to assert that:

The greatness of Connolly's intellect, the reality of his convictions, the heroism of his death have seized the attention of an Ireland awakened to the forced economic truths by the pressure of the present world-war. We, who reap where he and Jim Larkin have sown, are deeply concerned to take advantage of the present popularity and growth of the Union to put our organisation thoroughly into line with this, the only scientific solution of the labour question that has ever been put before the country. We must therefore see to it that the present and future development of this Union shall be based on a system which will need no alteration when at length THE ONE BIG UNION has been accepted by Irish labour as the effective instrument it needs to achieving its final emancipation from the bondage of wage slavery.[10]

The main body of *The Lines of Progress* sets out a simple and straightforward OBU organisational schema, very much along the same lines as Connolly's exposition in *The Axe to the Root* (sometimes published under the title *Socialism Made Easy*). Indeed, in an edition of *The Axe to the Root* published by the ITGWU in 1921, the Union's introduction states explicitly that 'The plan, the methods and the aims of the ITGWU are those set forth in this, the most popular of James Connolly's works,' and goes on to conclude that the work was 'but one portion of the legacy of thought and example Connolly has bequeathed to us. It is our duty to work out in action the principles for which he lived and died.'[11]

The first issue of *Irish Opinion: The Voice of Labour,* which later became the official organ of the ITGWU, appeared in December 1917. The whole front page was devoted to a reprint of one of Connolly's articles.[13] Indeed it was a rare occurrence for an issue of this paper, or indeed any labour paper, to appear without a reprint of one of his articles, short quotations subtracted from his writings or at least some reference to his life and work. Given the ITGWU's commitment to syndicalism, it is not surprising that in publications over which it had some influence, Connolly's name and writings were constantly used to promote syndicalist objectives. In January 1918, for example, an article appeared in *Irish Opinion,* which, after making the point that capitalists organised themselves into One Big Union, went on to assert that 'the ideal of James Connolly was One Big Union for all Labour in Ireland, and we shall strive to bring that ideal to fruition. It is worth striving for, as within such a Union the power of the worker can be truly focussed.'[14] Thomas Foran was in a combative mood in the next issue, and stated that the ITGWU's 'enemies', who 'boasted that the absence of Larkin and the death of Connolly had killed the Transport Union', were in error because in point of fact the 'militant spirit of their leaders had been bequeathed to everyone of the rank and file'.[15]

It was not only 'militant spirit' which Connolly had bequeathed the Union, although certainly in the eyes of some members, the ITGWU had been 'made sacred by his lifeblood bravely offered up for Ireland'.[16] In August 1918 in an article entitled 'The Programme of Labour' a writer—probably Cathal O'Shannon— made the point that:

If Irish Labour is to be aroused to self consciousness a widespread distribution of literature must be undertaken and nothing better can be found for
the start of definite effort than that admirable credo by James Connolly on
the front page recently. The Transport Union has ordered 10,000 reprints
with their own imprint, and we have no doubt they will want more.[17]

Clearly Connolly's syndicalist-orientated writings were perceived to be of major
educational and propaganda importance by the leaders of the Irish Labour
movement and more particularly by the leaders of the ITGWU, many of whom
had a long standing commitment to syndicalist strategies. This assessment of the
importance of Connolly's writings was not based on mere sentiment or nostalgia
but on a hard-headed analysis of the effectiveness of Connolly's written work in
promoting syndicalist ideas. Indeed, one commentator noted in September 1918
that it was 'largely through the writings of the late James Connolly' that the
'importance of industrial control is becoming more understood in Labour circles'.[18] Although it would be true to say that educational and propaganda work in
Ireland in favour of the 'One Big Union' movement was almost exclusively based
on promoting Connolly's brand of syndicalism—indeed the OBU was often
referred to as 'Connolly's ideal' in contexts which suggested that the OBU strategy was Connolly's own personal invention[19]—there were some attempts to break
out of this somewhat restricted and parochial pattern. On a few occasions the
'Preamble of the Industrial Workers of the World' was published in the Labour
press[20] and on one occasion the *Watchword* reprinted a chapter of Justus Ebert's
book *The IWW in Theory and Practice*.[21]

Whilst maintaining its commitment to OBU industrial development, the
ITGWU and indeed to some extent the Irish labour movement as a whole went
through a period of intense sympathy with and support of the Russian Revolution
and the new Soviet Government. This infatuation with Bolshevism was reflected
in meetings organised to express support for the Revolution and a good deal of
pro-soviet writing, including translations of articles by Soviet leaders, published in
the labour press.[22] The first and in some ways most impressive pro-Soviet meeting
took place in Dublin early in 1918 when 'an enormous crowd' attended a meeting
held in the Mansion House to 'congratulate the Russian people on the triumph
they had won for democratic principles'. With O'Brien in the chair, Union officers
O'Shannon, Foran and Coates amongst the platform speakers,[23] and an audience
which we can safely assume had a sizable ITGWU component, it is hardly
surprising that Coates evoked a sympathetic response when he said—only half in
jest—that they should 'transform the Viceregal Lodge into the head office of the
Irish Transport Workers'. O'Shannon successfully proposed the major resolution,
that the 'people of Dublin were at one with the Bolsheviks' and that the 'Russian
interpretation of the democratic principle was the only one that would be accept-
able to the people of Ireland'. O'Shannon's resolution went on to assert that
'political freedom would not suffice for this country, and that what they wanted
was a social revolution'.[24]

Given the interest in, and level of support for, Soviet ideas, it was perhaps inevitable that some sections of the Labour movement would attempt to emulate the Russian Soviet example. Soviets, mostly short lived, were established in a number of places including Limerick, Broadford, Knocklong, Bruree and Arigna.[25] The most important and well documented of these attempts to establish Soviets was the Limerick Soviet established in April 1919. For a few years prior to the establishment of the Soviet in Limerick, the town had been a noted centre for left-wing activities; indeed, the area had for a time been served by a colourfully radical and cheerfully aggressive Labour paper called *The Bottom Dog*—a fact which may have played some part in later developments in the city. *The Bottom Dog* reprinted a number of Connolly's writings and often contained exhortatory comments regarding the example Connolly had set by his leadership in 1916.[26] Some local Labour activists had a closer connection with Connolly than through his writings. An article in *Irish Opinion* in February 1918 entitled 'Connolly's Ideal for Limerick' noted that the Secretary of the ITGWU no. 3 Branch had told an ITGWU meeting that 'as one who had fought in Dublin, he believed in Connolly's ideal, that a free Ireland must mean freedom for Irish workers'.[27]

A general strike was declared in Limerick on April 13, 1919, sometimes referred to as the 'permit strike' as it was called in response to a military ruling that permits would be required to enter or leave the City. On the previous day the *Voice of Labour* published an article, most probably written by O'Shannon, but certainly reflecting the opinions of the whole ITGWU leadership. The following comments were made on the 'Soviet idea':

> We give it as our deliberate and carefully thought-out opinion that the best and most effective answer Ireland can give to MacPherson and the Government he represents is the establishment here and now of Soviets in Ireland . . . To-day the Soviet idea is sweeping westward over Europe . . . The Soviet has shown itself the only instrument of liberation in Europe . . . Ireland's best and most effective answer is the immediate establishment of the Soviets, the instruments which will bring about the dictatorship of the Irish proletariat.[28]

There can be no doubt that the leadership of the ITGWU had played a substantial part in promoting the Soviet idea to the workers in Limerick and that the influence of Connolly's ideas and example exerted a considerable influence on the radical direction which the strike took. The strikers' newspaper, the *Workers Bulletin,* which proudly proclaimed that it was 'Issued by the Limerick Proletariat', noted that 'James Connolly has not died in vain. His spirit is with the workers of Limerick today, and we shall not forget.' The same issue proclaimed that 'To the memory of our great Martyr—James Connolly—we pay the greatest tribute that workers can, viz:- by carrying on the struggle against tyranny and oppression.'[29]

Despite promises of extensive support, the Limerick strikers found that the ILPTUC leaders were slow to come to the scene of the strike, and that when Tom Johnson did appear, representing the ILPTUC, the promised assistance consisted almost entirely of verbal and moral support. The ILPTUC failed to provide the financial and logistical support necessary to sustain the strike and was unable to agree upon the calling of a national general strike in support of the Limerick strike. The strike effectively collapsed on April 24 when the Roman Catholic Bishop of Limerick and the Mayor of Limerick sent a joint letter to Limerick Trades Council requesting its immediate abandonment.[30] Although this intervention was clearly responsible for the timing of the strike's end the lack of support, the national labour movement had ensured that the strike was a lost cause long before the final blow was dealt.

In the aftermath of this failure, the *Voice of Labour* somewhat optimistically noted that 'one result of the Big strike being handled efficiently by a central committee is a lesson in unity and action and a decided impetus for the OBU ideal'.[31] In fact the reverse was the case: the failure of the strike, and more particularly the failure of the national leadership of the labour movement to offer effective support to the strikers, was generally recognised. At the 1919 Congress of the ILPTUC, T. Foran (President of the ITGWU) described the Limerick strike as a 'very perfect illustration of the inadequacy of the present methods' and went on to argue that 'if they had had the One Big Union, decisions would have been more satisfactory at Limerick'.[32]

The 1919 Congress in fact devoted a very large part of its time to discussing how best to organise such a One Big Union in Ireland. One speaker noted that 'there were few present who did not recognise that the One Big Union was the desirable goal and that it was inevitable some day'.[33] In the light of the fact that other attempts by workers to establish Soviets continued to be denied real support by organised Labour, it is arguable that the concentration on organisational problems was in large part a reluctance to face the fact that the leadership's support for the Soviet ideal and for the establishment of Soviets in Ireland was a purely theoretical commitment. In practice the leaders of Labour lacked the resolve and indeed the nerve to effectively support the radical, even potentially revolutionary, actions of sections of the rank and file.

On two occasions the *ILPTUC* called for and successfully directed general strikes, an anti-conscription one-day strike in April 1918 and a two-day general strike demanding the release of republican political prisoners in April 1920. Other major industrial campaigns falling short of full general strikes included the Motor Permits and Munition Transport strikes in 1920. All of these had in common the fact that they were organised around a specific issue and clearly limited in their scope and objectives. Following Connolly's opposition to the general strike, and their own inclinations to avoid large scale open-ended confrontational situations, the leadership of the labour movement rejected the classic syndicalist vision of the general strike as a revolutionary vehicle for the destruction of capitalism. It is also noteworthy that all the major political strikes owed more to the struggle for national independence than to socialist objectives. Many years later, William O'Brien, in reference to the 1935 tram and bus strike in Dublin, expressed his long-held view on more ambitious general strikes when he stated that general strikes were 'foolish' unless a 'revolutionary situation had arisen'.[34]

James Larkin returned to Ireland in April 1923. He had been in America since 1914, during which time he had spent some years in prison after being found guilty of a charge of criminal sedition. During his years outside Ireland, Larkin had retained his position—and wage—as General Secretary of the ITGWU, the Union he had founded in January 1909. An immensely attractive and inspirational man, Larkin displayed throughout his life an unquenchable and undeviating (although often misdirected) commitment to the working class struggle. In many ways a larger than life figure, a legend in his own time—and unfortunately in his own mind—Larkin's faults, his egotism, his tendency to play fast and loose with facts and figures and his poor administrative skills, were to prove extremely destructive to the ITGWU and indeed to the Irish labour movement as a whole.[35] As early as 1909 a Belfast delegate to the ITUC, speaking in opposition to the ITGWU's request for affiliation stated that he 'knew Larkin's ability as an organiser, but he also knew that unless he was boss he would always be an opponent'.[36] These were prophetic words.

During Larkin's absence, his sister Delia, who had at one time been in charge of the Irish Women Workers Union (IWWU), had perhaps given the ITGWU's leadership a foretaste of things to come, when, after becoming estranged from both the IWWU and the ITGWU, she devoted her not inconsiderable energies and invective to attacking the ITGWU. In July 1919 the fiery Miss Larkin was quoted as having said that 'if justice were done there would not be lamposts enough in Dublin to hang the scoundrels who were running Liberty Hall'. Commenting on this somewhat intemperate attack, a Union spokesperson noted 'we do not believe Miss Larkin made such a statement, but her colleague Mr. Michael Mullen did' and went on to reflect that 'The Transport Union knows how hard it is to fight on the industrial or agricultural field when it is attacked on the flank by professing friends'.[37]

Delia Larkin's enmity was merely an annoyance to the ITGWU leadership. The enmity of its General Secretary, a man worshipped by large sections of the Dublin working class and an object of particular devotion to the Dublin-based old guard of the Union, was a threat of a very different order. Before Larkin left for America, he had been very much an autocrat at Liberty Hall; he had made all the decisions and in effect acted as a one-man Union executive. On his return to Ireland he found a radically altered situation. When he left Ireland the Union had a few thousand members, huge debts and lacked even a rudimentary democratic structure. In the intervening eight years the Union had enlisted almost 100,000 members, accumulated substantial financial resources and established a democratic organisational structure. Although 'nearly five thousand enthusiastic admirers' greeted Larkin when he returned to Dublin, it would be fair to say that the crowd's enthusiasm was by no means shared by the men who had assumed the leadership of the ITGWU since his departure.[38]

The details of the extremely acrimonious, and occasionally violent split, which occurred between Larkin and his supporters, and the 'new guard' at the ITGWU has been well documented and need not be recounted in detail here.[39] Suffice to say that both sides were intransigent and that although the anti-Larkinite leadership, which easily held control of the Union, had the best arguments (and more importantly had the 'numbers' to defeat and eventually to expel Larkin), Larkin also had some cause to feel aggrieved particularly after he discovered the fact that union officials had surreptitiously withheld 7,500 pounds from him during the 1913 Lockout.[40] Whatever the rights and wrongs of the dispute, the end result was clearly a great blow to the ITGWU and indeed to organised labour as a whole. After his expulsion from the ITGWU, Larkin precipitated lengthy, expensive and very damaging legal actions and also founded a new OBU—The Workers Union of Ireland—a Union which attracted a substantial number of the ITGWU'S Dublin-based membership. Although never approaching the ITGWU's strength or power, the WUI was a constant thorn in its side. The ITGWU, Ireland's own OBU organisation had produced an unwanted offspring in the form of a rival OBU—a fact most damaging in its attempts to make successful propaganda in favour of Irish labour as a whole organising into the OBU. The ITGWU itself admitted that its 'internal crisis' had left it 'with somewhat diminished power and prestige'.[41]

Throughout the struggle for the leadership of the ITGWU, the Union 'new guard' (or, to be more precise, William O'Brien) made masterly and ruthless use of Connolly's name and reputation. O'Brien had become Connolly's literary executor by default after the murder of Francis Sheehy-Skeffington in 1916, and he had no compunction about using his privileged access to Connolly's private correspondence—including his private assessment of Larkin and his character— to discredit Larkin. Even Connolly's wife Lillie was brought into the fray.[42] The front page of the ITGWU's pamphlet 'Some Pages From Union History' provides good example of O'Brien's tactics. Under the heading 'Connolly's Opinion of Larkin,' the following extracts from Connolly's private letters regarding Larkin are printed: 'The man is utterly unreliable—and dangerous because unreliable'; 'He must rule or will not work'; 'He is consumed with jealousy and hatred of anyone who will not cringe to him and beslaver him all over'.[43] Connolly's personal opinions of Larkin during the years when they worked together combined with detailed comparisons of Larkin's years as an active leader of the ITGWU and Connolly's leadership after Larkin's visit to America—comparisons, one need hardly add, which reflected very badly on Larkin—were used as weapons in the successful effort to oust Larkin from the ITGWU. Ownership of Connolly's personal papers clearly was a factor of great advantage to O'Brien during the Larkin dispute.

Until 1930 the labour movement enjoyed an unusual and in syndicalist terms, potentially extremely valuable unity. The Irish Labour Party and the Trade Union Congress were united within one body the ILPTUC. Up until 1918 this organisation had been called Irish Trade Union Congress and Labour Party, but the order of precedence was thereafter reversed due to a 'growing realisation of the need for effective political organisation'.[44] At the 1924 ILPTUC William Norton moved a resolution calling for the establishment of a special Committee to 'consider and report on the desirability of separating the Industrial and Political sides of the movement into two independent and autonomous bodies'.[45] This committee was established and it reported its findings to a Special Congress early in 1930. The Committee reported in favour of the separation of labour's political and industrial arms. In Norton's statement supporting the resolution he used Connolly's name and reputation to back his argument: 'I cannot help feeling', he asserted, 'having regard to all he has written that James Connolly were he alive today, would be the first to endorse the proposals now being submitted to Congress. He would have seen that the needs of today demand something more efficient than the needs of yesterday.'[46] After a brief debate, Norton's motion was put and carried unanimously. An amendment by members of the Irish Women Workers Union designed to retain 'the essential unity of the two organisations' was defeated.[47] It is hard to see this organisational division as anything other than a step away from the unified labour movement which was the essential goal of the whole OBU syndicalist strategy.

A special Trade Union Conference in April 1936 set up a Commission of Inquiry into Trade Union Organisation. The inquiry's wide-ranging terms of reference centered upon a review of the desirability and feasibility of 'the amalgamation of groups of Unions analogous to or associated with special industries or occupations'[48]—in essence an inquiry into Industrial Unionism. It was to be February 1939 before this Commission presented its report to a 'conference of Trade Union representatives'. Despite its lengthy gestation the report highlighted the deep divisions within the movement and failed to reach any definite conclusions. Of the twelve people appointed to the Inquiry (Eamonn Lynch acted as Secretary) William O'Brien and four others—one of whom had deep reservations[49] supported a 're-casting of the whole Trade Union Movement' into industrial groupings; another group of five fronted by Samuel Kyle felt that the O'Brien proposals were 'much too far reaching' and that 'the suggestion that the entire Trade Union Movement in Ireland should be scrapped and that there should be substituted ten Industrial groups is quite unworkable'.[50] The leader of the Labour Party, William Norton, in his own one-man report stated that while he 'ardently' supported the 'principle of Trade Union amalgamation', he felt that it would be a 'disaster if an effort is made to attempt a large scale grouping of unions before the necessary psychological atmosphere has been created'.[51] The final member of the Commission, not included in either of the three memoranda presented, did not make any formal presentation of his opinion and thus in effect supported the *status quo*.[52]

Due to O'Brien's position within the trade union movement and his vast experience and expertise in such matters, he managed to get his minority memorandum presented as the majority position when a conference was held to discuss the Commission's Inquiry in Dublin in February 1939. But despite all of O'Brien's formidable influence and political skills, he failed to force through his blueprint for union re-organisation. The fact that one of his old enemies P.T. Daly was in the chair at the conference did nothing to improve O'Brien's chances of success, nor his temper. When it eventually became clear that all chance of success for his memorandum had vanished, an angry and disappointed O'Brien withdrew from the meeting in protest against one of the chairman's rulings.[53] Whatever else may be said about O'Brien, there can be no doubt that he remained true to, and tried to actively pursue, the syndicalist ideas which Connolly had taught him when he was little more than a boy during the early years of the ISRP.

O'Brien's failure, despite all his power, influence and organisational brilliance, to achieve a major restructuring of Irish Trade Unions along industrial Union lines—'the lines of progress'—is an appropriate note on which to conclude this chapter. The OBU movement in Ireland was a powerful and at times persuasive force within the labour movement, yet, in the final analysis it was a failure in its own terms. The ITGWU is of course the central factor in any assessment of Irish syndicalism. Arguably its very size, dwarfing as it did all other unions, was in itself a threat, the union being perceived to be a poacher of other unions members and as being staffed by empire builders rather than an inspirational and attractive force. This perception of the ITGWU as an aggressively expansionist rather than idealistically committed organisation was not helped by the leadership of the ITGWU using the term OBU rather loosely, the term being used to describe both the ideal as an objective for the labour movement as a whole, and as a description of the ITGWU. This suggested to some trade unionists outside the ITGWU that the OBU objective was simply the ITGWU pursuing a monopolistic control over Irish labour. Problems also existed within the ITGWU. The Larkin split and its bitter aftermath was extremely damaging but probably even more damaging was the fact that many, probably most, ITGWU members saw the union as 'a mere wagegetting machine' rather than as an organisation committed to an OBU economic and political strategy. Finally, although the union leadership cannot be accused of lacking intellectual commitment to the OBU, O'Brien, O'Shannon and the other leaders were dedicated to Connolly's teachings and were moreover men of real ability and courage they lacked the revolutionary fire, the wild opportunism which might have allowed their beliefs to be translated into concrete form.

CHAPTER 12

Socialism and Nationalism

Of James Connolly, one of whose oldest friends in the Labour movement I can proudly claim to be, I am bound to say this: his life and his death were the inspiration to which are due the splendid enthusiasms, the strong determination, the manly independence, and in a large measure the wholehearted allegiance of the many thousands of workers who have joined our ranks within the past two years. His are the ideals we follow, his the principles we adopt, his the plans and methods upon which we organise, his the memory and the inspiration from which we draw our strength and our place in the forefront of the fighting army of Labour and in the battle for the freedom and justice in this and all other lands. May the sod rest lightly upon you, old comrade, murdered at the hands of a tyranny, and may peace be your's in death . . . You have given us the most precious of legacies and we who remain to carry on your battles promise you that we shall not lower your flag, but through success and reverse shall travel the road you cut out for us, and battle on until we have built up in Ireland that worker's Republic for which you worked and fought and died.

William O'Brien, ITUCLP, 1918.[1]

A FEW HOURS before facing the firing squad, when speaking to his wife and eldest daughter for the last time, one of Connolly's questions to his daughter was 'have you seen any of the Socialist papers?' When his daughter replied in the negative and questioned his interest, Connolly responded: 'they will never understand why I am here, they will forget I am an Irishman'.[2] Despite his appalling situation—badly wounded and facing a violent death; despite the almost unbearable emotional intensity of seeing his wife and child for the last time; despite all the distractions and excitements of the previous weeks; Connolly the veteran socialist was concerned about how the socialist press was reporting upon and analysing the Rising. His concern that his fellow socialists would not understand his involvement in a 'national' insurrection was shown, in the weeks, months and years that followed, as being based on a sound understanding of their perspectives and limitations.

John Leslie was Connolly's earliest and perhaps most important political mentor. A socialist with strong Irish nationalist sympathies, Leslie 'had the honour of welcoming James Connolly into the Socialist Movement' and had been Connolly's comrade and personal friend for over twenty years.[3] Writing in *Justice,* the organ of the British Social Democratic Federation, in May 1916, Leslie stated that attempting to explain Connolly's participation in the 'deplorable Dublin Tragedy', which he describes as a 'sad, bad and mad outbreak', was 'perhaps the most difficult task' he had ever undertaken. He noted that in his most recent conversation with Connolly he had detected a 'growing Irishism' and concluded from this that if Connolly had 'influenced Sinn Fein the influence had been mutual and reciprocal and that Sinn Fein had made its mark on him'. In Leslie's view, however, 'Sinn Fein' influence on Connolly was only a partial explanation for his involvement in the Rising. He presents 'his own opinion for what it is worth' when he writes:

> I have reason to believe that Connolly did not place a very high estimate upon the Labour or Socialist movement here. Knowing the man, I say it is possible that, despairing of effective assistance from that quarter and indeed believing that it would act as a drag upon his efforts to form an Irish Socialist Party, he determined at all costs to identify or to indissolubly link the course of Irish Labour with the most extreme Irish nationalism, and to seal the band of union with his blood if necessary. [4]

When he made this assessment of the Easter Rising, Leslie was confused about the origins of the Rising and had only a sketchy idea of Connolly's role. At this stage he could not foresee the catalytic effect the Rising was to have on Irish opinion and the development of Irish nationalist sentiment. His assessment of Connolly's aims and objectives, on the other hand, is exceptionally shrewd and penetrating. Leslie clearly knew his man well. Back in Ireland, in the aftermath of the Rising, labour was in a state of disarray. Connolly, Richard O'Carroll, Peter Macken, Francis Sheehy-Skeffington, Michael Mallin and a number of other prominent labour men had either been killed in the fighting or executed after they surrendered. Almost all the other notable figures in the movement, including O'Brien, O'Shannon, P.T. Daly and Thomas Foran, were, as a direct result of their prominence, incarcerated in British internment camps. The leadership vacuum brought about by the failure of the Rising was exacerbated by the fact that ITUCLP records and papers were in the hands of the military and that Liberty Hall, the headquarters of the ITGWU, was in ruins after receiving particular attention from British artillery during the Rising because of its reputation as a centre of rebellion. Labour had paid a very high price for its involvement in the Rising.

It is perhaps ironic that the vacuum created by Connolly's execution and the destruction of labour organisation in Dublin was in large part filled by Thomas Johnson an English-born Protestant based in Belfast. A man of strong pacifist inclinations who nonetheless tended to support the Allied war effort, Johnson had very little understanding of Irish nationalism, being at best a somewhat mild supporter of Home Rule.[5] Johnson was no Johnny Come Lately. He had achieved high office in the Irish Labour movement prior to 1916 (Vice-Chairman of the ITUC in 1913, Chairman in 1914) and despite their political differences, he had enjoyed a harmonious relationship, based on mutual respect and tolerance with Connolly when Connolly worked in Belfast as an ITGWU organiser. Johnson was a dedicated socialist and had an immense capacity for hard and effective work. He was also a decent man who impressed both his colleagues and his opponents with his integrity and seriousness of purpose. He was, however, not a labour leader in the Connolly mould. Fabianism rather than Fenianism[6] coloured Johnson's socialism and this fact was to exert an important influence on Irish labour after the Rising.

The ITUCLP Congress held in Sligo in August 1916 was one of the first major public meetings to be held after the Rising. Labour was at this time clearly faced with both great opportunities and great dangers. It is arguable that labour had a chance to seize the initiative and place itself at the head of the national movement, as Connolly had done. Indeed, Connolly had died establishing labour's right and providing its opportunity to do just this. Such an action would of course have resulted in an immediate attack by the forces of the Crown on the already depleted, badly shaken and poorly prepared labour movement. These forces were already, and with some justice, disposed to view Irish labour (with the exception of the Protestant enclave in the North-East) as rebels of the darkest hue. What in fact took place in Sligo, however, was what one commentator has called a 'facing both ways'[7] stance. As President of Congress Johnson had responsibility for making the initial keynote address, although we can safely assume that he discussed its contents with other labour leaders (both O'Brien and O'Shannon had been released before Congress met). Johnson saw the task as one calling for healing words and defensive rather than revolutionary attitudes.

In his speech to Congress, Johnson frequently referred to Connolly, stating at one point that:

> We who know him must feel that in his death the working class of Ireland has lost a champion they could ill afford to lose. We looked forward to seeing him take a very active leading part in the direction of the Labour Movement in the civil life of this country under a new regime, but he conceived his duty lay in another direction. We mourn his death, we honour his work, we revere his memory.[8]

We have no reason to doubt Johnson's sincerity when he publicly proclaimed his respect and admiration for Connolly, but it was clearly to Connolly the labour man, rather than Connolly the political theorist and revolutionary, to whom he paid his respects. Johnson's speech, which was widely acclaimed and later published in pamphlet form under the title *The Future of Labour in Ireland*,[9] was almost the exact antithesis of Connolly's aggressive revolutionary socialist political position. This was clearly evident when he told Congress that 'As a Trade Union Movement we are of varied minds on matters of history and political development, and, consequently, this is not a place to enter into discussion as to the right or the wrong, the wisdom or the folly of the revolt.'[10]

Given that Johnson's prime concern was to maintain the unity of labour in Ireland—the North-East being not only Ireland's Unionist stronghold but also the area with the greatest concentration of industrial workers—it is perhaps not surprising that he should refer to the war in France and ask Congress to remember those 'who have laid down *their* lives in another field, also for what they believed to be the Cause of Liberty and Democracy and for Love of their Country'.[11] What is surprising is that in concluding his preamble on the Rising he should cite Connolly's reputed last words, 'I pray for all men who do their duty according to their lights', and then state that 'In that spirit I ask all, whatever their views may be in regard to the war or the rebellion, to rise for a moment in token of respect for all our comrades who have been brave enough to give their lives for the cause they believed in.'[12] For the first but by no means the last time, Connolly's words were being used to justify political positions which he would in fact have vehemently opposed.

In his informative study of the ITGWU, Greaves notes that Johnson's 'facing both ways' stance became the Irish labour movement's 'strongest precedent' and expresses the view that it was 'surprising that at this crucial test of Irish Labour, no voice was raised to avow Connolly's programme of revolutionary opposition to the war'. Greaves argues that the Congress leaders 'lacked Connolly's tumultuous imagination. They felt he had failed, just when he was about to be justified. They wanted to play safe. And perhaps at a time when Dublin lay in ruins and the jails were full it was understandable.'[13]

An opportunity to follow Connolly's political line was missed at the 1916 ITUCLP Congress. Most political commentators have noted that Ireland was in a state of political flux at this time, and that people were looking for leadership, nationalist leadership, leadership with courage and vision which would build on the groundwork laid by the Easter Rising. The labour leaders at Sligo were too indecisive, too inward looking, to provide the type of clear and compelling direction which could have established labour as the vanguard of the national struggle for independence.

Following the Sligo Congress, the leaders of the labour movement had to face the daunting task of rebuilding the labour organisations which had been all but destroyed as a result of the Rising. Pressing and extremely demanding internal concerns, not the least of which was the problem of how to maintain an all-Ireland labour unity in the face of the clear and deeply rooted divisions which existed between nationalist and unionist workers, may to some extent have distracted them from recognising the immense political changes, realignments and opportunities which were taking place around them.

William O'Brien, who had closer contact with the non-labour nationalists than most of the other labour leaders,[14] attended the Plunkett Assembly in April 1917. Here he was elected onto the organising committee, on the proposal of Arthur Griffith, as a 'representative of Labour'. O'Brien was then persuaded 'very reluctantly to accept the Chairmanship of the committee'. As it transpired, the Plunkett Assembly was not a particularly successful initiative, but O'Brien's rise to prominence is worth noting as an example of the opportunities which existed at this time. The background to O'Brien's rather unconvincing reluctance to participate in the work of the Assembly is worth noting also.[15] O'Brien was attending the

Assembly as a delegate of the Dublin Trades Council and had been instructed by this body to inform the Assembly that 'as a component part of the Irish Trade Union Congress and Labour Party, which is organised to obtain control of the country for the workers, we cannot send delegates to any but a Labour conference.'[16] Again we see evidence of insularity and restricted vision promoting a policy which was at odds with the teaching and practice of Connolly which the labour movement claimed to adhere to.

Nor was the labour movement officially represented at the Sinn Fein reorganisation meeting held in October 1917, although two ICA members, Constance Markievicz and Dr. Kathleen Lynn, were present and indeed were elected to sit on the Sinn Fein Executive. Commenting on the outcome of this important watershed in Irish politics, Peadar O'Donnell, displaying his customary acuity and forcefulness, noted that:

> Nobody noticed that Connolly's chair was left vacant; that the place Connolly purchased for the organised Labour movement in the leadership of the independence struggle was being denied or reneged. It was made easy for De Valera to call Griffith in and shut Labour out, for the Irish Labour Party did not want a share in the leadership. James Connolly's work, teaching, martyrdom, left no imprint on the policy of Irish working class movements. Dublin workers uncovered at every mention of his name at a meeting but nobody preached Connolly to them.[17]

O'Donnell's argument may perhaps be a little overstated but it does reflect a basic truth in as much as labour, in the period immediately following Connolly's death, was failing to capitalise on his theoretical insights, his practical example and his growing public reputation as a national hero.

In December 1917 the labour movement was, for the first time since Easter 1916, able to re-establish a labour newspaper. In its first issue this paper, published under the title *Irish Opinion,* proclaimed that 'We shall oppose any exploitation in the words of James Connolly whether of class by class, of sex by sex or of nation by nation'.[18] Later in the same issue, in a further attempt to delineate the paper's political perspective, one writer noted:

> Since the death of James Connolly it is impossible to divorce national and Labour problems in Ireland although the desire to return to our earlier insularlty has been evident in the disposition in certain quarters to shelve Connolly and to maintain silence on precisely those questions which lay nearest to his heart . . . it is our intention in this place to keep alive not merely the memory, but, above all the ideals of James Connolly. [19]

While the publication of *Irish Opinion* was a sign of the labour movement's recovering fortunes, the paper was by no means an immediate success. It not only failed to achieve the level of support from organised labour that had been expected but received a blow to its credibility (and indeed the credibility of the whole labour movement) when it emerged that the paper was being funded from an

English anti-Sinn Fein source.[20] Given that in nationalist eyes Tom Johnson was already extremely suspect because of his nationality and religion, it was especially unfortunate that he was the labour leader chosen as a conduit for transferring the funds from England to Ireland. The money had been offered to Johnson by J.M. Lyon to assist in funding an Irish labour newspaper which would promote 'a definite Irish Labour policy of a constructive character'.[21] Johnson rather naively believed that in financing the paper, Lyon and Edward Aston, the agent acting on his behalf in Ireland, were extending a purely altruistic assistance to Irish labour. As it transpired, Lyon and Aston proved to be vehemently opposed to *Irish Opinion* publishing any material which tended to ally labour with Sinn Fein or to present pro-Bolshevik or pro-republican material.[22]

When information about *Irish Opinion*'s dubious financial support became public, Frank Gallagher (later to achieve fame as a writer), who was working on the paper at that time, resigned and the paper's editor L.P. Byrne (under the *nom de plume* of A. E. Malone) was deeply troubled. Byrne refused to follow Lyon's instructions and continued to present a pro-Sinn Fein line in the paper. This resulted in his removal. Cathal O'Shannon, who as we have seen was an out-spoken socialist republican, took over as editor in March 1918, but it was not until August of that year that Lyon—disgusted with the paper's bolshevism and nationalism—finally withdrew his financial support. In the absence of Lyon's support, the paper was uneconomic and only survived as a result of ITGWU inter-vention. Under the title *Irish Opinion: The Voice of Labour*, the paper eventually became the official organ of the ITGWU.

In Johnson's favour, one could cite the fact that Connolly himself accepted fifty pounds from Keir Hardie, the British labour leader, when he was starting the *Workers Republic*,[23] as a precedent for accepting English—or, in Connolly's case, Scottish—money. Yet the circumstances behind Johnson's acceptance of English monies were very different, and reflect little credit on any of the parties involved. That the first Irish labour paper since Connolly's death should damage rather than build upon Irish labour's standing within the nationalist community reflects a willingness to compromise which was very much at variance with the attitude Connolly had tried to instil in Irish labour. Johnson's *faux pas* in accepting 'tainted' money was not quickly forgotten. A letter to the *Daily Bulletin* in 1923 refers to Johnson receiving money from Lyon and describes Lyon as a 'British spy'.[24] James Larkin in his *Irish Worker* often harked back to Johnson's dealings with Lyon. Larkin, who made a point of referring to Johnson by descriptions such as that 'pestiferous Englishman'[25] and the 'English anti-Irishman',[26] noted in one issue that Johnson had been paid seven hundred pounds to publish British propaganda by Lyon who is referred to as a 'British Government agent'.[27]

In 1918 the Labour Party was therefore in an unenviable position with regard to the national question, the issue which had become of paramount importance within Irish political life. Even before the 1918 election, the Party had encountered real difficulties in this area. For example, when labour took an active and promi-nent part in the successful anti-conscription campaign and organised a twenty-four hour general strike on 23 April 1918, the unionist workers in Belfast and even some members of British-based unions in the South refused to heed the ITUCLP's strike call. This partial failure provided confirmation for the leaders of the labour movement, if any confirmation was needed, that on issues relating to the national question they were attempting to provide leadership for a working class which was deeply, and apparently irrevocably, divided. Mitchell is surely correct when he writes that the overall political outcome of labour's anti-conscription campaign was that 'thereafter, when leaders attempted to strike a middle position to appease both nationalist and Unionist workers, it lost the political support of the nationalists and failed to gain the backing of the Unionists'.[28]

By the time Lyon finally despaired of the political efficacy of financial support for *Irish Opinion,* the ILPTUC was on the verge of making a decision which has been generally recognised as being Irish labour's most self-sacrificing contribution to the cause of Irish nationalism. This great opportunity for self-sacrifice arose out of the General Election that had been called for 14 December 1918. As late as October 1918, the ILPTUC held high, and not altogether unreasonable, hopes, that labour could make a real breakthrough and succeed in winning sizable labour representation. On 5 October 1918 *Irish Opinion: Voice of Labour* contained a three-page election manifesto addressed to 'the workers of Ireland'. This manifesto argued the absolute necessity of labour candidates standing in the election, and echoed Connolly's contention that labour should do battle in every possible arena of struggle, including the parliamentary arena. Page one of the manifesto is quite unambiguous and reads in part:

> We have been taught by experience not to allow the victories of Trade Unionism to be brought to nought by laxity in politics—by leaving the political machinery of the state in the control either of Labour's enemies or of professing friends, who are not themselves of the working-class. We must support our Trade Unionism by our politics; we must be ready to use every weapon that has been placed in our hands, to avail of every opportunity which comes in our way to strike blow upon blow in the age-long fight for liberty. Hence it is that the Irish Labour Party announces itself as a combatant in the coming electoral struggle.[29]

Sinn Fein was clearly going to be the major factor in the election. The National Executive of the Labour Party was confident Sinn Fein would be willing, indeed anxious, to come to mutually beneficial agreements with Labour over electoral candidacies. Their manifesto, however, contained a statement which was in itself more than enough to make any Labour-Sinn Fein electoral alliance most unlikely. The manifesto stated that the National Executive had decided 'by a unanimous vote' not to attend the House of Commons. To this point Labour was in line with Sinn Fein policy, and nationalist sentiment in general. However, a crucial, and surely rather pointless, qualification was added as a rider to Labour's abstentionist policy; the ILPTUC noted that it was 'conceivable that altered circumstances and the interests of the workers and democracy may however warrant a change of policy which shall be determined by a special National Congress'.[30] Labour's statement, while admirably honest, was a political blunder. At a time when wholehearted separatism was very much the order of the day, Labour was guilty of prevarication in as much as it failed to commit itself to an irrevocably abstentionist policy. Even those nationalists who were sympathetic to Labour must have found it hard to avoid the conclusion that Labour's abstentionist policy was a matter of short-term expediency rather than political principle.

The front page of the next issue of *Irish Opinion: Voice of Labour* consisted of an article entitled 'Back to Connolly', an article which, as the name suggests, consisted of an exposition designed to show that the Labour Party's decision to contest the General Election was based directly upon Connolly's teaching and practice. The main body of the article consisted of a series of quotations from Connolly but its basic argument is contained in a passage which reads:

> Back to Connolly then is our advice. James Connolly was no dreamer or visionary and never was so regarded in his lifetime. He was a scientific thinker, who deduced theories, only from facts, not from fancy. Those who declare that Labour should not meddle with politics—and there are many such attached to the political parties of the day—and those who demand that Labour should adopt the methods of this non-working-class party or of the other, should calmly study those essays in politics and working-class tactics which are Connolly's precious legacies to the Irish working-class he loved. To him political action—the entry of an organised party of workers upon the struggle for the control of the powers of government—was an historical necessity.[31]

Through the columns of *Irish Opinion: The Voice of Labour,* the National Executive continued over the next few weeks, to most vigorously defend its decision to field candidates in the forthcoming election and continued, moreover, to lay great emphasis on its contention that this stance was based upon the party's faithfulness to the principles of Connolly. A front page article in *Irish Opinion: Voice of Labour* on 19 October[32] was particularly forthright, especially when it took issue with those who were suggesting that 'Labour's approach to politics is a deadly insult to Connolly's memory and quite contrary to his teaching, and that the nomination of Labour candidates is an entirely new plan devised by William O'Brien, Thomas Johnson, and a few other prominent Labour men'. Without mincing words, the article claimed that many of the critics who invoked Connolly's name were in fact his 'bitterest critics in life', would 'fain blot out his memory and teaching', and were 'slandering the dead by innuendo and misrepresentation.' The writer noted that he could find no excuses for these 'perversions'. After once again advising readers to 'go back to Connolly direct' and reasserting that the party was simply 'carrying out the policy that Connolly initiated', the writer posed a question, which in the context is obviously meant to be rhetorical: 'Is there a line in Connolly's writings that would justify the workers of Ireland in abandoning to middle-class theorists, to lawyers, politicians, farmers and shop-keepers, the choice of political representative?'.

Notwithstanding the depth and fervour of their faithfulness to Connolly's teachings, a special Congress of the Party which met on 1 November voted by a large majority to accept a National Executive recommendation for the 'with-drawal from this election of all candidates'.[33] The National Executive's statement which, not surprisingly in the circumstances, avoids mentioning Connolly's name—stated that the party's *volte-face* was undertaken

> in the hope that the democratic demand for self-determination to which the Irish Labour Party and its candidates give its unqualified adherence will thereby obtain the greatest chance of expression at the polls. We shall show by this action that while each of the other political parties is prepared to divide the people in their effort to obtain power, the Labour Party is the only party which is prepared to sacrifice party in the interests of the Nation in this important crisis in the history of Ireland.[34]

Perhaps in an effort to convince itself that the Labour Party really was a political party, this same Special Congress also decided to alter the emphasis of its title by changing it from Irish Trade Union Congress and Labour Party to the more poli-tical sounding Irish Labour Party and Trade Union Congress.[35] In the following chapter we shall explore the political background and ramifications of the Labour Party's decision not to contest the 1918 election. For our present purposes it is enough to note that the Party failed to recognise that its fence-sitting on abstention from Westminster effectively precluded an electoral 'deal' with Sinn Fein—a 'deal' which had been discussed as early as December 1917.[36] As late as October 1918 Sinn Fein was still anxious to come to an electoral arrangement with Labour provided that Labour candidates would agree to take an oath which bound them to resign their seats if they were at any time 'ordered by the Labour Congress to attend the English Parliament'.[37]

The Labour Party had swung almost overnight from a stance on the national question which was unacceptable to many nationalists to an ultra-nationalist 'holier than thou' position of withdrawal from the election. The Party's erratic behaviour at this important juncture in Irish political life clearly reflects the disunity and confusion created by the nationalist question within the party. The decision to retain the option of attending Westminster at some future date was designed principally to impress the Unionist working class of the North East. When it became apparent that the Party's attempt to face both ways at once was causing great damage to its standing within the broader community, the Party lost its resolve and, in the face of what increasingly appeared to be an unwinnable situation, opted out of the electoral contest and replaced its previously proclaimed, Connolly 'sanctioned', policy with lofty but transparently vacuous rhetoric.

After its disappointing electoral non-performance in 1918, the Labour Party took some measure of solace in the fact that 'during the election much use was made by Sinn Fein of an extract from an article by James Connolly in the *Workers Republic* of April 8 1916' and contended that 'the use of Connolly's writing' was an 'endorsement by the national organisation of the policy expressed in it'.[37] One would have thought that Labour's own recent experience of using Connolly's imprimatur to support a policy which it later reversed would have had a cautionary effect, perhaps even caused them to reflect upon the old adage regarding 'people in glass houses', before indulging in thinly veiled criticisms of Sinn Fein's commitment to Connolly's political legacy.

In April 1918 an editorial comment appeared in *Irish Opinion: Voice of Labour* explaining the paper's response to the heavy-handed attentions of the Press Censors Office. The editorial noted that 'the penalty of disobedience to their orders might be entire suppression so our motto is 'Better a live dog than a dead Lion'.[39] In the next issue a reader who had taken issue with what he termed the 'metaphysics' of the issue in which the 'live dog' explanation appeared was informed

> We can only say bluntly that this is not April 1916, but April 1918. Unfortunately *The Voice of Labour* is not *The Workers Republic* and more unfortunately still we are not James Connolly. But one never knows how soon we may become at least, the former; it is beyond anybody in Ireland to become the latter.[40]

Clearly as long as the *Voice of Labour* accepted the role of 'live dog' it could not hope to become another *Workers Republic*. Connolly, who fulfilled the dual role of 'dead lion' and lionised dead for the Irish Labour Movement, had devoted his whole life to raising the working class from its knees. He never under any circumstances resorted to a 'live dog' attitude in any of the numerous radical papers which he edited over the years.

Despite its somewhat inglorious attempt to act the 'live dog', the *Irish Opinion: Voice of Labour* was suppressed in September 1919 after it published an advertisement for the Dáil Eireann National Loan. The *Watchword of Labour,* which succeeded the *Voice*, proclaimed in its first editorial:

> The life and teaching and final oblation of James Connolly it will be our duty; as it is our inclination, to set before the workers of Ireland as an examplar and model, in patience, of study and reflection, in exactitude of thought, and promptness to act and readiness to sacrifice.[41]

Fine words indeed, but it is noticeable that the writer tended to emphasize Connolly's intellect rather than the revolutionary socialist republican militancy which inspired and directed his writings, beliefs and character. In effect, this emphasis reflects a move away from Connolly's absolute commitment to establishing an Irish socialist republic.

As we have seen, caution and political indecisiveness within the Labour movement created political windfalls for Sinn Fein. This in turn led Sinn Fein leaders to view Labour with a fair amount of goodwill. Labour was clearly neither a serious threat nor a demanding ally. Six months after he had been elected President of Dáil Eireann on 1 April 1919 (a somewhat inauspicious date), Eamon de Valera gave a speech on 'The Irish Patriot James Connolly' during the course of which he noted:

> In the Labour world the Irish patriot James Connolly, whom many of you knew personally, was known as a Socialist. There is nothing inconsistent with his

economic idea in his life and fight and death as an Irish Republican—an Irish Nationalist. His position is very much our position. Connolly's story is broadly the story of Irish Labour throughout history . . . the Irish worker, ever true to Irish National ideals, has declared himself unmistakably, and finds no clash between his interests as an Irishman and his class interests as a worker.[42]

De Valera's speech, no doubt sincere and well meaning enough in its own fashion, highlights some of the problems the Irish labour movement faced after it had relinquished political initiative to Sinn Fein. De Valera and other Sinn Fein leaders were able, with a certain amount of justification (particularly in the light of the growth and increasing aggressiveness of the IRA), to claim that Sinn Fein was the most militant force and true custodian of the national struggle. The Sinn Fein claim that the national struggle not only superseded, but also contained within it, the interests of all sections of the community, struck a responsive chord. Labour's insistence on a class analysis of society and on separate working-class organisations and objectives tended to look, and could certainly be presented as being, petty and self-interested, when held up against the call of simple 'apolitical', romantic patriotism, of the kind which Sinn Fein represented. De Valera's assertion that Sinn Fein was in effect Connolly's political legatee, a claim which was strongly, persistently, and for many workers convincingly made by Sinn Fein, was a piece of political usurpation which boded ill for labour's ability to mobilise working-class nationalist support.

Although the labour movement had many close contacts within the non-labour nationalist movement and many labour supporters and labour sympathisers were active within the IRA, there nonetheless existed a tension between the two movements.[43] As obvious rivals for working-class support, this watchfulness, even distrust and animosity, was probably inevitable. From labour's point of view, class factors played a central role in the formation of their attitude towards Sinn Fein. The labour movement was deeply suspicious, on class-based grounds, of many Sinn Fein activists. On a number of occasions the labour press attacked Cathal Brugha, a man whose physical courage and dedication to the Irish Republic had won him an exalted position within the nationalist community. The labour press claimed that Brugha was a bad employer—charges which were in fact later retracted.[44]

During the War of Independence and Civil War period a constant stream of complaints regarding Sinn Fein's right-wing anti-labour tendencies appeared in the labour press. The basic thrust of these complaints and recriminations was that Sinn Fein was 'showing that they are the old gang with different headdress'.[45] In October 1920 a correspondent to the *Watchword of Labour* argued that it was 'foolish and disastrous for Republicans who have the power to improve working-class conditions to allow their judgement to be warped by class bias and prejudice'.[46] Later in the same year the *Watchword* had cause to reflect that while:

> Labour in large part, sank much of its own interests in these elections (County and District elections held in June 1920) in order to secure political unity in the

many crises facing the country. The workers now find themselves scurvily repaid by the Sinn Fein majorities in some of the councils. The philosophy of Sinn Fein is based on sacrifice but some Sinn Feinidthe appear to imagine that the sacrifices are to be exclusively made by one class in the community.[47]

In November 1921 William O'Brien felt obliged in his capacity as Secretary of the ITGWU to reply to a letter received from the officer commanding the Dublin City Brigade of the IRA informing him that the ITGWU 'do not think it desirable that your organisation should interfere in a purely domestic Trade Union matter'.[48] In the same month the *Voice of Labour* noted in an article criticising the Sinn Fein chairman of Dublin County Council that he 'typifies an element likely to develop amongst present-day ardent young Irish patriots of his school', and argued that this was an 'element whose ardent patriotism, admirable as it is, lifts them so cloudward that the wrongs of the toiling masses below are unchampioned by many a valorous sword'[49] In January 1922, when the IRA proclaimed martial law in Kilmallock in an attempt to control a strike by farmworkers, the *Voice of Labour* noted astringently that 'it was *not* for martial law to down strikers that James Connolly died as first Commandant General of the Army of the Republic'.[50] In the same issue of the *Voice* an editorial, almost certainly written by Cathal O'Shannon noted:

> The nearest path to political independence as to social freedom is through the Workers Republic. Vague generalities will cut no ice for the workers. Yet we would be friends and more to the political Republicans if they are prepared to follow their generalisations to a logical conclusion. Towards that end we invite them to do two things. The first is to study and to print in their organ the socialist as well as the nationalist teachings of James Connolly.[51]

Clearly, organised Labour were disenchanted with aspects of Sinn Fein and the 'New Ireland'. In February 1922 William O'Brien somehow managed to get hold of a copy of a letter addressed to the Minister of Defence, Dáil Eireann, from the manager of a flour mill in Mallow, which bluntly and appreciatively stated that 'We beg to enclose cheque for 50 pounds as a subscription to the IRA funds and take this opportunity of thanking you for the protection you offered us during the recent Labour trouble here.'[52] This correspondence and other incidents of a similar kind could not help but create distrust and indeed bitterness. Despite misgivings about Sinn Fein's economic and social perspective, organised labour did support the War of Independence, but increasingly in a secondary capacity. L. J. Duffy, an important labour leader at the time, reflected upon the period in 1924:

> Sinn Fein sought, secured and acknowledged the ready co-operation of the Labour Movement during the Anglo-Irish war. But the Labour Movement entered into the compact as a vassal rather than a co-partner. Let us not blame Sinn Fein for that position. Congress is responsible entirely for the position that grew up around the struggle with England.[53]

Labour's own political mistakes played an important part in diminishing its influence and importance during the war years, but the nature of the struggle, and of the character of the Irish working class itself may have militated against labour. Ernie O'Malley, an important and widely respected IRA organiser, travelled extensively throughout the country during the war years. In his two published works dealing with those years he presented an intelligent and observant analysis of Irish social and military conditions, including comments on labour's position in the national struggle. After noting that 'few of the boys I met had studied Tone, Fintan Lalor or James Connolly', he went on to make the point that 'since the execution of Connolly there has been no revolutionary leader, no one made contact between extreme Labour and the Separatists'. O'Malley's explanation for this lack of 'contact' was that the 'Volunteer spirit in essentials was hostile to Labour, afraid that any attention to its needs or direction would weaken the one-sided thrust of force'.[54]

One might have expected that, with its commitment to a Workers' Republic, organised labour would have been solidly and militantly on the Republican side in the division which split Ireland over the Treaty with Britain. Labour adopted a 'plague on both your houses' stance', a stance which did not make Labour very popular: a correspondent in the *Voice,* noting in July 1922 that 'many people on both sides are displaying the most venomous enmity to the Irish Labour Party'.[55] In effect Labour was pro-Treaty. In an article entitled 'Labour and the Republic' which appeared in the *Voice of Labour* in late December 1921, it was noted, in reference to Ireland having a resident Governor-General, that 'we have little objection to a representative of the King of England as a sort of liason officer if he keeps his place—but there must be no imitation King and Court business allowed'.[56] This willingness to accept a 'representative of the King' in Ireland— Labour's reservations appeared to be directed at the superficial appearance of the Office rather than its political and legal implications—placed Labour well outside the Republican camp and a long distance from Connolly's publicly expressed 'hatred' for the monarchy.[57] Labour's decision to enter the Free State Parliament provided the Treaty Party with a much needed face saving opposition and confirmed Republicans in their belief that Labour was a pro-Treaty party.

Most labour leaders took a pragmatic approach to entering the Dáil. This attitude towards an enforced Oath of Allegiance to the British Crown was consistent with Connolly's view on the matter, for despite his anti-monarchial views, he believed that such an oath was 'a mere formality—a declaration not regarded as binding upon the conscience of any man to whose political opinions the allegiance required is opposed'. Connolly made light of the oath—a thing which of course many religious people could not do—referring to it as 'mummery' and 'indecent foolery'.[58] Similarly in 1914, when he wished to get in contact with the oath-bound Irish Republican Brotherhood (Fenians), he is reported to have said: 'never mind about the formalities—in this business at this time I'm willing to take a score of oaths if they want me to'.[59]

While a good many people on the left of Irish politics opposed the Treaty with Britain, and cited Connolly's political legacy as an explanation of their rejection—

Markievicz for example, in her speech in the Dail during the Treaty debates, noted that she stood for 'James Connolly's ideal of a Workers Republic'[60] what might be termed official labour took a more pragmatic, and in the eyes of many nationalists, a less heroic position. Speaking in the Dáil on behalf of the Labour Party in 1922, Cathal O'Shannon noted that 'the Treaty was not to our liking. Many of the clauses in the Treaty were not to our liking, but we recognised the situation and the conditions governing the Treaty.' O'Shannon went on to make the rather unimpressive admission that 'to us the Treaty was accepted under duress and under nothing else but duress'.[61]

Labour's pragmatism and caution were traits which it certainly had not copied from Connolly and these traits were not attractive to young militants. Commenting on the June 1922 elections, the *Voice of Labour* noted sadly that in the election Labour had attracted:

> no bigger or better supporters than the women of Ireland, but they were not the young women: the young women of Ireland had followed another flag. Labour now asked them to come in with them and had shown them what they could do. The people who had worked for them in this election were the men and women over 30. The young men and young women who ought to have been with them were working for someone else.[62]

That young activists had ignored, or, worse still, deserted the labour camp in the election was symptomatic of the fact that the anti-Treaty Republicans had established themselves as the radical element in Irish politics. It boded ill for labour's future success that the most active and militant section of Ireland's youth and young manhood had opted for the non-labour Republican movement.

The fact that the Labour Party recognised the Free State and entered the Dáil caused great bitterness. Labour perhaps rather unfairly was held responsible, more by association than any direct guilt, for the extremely severe, indeed barbarous, policy of military courts and 'hostage' type executions of imprisoned Republicans for 'crimes' commited by their fellow Republicans. This attitude is clearly reflected in a letter written by Liam Lynch, chief of staff of the anti-Treaty IRA, to Tom Johnson, in which he stated that:

> You, as spokesman, have given the approval of your Party to the present policy of the so-called Provisional government. We are satisfied that your attitude does not reflect the overwhelming opinion of Labour in this country. You must know, however, that your action gave sanction to the executions . . . The continuing participation of your Party in the proceedings of this illegal parliament can only be construed by us as intentional co-operation with enemy forces in the murder of our soldiers, a great proportion of whom are drawn from the ranks of Labour.[63]

Early in 1923 an interesting and instructive indication of how Republicans had come to view Tom Johnson, and by implication, the labour leadership in general, appeared in the *Daily Bulletin*, a Republican newspaper:

There are many Englishmen like you, Mr. Johnson, living as you do, in the Rathmines suburbs, and the majority of them, no doubt, share your political opinions. But they are not the opinions of the workers of Ireland . . . They found their inspiration in James Connolly and not in you, who climbed into power as a result of his sacrifice, having helped to send recent martyrs, workers of Ireland to share his noble company.[64]

In the next chapter we shall examine Connolly's influence on the formation, structure and objectives of Irish political parties and organisations. Saor Eire and Republican Congress, two major left republican initiatives in the 1930s, will be discussed at some length. In this present chapter, however, it is pertinent to note that Connolly's aim of creating a unity between the forces of organised labour with the forces of advanced nationalism was not attained after his death. This failure was not due to ignorance of his ideas. Maeve Cavanagh in 1918, clearly in an optimistic frame of mind, wrote:

Ireland is bringing her own sane and idealistic mind to bear on her Labour question. The reverent disciples of James Connolly are among those who hold aloft the flag of Labour in Ireland—they march among the ranks. With those men and women, to whom his gospel is a religion, the cause of Labour and nationality is safe. May they ever be as closely linked as he left them—one splendid and lasting monument of his great life work.[65]

A decade and a half after Cavanagh's statement, a meeting of left-wing IRA officers and 'others prominently active in the republican and Labour organisa-tions' met in Athlone and drafted a Manifesto which in part stated: 'We believe that a Republic of a united Ireland will never be achieved except through a struggle which uproots capitalism on its way.' The Manifesto went on to quote Conolly's famous statement, 'We cannot conceive of a free Ireland with a subject working class, we cannot conceive of a subject Ireland with a free working class,' and assert that 'This teaching of Connolly represents the deepest instinct of the oppressed Irish nation.'[66] Despite their interest in Connolly's political ideas, the leaders of the Republican Congress, the organisation which grew out of the Athlone meeting, were deeply suspicious of, if not actually hostile to, the Irish Labour Party. Speaking on behalf of the organising Bureau of Republican Congress, Michael Price, in his comments to a trade Union meeting, highlighted how deep the split between organised labour and radical republicanism had become, when he said, with regard to the formation of Republican Congress, that 'the Labour Leadership is not being invited. The Irish Labour Party betrayed the Connolly teaching and tradition in 1922, and its stand on the Republican issue today is not at all an amend for that betrayal. As a matter of fact the Irish Labour Party is shifty on the Republican issue, and they are certainly not leading any struggle for the overthrow of capitalism.'[67] These are harsh words to describe a party founded by Connolly.

Connolly attempted to establish the Irish working class as the centre of mili-tancy, the vanguard of Ireland's struggle for independence. He wished to make socialism a synonym for Irish nationalism. He believed that socialism was the highest form of—indeed the only true—patriotism. His successors shared his nationalist, and to some extent his socialist views, but they never managed to combine the two in a single, purposeful and dynamic synthesis. In order to follow the path laid by Connolly the Irish left would have had to force themselves to the forefront in every aspect of the national struggle, always taking the high ground when principle was at stake and the front rank in every confrontation with the nation's oppressors. Connolly believed that the cause of Ireland and the cause of labour were one and that they could not be 'dissevered'. In this instance he was a poor prophet, for in the years after his death labour became increasingly and fundamentally severed from the 'cause of Ireland'.

In concluding this chapter it is hard to go beyond the analysis of George Gilmore, senior IRA officer and left-wing activist, who in his fascinating study of Republican Congress (an organisation within which he was a major figure) concluded that:

> The great weakness in the Republican movement ever since the death of James Connolly in 1916 has been the abandonment by organised Labour of the Connolly concept of the reconquest of Ireland by its people, and the substitution for it of the comfortable doctrine of reformism within the imperial system.[68]

CHAPTER 13

The Revolutionary Party

Unity is a good thing, no doubt, but honesty is better, and if unity can only be obtained by the suppression of truth and the toleration of false-hood, then it is not worth the price we are asked to pay for it.

James Connolly.[1]

Be not afraid of allying yourselves with whomsoever can contribute to the strength and power and directing capacity of whatever local authority you set up. To work then, brave hearts, and with you be the memory, the inspiration and the example of your master and ours, the inspiration and the example of James Connolly. Would that we had him to-day!

Irish Opinion: Voice of Labour, 1918.[2]

A RECENT COMMENTATOR on Irish literary and political life in the 1920s and 30s has noted that 'the poetry of revolution makes the prose of constitutional politics look shabby'.[3] In regard to the subject of the present chapter, it would certainly be easy to respond positively and uncritically to the men and women in post-1916 Ireland who took what might be seen as the political high ground in their total and undeviating support for the Irish Republic. Constance Markievicz, speaking in opposition to accepting the Treaty, during the Treaty debate in the Dáil in January 1922, expressed her total commitment to the 'Workers Republic for which Connolly died' and explained her position when she told the Dáil, 'I have seen the stars and I am not going to follow a flickering will-o-the-wisp'.[4] Markievicz was by no means alone in her passionate and visionary, near religious, faith in 'the Republic'. Ernie O'Malley, himself once described as 'one of the bravest soldiers who ever fought for the Independence of Ireland',[5] noted in his autobiography that for many individuals acceptance of the Republican ideal meant that 'a strange love was born that was for some never to die till they lay stiff on the hillside or in quicklime near a barrack wall'.[6]

It is important to recognise the power that the republican ideal exerted and to be aware of the depth of commitment, and sheer passion, involved in the struggle for the Republic. The 'Republic', a term which in purely political terms has a straightforward definition, became a sacred object and goal, sanctified both by the higher meaning invested in it, and by the blood sacrifices of the men and women who had died for its establishment. This emotional, indeed spiritual, aspect of the struggle existed not only amongst the purely nationalist inspired republicans, but also within those republicans committed to establishing a Workers' Republic—given Connolly's exalted position in both labour and republican martyrology this is hardly surprising. Perhaps above all else this fact underlies the bitterness, disunity, and personal animosity which we shall encounter in the following pages, as we examine the development (or as is most often the case the lack of development) of Party organisation within the Irish Left. After the 1916 Rising the 'Republic' was not just a high ideal it was also a source of great disunity and animosity.

In previous chapters we have examined various aspects of the Irish Labour Party's development and have noted the problems which the Party encountered both in interpreting Connolly's political legacy and in its attempts to translate his theoretical constructs into practice. We have observed that despite the constantly repeated claims by the Labour Party that there could 'never be enough Connolly' and that Irish Labour would 'never cease to preach Connolly, the complete Connolly',[7] the Party in almost every area other than pure rhetoric moved increasingly and fundamentally away from Connolly's teachings and practice. The movement away from Connolly was invariably in a rightward—direction, as the Party edged ever closer to its ultimate position as a mildly reformist and sometimes rather reactionary, constitutional Party. The Labour Party, in fact, despite proudly claiming Connolly as its founder, inspiration and guide, became a Party of a type which Connolly himself had abhorred and had castigated in his speeches and writings with all the not inconsiderable vehemence and invective at his command.

There can be little doubt that Party organisation played a substantial part in the Labour Party's move from revolutionary socialism to mild reformism, Connolly's own position with regard to the revolutionary party was explored in chapter five. His move from a revolutionary strategy centred upon a vanguard-type party, towards a more diffuse and in some ways opportunist strategy which relegated the party to a secondary role, the primary revolutionary vehicle being the ITGWU-ICA. The move was to a large extent forced upon him by his failure to develop the type of uncompromising, exclusive, tightly disciplined party which had been his objective during most of his political life. While Connolly's changed perspective on the role of the party was primarily a pragmatic response to his inability to create a revolutionary party, it is nonetheless true that he was unable to establish any theoretically coherent, self-directing organisation, or even any effective cells within non-revolutionary organisations, which were capable of understanding and continuing, let alone developing, his revolutionary strategy. We have already seen in earlier chapters how the ITGWU and the ICA failed to realise their revolutionary potential. If Connolly's primary revolutionary vehicles lacked direction and coherence, the two organisations which he had assessed and therefore treated as being of secondary importance, namely the Socialist Party of Ireland of the Irish Labour Party, were clearly facing an uphill battle after his death.

When studying the Socialist Party after Connolly's death it is important to recognise that during the politically crucial four or five years after 1916 Irish

Labour had very little theoretical guidance or practical example upon which to base its organisational schema.[8] A commentator on the British left and it should be noted that the British left had if anything closer links with the European socialist parties than the Irish left—has argued that 'it is very doubtful whether, by the time of the formation of the Communist Party in 1920–1, any substantial proportion of its members or leaders had grasped the Bolshevik idea of the Party or would have approved of it had they done so'.[9] Certainly the success of the Russian Revolution was enthusiastically welcomed by the Irish left. A large public meeting was held in February 1918 to 'hail the Russian Revolution'.[10] D.R. Campbell and W. O'Brien had met Litvinoff in January 1918 and had been very pleased when he 'showed himself to be well informed about Irish affairs, and mentioned that both Lenin and Trotsky were conversant with the writings of James Connolly', whose name, according to Litvinoff, 'was favourably known to the Russian Revolutionary Movement'.[11] Connolly was of course adopted posthumously by the Communist International. Nevertheless, it was to be some time before anyone on the Irish left recognised the importance of Lenin's concept of the revolutionary party. A number of Irish labour's most influential leaders still carried painful memories of Connolly's unsuccessful attempt to turn the ISRP into a disciplined vanguard party and resisted a course which had already been tried and found wanting. Knowledge of and acceptance of the Leninist concept of the party came relatively slowly to Ireland and was largely limited to very young left-wing activists of whom Connolly's son Roddy—himself an Easter Rising veteran—was a leading light.

For some years after 1916 the Socialist Party of Ireland (see chapter 5 for details of this party's origins and development) existed as a virtual adjunct of the ITUCLP. O'Brien and O'Shannon, while devoting their main energies to the ITUCLP and the ITGWU, continued to control the SPI. Their motive for keeping the Party alive would appear to have been based more on sentiment than on any real political vision or commitment. The SPI claimed direct descent from the ISRP and this, combined with the Party's links with Connolly, appears to have been enough to ensure that it would be kept alive, albeit in the shade of the ITUCLP and in a rather moribund state. On occasion the SPI would start to take itself seriously and attempt to increase membership and political influence. In February 1918, for example, the Dublin branch proclaimed that it 'was preparing for a forward move in Socialist propaganda in the city and the outside', and noted that 'the formation of branches in the country is urgently needed to ensure the growth of the Connolly ideal'.[12] This 'forward move', which aimed to 'link up in the ranks of the party the growing number of Socialists in Ireland',[13] made little if any headway and the Party remained small and largely ineffective, as indeed it did after other such 'forward moves'.

Writing a lengthy report on behalf of the SPI after the postponement of the Socialist International Conference, which was to have been held in Stockholm in 1917, Cathal O'Shannon presented a somewhat optimistic picture of the strength and potential of the SPI, but was at least honest enough to acknowledge that the Party might be seen as being 'weak and of little or no account'.[14] O'Shannon's

characteristically well-written and reasonably well-balanced report was sanctioned by the Party and can thus at least be said to have reflected some level of
political unity and purpose within the Party's small membership.

A few years later the Amsterdam Sub-Bureau of the Third International
received a report from Ireland which it circulated widely under the title 'The
Political and Working Class Organisation in Ireland'. This report clearly emanated
from left-wing elements who were either members of the SPI or who had only
recently left the Party and were attempting to form a new Party under the name of
Workers Communist Party. The report, while undoubtedly somewhat intemperate
and frequently inaccurate, nonetheless contained interesting, and, one suspects,
not altogether baseless critical analyses of the Irish political and military situation.
The section of the report which dealt with the SPI was completely negative and
indeed constituted a ferocious attack on the SPI's leadership. The report described
the SPI thus:

> This once active organisation is now nearly defunct . . . It is now practically
> in the hands of the Office Staff of Liberty Hall, ITGWU Head Office who are
> anything but Socialists. An attempt was made to transform it into a Revolu-
> tionary movement some months ago, and partially succeeded, but it was finally
> killed by the opposition of the Press, Clergy, Sinn Fein and the Transport Union
> Officials led by William O'Brien, who was once Chairman of the Party, but was
> never a Socialist. It wields no political or any other power, and is merely used as
> a debating Society, and will continue to be used as such while it is controlled by
> men who are Trades Union officials first, anything else second, last (and very
> least) Socialists.[15]

The SPI Leadership were outraged when they received a copy of the report from
'our Comrade Nora Connolly' (Nora, Connolly's eldest daughter, might have had
a very early sighting of the report as her brother Roddy, a prominent member of
the SPI's left-wing, may well have had a hand in its preparation.) In a fiery reply
to the International, the SPI leadership claimed that 'far from defunct, the Socialist
Party of Ireland hitherto confined to Belfast, Dublin and Cork, is opening local
branches in the country towns and increasing the circulation of its literature'. The
reply castigated the Amsterdam Sub-Bureau for its 'un-comradely, indeed das-
tardly conduct' in circulating the document, argued that the document probably
originated in Dublin Castle and noted rather threateningly that one of the Castle
'employees' who was closely associated with several *soi-disant* communists of
bourgeois origin in London' had 'met a well deserved fate recently in Dublin' and
that some of his associates were 'under observation' by those 'whose concern it is
to keep the working class movement clean'.[16]

Clearly, despite the fact that the SPI members shared not only a political
commitment to the 'Connolly ideal', but also in many cases had close personal
and familial links to the man himself, all was not harmony and light in the SPI.
At an SPI meeting in September 1921 the leadership challenge foreshadowed
in the communication to the International the previous year finally succeeded.

Roddy Connolly (President) Nora Connolly (Treasurer) and Walter Carpenter (Secretary) were elected to the executive positions in the Party. Within a few weeks the party passed a resolution expelling William O'Brien and Cathal O'Shannon (both of whom had enjoyed longstanding political and personal friendships with James Connolly) 'on the grounds of reformism, consecutive non-attendance at the Party, and consistent attempts to render futile all efforts to built up a Communist Party in Ireland'.[17] A detailed explanation of the expulsion appeared under the title 'Clearing the Decks' in the *Workers Republic*. This article, which showed clear signs of being influenced by Bolshevik ideology, claimed that the chief fault of these two members was the fault of omission.

> For several years they have been content with calling themselves Socialists, devoting their whole time to the Labour Party and Unions—not, however in the spirit of Socialists, but in the spirit of the old second International Labourites, and, naturally, did absolutely nothing to build up a strong Socialist Party to direct the—Labour movement. They preferred to direct this movement as personalities themselves, not as directed and assisted by any organised body of Socialists.

It was further charged, and this was clearly the crucial point, that 'despite the knowledge that the development of the World Proletarian Revolution, that the development of Communism in every country demands a strong centralised, disciplined Communist Party, they did nothing towards the creation of any such body in Ireland'.[18]

In November of the same year the SPI formally resolved to change its name to the Communist Party of Ireland. Roddy Connolly was in fact opposed to the speed with which the SPI was moving towards transforming itself into a fully fledged, Comintern-affiliated, Communist Party. Echoing the views which his father expressed on party organisation and development during the latter years of his political career, Connolly argued that a 'collaboration' within the existing SPI between 'Communists', 'pseudo-Communists', 'Socialists' and 'Labourites' should be encouraged, at least until the Party had advanced to some degree.[19] Despite his position as Party President and the weight which his name added to his views, Connolly was unable to exert any delaying influence on the establishment of the first Irish Communist Party. Enthusiasm for this step was simply too great and urgent amongst the mainly youthful SPI activists.

The newly established Communist Party of Ireland declared that its 'Object' was the 'establishment of the Workers Republic' and that the 'Means' to achieve this object was the 'formation of a strongly disciplined Communist Party'.[20] Roddy Connolly, who, as we have seen, had opposed the timing, if not the principle, of setting up the CPI, accepted the majority decision and became deeply involved in establishing the new Party through his position as Party President and editor of the *Workers Republic*. The paper, which claimed on its bannerhead that it had been 'founded by James Connolly August 1898', sought to build up the Party and ensure that 'the difference between a loosely formed Socialist Party and a strictly disciplined Communist Party' was 'gradually driven home to the members'.[21] At this stage of his career Roddy Connolly was a most unconvincing gradualist.

Given the fact that the CPI had only 'twenty or so active members',[22] one might have thought that creating a centralised disciplined party would not have been a particularly difficult task. This was not in fact the case. From the inception of the Party there was copious evidence in the pages of the *Workers Republic* that internal discipline was a serious and divisive problem. As early as 3 December 1921, it was noted that 'a few of the so-called intellectuals are finding it difficult to rid themselves of old ideas despite their loudly protested adherence to and pretended understanding of Communist policy'.[23] A week later the political temperature had risen somewhat and the 'so-called intellectuals' were being described as 'always beautifully smelling . . . petty bourgeois fops'. Those who would not accept the 'acid test' of Party discipline were described as 'pseudo-revolutionists' and the necessity of clearing the Party of such 'useless material' was being urged.[24] In these early days the Party even found it necessary to institute a probationary period for selected members and expulsions were clearly in the air. The main point made by those Party members who opposed the Party's strong line on discipline was the familiar—and often justified—argument that the Party's disciplinary demands were preventing 'members fully participating in Party life'.[25] The similarities with the internal ructions which had occurred with the ISRP almost two decades before are obvious.

The CPI's early months coincided with a period of great turbulence in Irish politics. The whole issue of the Treaty was being fiercely debated throughout the country and it was becoming clear that the issue might well be settled by force of arms through civil war. The CPI was in fact the first organisation in Ireland to express publicly its opposition to the Treaty.[26] It is worth noting that the Communist Party of Great Britain also took an active interest in Irish affairs at this time. William Gallacher (later CPGB MP for West Fife, 1935–51), a member of the CPGB Executive, visited Ireland during the Treaty negotiations in London to warn senior republicans that Ireland's plenipotentiaries had accepted partition. Gallagher's advice, which went unheeded, was that the Irish representatives should be arrested as soon as they returned to Ireland and their agreement renounced.[27] The CPI members were annoyed that the CPGB had ignored Ireland's own 'Official' Communist Party throughout the whole exercise and relations between the two Parties were strained for some time.

The CPI stood unequivocally against the acceptance of the Treaty and gave the anti-Treaty republicans what support they could during the Treaty debate and subsequent civil war. Given the Party's limited resources, support was largely based on the outstanding republican reputations which a number of CPI leaders enjoyed. Connolly, his father's son and himself a 'boy' veteran of 1916, Sean McLoughlin,[28] promoted to Commandant during the Rising at the age of fifteen, Walter Carpenter, ICA o/c Boy Corps GPO, and Seamus McGowan,

Sergeant and Assistant QMG, GPO,[29] were CPI leaders with notable 'national' records. As might be expected, CPI members took an active part in the military struggle. When McLoughlin accompanied Roddy Connolly on an unsuccessful CPI mission to IRA Chief of Staff Liam Lynch, he was offered and accepted the rank of Commandant in the IRA.[30]

The CPI's concentration upon and commitment to the Republican side in the Civil War, came under question when Roddy Connolly and George Pollock (alias McLay) attended the Fourth World Congress of the Comintern towards the end of 1922. On his return to Ireland Connolly published a series of articles in the *Workers Republic*.[31] These articles argued the need for a new direction in CPI policy; the Party was urged to focus on labour issues in order to build up its strength and influence in the industrial field rather than continue to devote its energies to supporting the Republican struggle. In January 1923 Connolly went even further and published an article in the *Workers Republic*[32] in which he urged the IRA to accept that it had been defeated in the field (at least temporarily) and advised the leaders of the IRA to draw the armed struggle to a close, allow imprisoned IRA members to sign the non-aggression undertakings, which the Free State Government insisted upon before release, establish a new Republican Party and even to take the oath and enter the Dáil. Connolly's advice was in many ways sensible and realistic and indeed in time all of the steps which he recommended were accepted—or rather forced upon—the republican leadership.

In the short term, however, Connolly's advice was not well received and at the CPI's First Congress in Dublin in January 1923 he failed to regain election to the Party Executive. In his authoritative study of Irish Communism, Milotte has noted that Connolly's call for an IRA ceasefire was not seriously contested at the Congress and has pointed out that 'the main point at issue was whether—as Connolly claimed but as Pollock denied—the Comintern had *sanctioned* Connolly's advice to the IRA'. According to Milotte this dispute 'caused more turmoil than the actual *substance* of Connolly's remarks and was a major factor in his downfall'.[33]

The CPI's change of direction was not reflected in any noticeable expansion of the Party's size or influence and Connolly was soon reinstated as a member of the Executive, in the first instance as director of propaganda and later as Political Secretary. But tensions and disagreements continued within the Party. The most basic split was between Connolly's faction, which continued to see one of the Party's main tasks as being the attempt to influence and guide the republican movement, and an opposing faction which considered that this policy was pointless and that the Party should use its resources to promote direct action and Marxist education.

By November 1923 the Party had made so little progress that it could no longer support the *Workers Republic* and the paper ceased publication. At this point the Comintern stepped in and ordered the Party's dissolution, an order which the Party accepted.[34] Although the CPI claimed descent from the ISRP and the SPI, it is clear from its response to the Comintern order that a distinct qualitative change in the spirit of independence had occurred over the years. It is inconceivable that James Connolly would have meekly accepted an order from outside the

Party—indeed outside the country—to dissolve any of the parties with which he had been involved. Milotte's explanation for the weakness and disunity of the CPI is that there was an 'ever-present tension within the party between those who saw the national question as the starting-point for all activity and those who sought to concentrate on economic issues'. The Party's real problem was that 'neither faction seemed to have grasped James Connolly's point that the two aspects were inseparable and that only an autonomous worker's movement, linking them together in theory and practice, could bring the struggle to a successful con- clusion'.[35] This analysis is borne out both in theoretical terms and in regard to the extra pressures which the CPI encountered through its wholehearted commitment to the International socialist movement and the directions of the Comintern. Autonomy was somewhat problematic when the very existence of the Party was dependant on the decisions of a body which met far from Ireland, was in many respects quite ignorant of Irish political conditions, and was by this period acting increasingly as an agency of Russian foreign policy.

The Comintern did not dissolve the CPI because of its disappointing progress nor because of its internal ructions, it had simply reacted to the fact that James Larkin stated on his return to Ireland in 1923, for reasons of his own, that he would have nothing to do with the CPI. After due reflection the Comintern decided that Larkin, with his high public profile and substantial personal support base, was the foundation upon which Irish Communism should be built. Larkin's importance as an individual to the future of Communism in Ireland superseded any claim that the CPI had on Comintern support. Thus the first Communist Party to be established in Ireland was simply ordered to self-destruct and its members were told to join, as individuals, Larkin's new political association, the 'Irish Workers' League (IWL). The IWL, which was more a support group for Larkin's paper, the *Irish Worker* than a political party, was recognised as the official Comintern section in Ireland. Larkin's status and political credentials were further enhanced in July 1924 when he was elected to the Executive Committee of the Communist International. Commenting on his election, Larkin noted that 'he had been elected by the working classes of 32 countries of the world, as one of the 25 Commissioners to rule and govern the earth'.[36] Modesty and a strict regard for the truth were not among Larkin's strong points. Superficially, and more particularly as viewed from afar, Larkin may indeed have appeared to have been an ideal leader for the Irish Communist movement. His record as a courageous, and incor- ruptible, militant labour leader, his magnificent oratorical power and ability as a newspaper editor, and his near-legendary reputation amongst Irish—or more particularly Dublin workers—made him appear an ideal choice. But despite his undoubted personal appeal and his great talents, Larkin could hardly have been less suited to lead a political party, let alone an effective Communist Party. In his sympathetic biography of Larkin, R.M. Fox noted that:

At no time in his life did Larkin advance any sharply defined view of the Labour struggle. He was always a field worker not a staff man, and he accepted the vague socialist ideas of a future harmonious society which young men of that time could hear from many Labour platforms. Sometimes he was inclined to speak with contempt of abstract theorists as Long haired men and short-haired women who wanted to demonstrate their own clever-ness instead of joining in the fight to end intolerable evils.[37]

Larkin's theoretical shortcomings might have been sustainable if he had recognised his weakness in this area and worked co-operatively within a well-defined party structure, but this was not and never had been Larkin's way. Emmet Larkin has noted that Larkin 'for thirty years had believed himself to be the Irish Labour movement incarnate'.[38] Larkin, unlike Connolly (who had found Larkin almost impossible to work with), did not have, and did not seek to have, comrades fighting alongside him in the labour struggle. His personality and level of political sophis-tication ensured that he would only attract and accept followers whose designated role in the struggle was simply to give him their total and uncritical support.

As Ireland's 'officially' recognised Communist organisation, the IWL was by no means a vibrant and successful organisation. Even if Larkin had perceived it to be an important and potentially revolutionary organisation, he had a number of other pressing demands upon his time and energies, not the least of which was the divisive and intensely bitter battle which raged between himself and the leaders of his old Union the ITGWU. He was building up a new syndicalist union, the Workers Union of Ireland (WUI), which he hoped would rival and eventually destroy the ITGWU—and was also editing his newspaper, the *Irish Worker*. The IWL suffered the same neglect as many of Larkin's other passing enthusiasms. Founded in September 1923, the League had originally been seen by Larkin as a support group for his newspaper, and although it did, at least in theory, become more akin to a real political party in 1924, it was not until 1927 that it became a 'full fledged political organisation'.[39]

Like all organisations which Larkin controlled, the IWL was at the mercy of his whim for its advancement and indeed its very existence. Milotte makes the point that 'meeting after meeting was cancelled on the grounds that Larkin himself was unable to attend'.[40] In 1926 a number of prominent Communists who despaired of the IWL ever becoming any sort of effective political organisation (its very exis-tence often appeared to be in some doubt) formed the Workers Party of Ireland (WPI). This Party had grown out of the small and largely ineffective Connolly Workers' Educational Club and included a number of well-known ex-CPI Leaders including Roddy Connolly (Party President and editor of the Party's paper *Hammer and Plough*), George Pollock and Seamus McGowan. After a promising start, the young Party received a major, and by now rather familiar, blow when its application to join the International was rejected and the Party told to dissolve. Although most of the Party's leading figures, with Connolly leading the way, accepted the Comintern's direction, some members decided to continue despite the Party's 'unofficial' status. The WPI suffered another damaging repudiation at the hands of the Comintern in 1927 when that organisation reaffirmed its recog-nition of the IWL as the only official Communist Party in Ireland. By the end of

1927 the WPI had ceased to exist. The Comintern's support for Larkin's non-marxist, poorly organised and largely inactive IWL, to the detriment and indeed destruction of an active Communist Party, demonstrated both the International's lack of accurate information on the actual political situation within Ireland and the dangers inherent in national communist parties accepting external control.

An IWL delegation accompanied by a few prominent members of the IRA attended the tenth anniversary celebrations of the Russian Revolution in Moscow in 1927. At this time links between the communist movement and the IRA—links which had always existed—were becoming stronger and more purposeful. In 1928 Larkin attended the Ninth Plenum of the Executive Committee of the Communist International and received instructions that he should build up the strength and influence of the WUI and use his influence to assist revolutionary workers within the existing trade unions to oust reformist trade union leaders. Larkin, who was experiencing considerable difficulties both in terms of membership and finance, in maintaining the WUI, made little or no progress in achieving the ECCI objectives.[41] By the end of the decade Moscow had belatedly concluded that Larkin was not after all the ideal man to head the Irish labour movement and henceforth he played only a minor, subsidiary role in their plans for Ireland.

By 1930 the Connolly Workers Club, which had been revived in 1928, the Labour Defence League (which had a substantial number of IRA members in its ranks) and the Friends of Soviet Russia provided the main impetus for the founding of a Preparatory Committee for the formation of a Workers Revolutionary Party (PCWRP). It was hoped that the PCWRP would provide a unifying focus for Communists and Socialist Republicans whose time and energy were being invested in a wide range of activities and organisations. A confidential police report to the Government, early in 1930, noted that 'the number of revolutionary organisations, all of which have something in common, is bewildering and each week, so to speak, gives birth to new ones'.[42]

A Department of Justice report dated 16 June 1930 noted the names of 72 people on the 'current list' of members of the Workers Revolutionary Party and drew attention to the fact that no less than 30 of those named were 'active irregulars', which in Free State terminology meant IRA men.[43] The report also makes the point that Peadar O'Donnell, a longstanding and high ranking left-wing IRA leader, had been making 'every effort' to 'entice members of the Irregulars to join the Organisation and in that respect he has been very successful.' The main purpose of the Report was to stress that it was 'obvious that the Worker's Revolutionary Party and the IRA are closely allied'. To this end the report noted that 'information received is to the effect that GHQ Irregulars have encouraged members of the Dublin Brigade to join the Worker's Revolutionary Party'.[44]

When James Larkin's son and namesake returned to Ireland in July 1930, after spending two and a half years attending the 'Lenin school for the development of political cadres' in Moscow,[45] he, like his father before him, brought instructions from the Comintern which, when put into effect, placed great stress on the Communist movement's association with the IRA. Larkin

Jnr's instructions, contained in a 'Draft letter to the Comrades in Ireland', drew attention to the IRA's 'decidedly petty bourgeois character' and stated that whilst 'the comrades' should certainly approach the 'IRA and An Poblacht' they should 'make it quite clear to the followers of the IRA that only a consistent revolutionary policy of the Communist Party can liberate the toiling masses of Ireland'. Communist tasks in relation to the IRA were to centre upon developing 'the process of differentiation within the IRA', exposing its petty bourgeois character and policies and increasing communist influences in its ranks.[46] This approach derived from the current Comintern policy of 'Class Against Class', in the expectation of an imminent revolutionary crisis and a consequent intention to discredit reformist in the labour movement.

The Comintern's new approach to the IRA was very aggressive and lacked either subtlety or any real understanding of the internal dynamics and personalities operating within the IRA. The new tactics placed Communists within the IRA in a difficult position and put relations between the Communist movement and the IRA under considerable strain. The main outcome of the Comintern's ambitious but rather misguided initiative was the exact opposite of what it had hoped to achieve. Communist influence within the IRA was reduced and the IRA withdrew from communist-inspired organisations such as the Labour Defence League. Over the next few years the WRP was reconstituted under the title Revolutionary Workers Groups (RWGs) and in June 1933 the RWGs formed the basis for the founding of Ireland's second, fully constituted, Communist Party. Despite these setbacks, the early thirties nonetheless were years in which the IRA—under intense pressure from its left-wing—became involved in a number of radical political initiatives, the most important of which were Saor Eire and Republican Congress. The formation of an IRA-supported left-wing political party under the name Saor Eire (Free Ireland) was first proposed at an IRA General Army Convention in January 1929. Despite a significant level of support, the Convention rejected the proposal and decided instead to establish a more traditional non-revolutionary party which it called Comhairle na Poblachta.[47] In February 1931 the Saor Eire concept was once again proposed at the IRA General Army Convention and on this occasion won acceptance.[48] Saor Eire's First Congress was held in Dublin in September 1931. Describing itself as being 'an Organisation of Workers and Working Farmers',[49] Saor Eire's objectives have been accurately described as being 'radical socialist goals' and it has been argued that its objectives were 'based on the writings of James Connolly, writings which only Labour supporters had bothered to read during the turmoil of the preceding decade'.[50]

On 19 October 1931 both Saor Eire and the IRA were condemned by the Catholic Bishops of Ireland. After describing Saor Eire as being 'frankly communistic in its aims', the statement went on to declare that Saor Eire and the IRA, 'whether separate or in alliance', were 'sinful and irreligious' and to proclaim that 'no Catholic can lawfully be a member of them'.[51] On the day after the appearance of the Bishops' statement, Saor Eire, the IRA and ten other radical Republican organisations were declared illegal under a Constitution (Declaration of Unlawful

Associations) Order.[52] To a certain extent Saor Eire had been forced upon a rather reluctant IRA leadership by the Army's left-wing militants. Lacking the strength or depth of support to survive an orchestrated attack by Church and State, it soon collapsed.[53]

Republican Congress had its roots in a debate at an IRA Convention in Dublin in March 1934. Here Peadar O'Donnell and George Gilmore presented a motion which called for 'a Republican Congress and a rally of Republican Opinion'.[54] The proposal was supported by a majority of the elected delegates but it was 'opposed by the Executive and Army Council and lost by one vote'.[55] O'Donnell, Gilmore, Frank Ryan, Michael Price and a number of other IRA radicals thereupon left both the Convention and the IRA. A Republican Congress preparatory Conference held in Athlone in April 1931, issued a Manifesto which proclaimed:

> We believe that a Republic of a united Ireland will never be achieved except through a struggle which uproots Capitalism on its way. 'We cannot conceive of a free Ireland with a subject working class: We cannot conceive of a subject Ireland with a free working class.' This teaching of Connolly represents the deepest instincts of the oppressed Irish nation.[56]

The 'Athlone' Manifesto urged that 'A Congress of Republican opinion must be assembled to make the Republic a main issue dominating the whole political field and to outline what are the forms of activity that move to its support'.[57]

At a Republican Congress rally held in Rathfarnham in April 1934, Michael Price pointed out that Congress 'would make Connolly's philosophy the basis for the achievement of the Republic'.[58] For Price the role of Congress was clear: Congress should, he stated, 'write upon the skyline the real conception, the James Connolly conception of the Republic'.[59] *Republican Congress,* the organisation's newspaper, constantly stressed the central importance which the organisation attached to Connolly's vision of an Irish Workers Republic. Price was quoted in one issue as having publicly stated that Republican Congress would become a 'Workers Revolutionary Party' and that 'anyone who thinks that this party will spend its energies in mere election work is mistaken. It will be a Revolutionary Party with Connolly's methods to achieve Connolly's objective.[60] Connolly's son Roddy and daughter Nora were regular and prominent contributors to *Republican Congress* and an attempt was made not only to present Connolly's ideas through the printed medium but also to set up 'Connolly Study Circles'.[61]

Republican Congress members were united in their regard for James Connolly and his teachings. The strength and depth of this unity faced its moment of truth, when Republican Congress held its first Congress in September 1934. A major split occurred at this Congress. Roddy Connolly, with the backing of his sister Nora, Michael Price and other delegates, proposed a resolution which 'demanded that Congress definitely declare that an Irish Workers' Republic be its slogan of action'.[62] Another resolution, proposed by Peadar O'Donnell and supported by George Gilmore, Frank Ryan and others, asked Congress to declare that the United Front be its slogan of action.[63] The United Front resolution was carried by 99 votes to 84.[64] The difference between the two factions was not merely semantic. The disagreement centred upon whether Congress was to be a tightly organised Workers' Republican Party or a fairly loose Republican coalition. Both sides could, and did, cite Connolly's life and work to support their arguments and to validate their political position. A majority of those who supported the defeated resolution ended their involvement with Congress. Republican Congress never recovered from this loss and the picture of disunity and factionalism which had been presented to the public. Republican Congress continued after the split but never regained the confidence and drive which it had displayed in its earlier months. The organisation's newspaper, largely written by O'Donnell, survived until December 1935 but gradually decreased in size, quality and regularity. With the demise of its newspaper, Republican Congress effectively ceased to exist.[65] For Republican Congress, a shared commitment to Connolly had proven an insufficient binding.

The second CPI established in 1933 fared little better than Saor Eire and Republican Congress. However, the party did take and active part in the struggle against Fascism, opposing the Blueshirts at home and providing what support it could to the Spanish Republic. The extent of those activities is well told by Michael O'Riordan, International Brigade veteran, and for many years Chairman of the CPI, in his book *Connolly Column*.[66] Milotte deals with the years 1934–39 in a chapter entitled 'The Unpopular Popular front', a title which in itself tells the essential story of the CPI in those years. Milotte notes that the 'Communist Party's twists and turns in the 1937–39 period had a devastating effect on party organisation—which virtually disintegrated', and he goes on to state that 'Party activity now consisted almost entirely of discussing what others were doing'.[67] Clearly the mid to late thirties were not years in which the Irish left made any significant advances.

The Labour Party has not been given a prominent position in this study of party organisation. This is in part due to the fact that aspects of the Party's development have already been examined in previous chapters, but is primarily because the Party never seriously or urgently addressed the question of its organisation or structure. In July 1925, Thomas Johnson, Chief Executive Officer of the ILPTUC and Chairman of the Party in the Dáil, noted in a letter to members of the Party's National Executive that 'the absence of a properly organised party in the country is perhaps an explanation of our failure'.[68] Some years later at the Party's Conference in 1930, William McMullen complained that the Party's 'Object' was 'pale pink, bourgeois and middle-class', and asserted that 'anybody could subscribe to them'.[69] The complaint was echoed by Cathal O'Shannon, who described the Party's political platform as being 'the absolute minimum any decent man should have' and urged that the Party 'organise as a fighting party' and 'pitch our banner a little nearer to the skies'.[70]

Over the years similar complaints were voiced within the Party about its platform and organisation. At the Labour Party's Tenth Annual Conference in 1941 a resolution was carried by 51 votes to 16 which stated that 'This conference is of the opinion that not enough is being done effectively to organise the Party throughout the country'.[71] Clearly little had changed over the years and the Labour Party remained dominated by and organised around the trade union movement. It had failed to expand either its political horizons or its support base. The Labour Party's vote in Irish elections between 1923–1938 reached a peak of 12.6% in 1927 and reached its lowest point in 1933 when it managed to secure a mere 5.7% of the vote. Overall, during this period Labour averaged around 9.72. In truth the Party appeared to find its position as an influential but minor Party rather comfortable. Despite regular resolutions to the effect that the Party was about to be re-organised and re-invigorated, very few positive steps were ever taken. The Party had neither Connolly's spirit, nor, despite frequent protestations to the contrary, did it have any real grip on his political legacy.

In truth Connolly's legacy with regard to party organisation was in itself a somewhat confusing one. During his political career Connolly moved from a strong belief in the necessity of establishing a centralised and tightly disciplined revolutionary party, towards an acceptance, albeit a somewhat enforced and grudging acceptance, that a more broadly based and loosely structured political party was necessary in the circumstances then prevalent. The tension between these two concepts of the role and organisation of the party was echoed in the years after his death and, as the preceding pages have shown, created a continuing climate of political disunity and stultification within the Irish left. This problem—which was of course by no means confined to the Irish left—was in the Irish context compounded by acute problems relating to the personalities of a number of labour leaders, most notably the indiscipline and volatile temperament of James Larkin Snr. These problems were in turn compounded and exacerbated by the often poorly researched and consequently misguided directions of the Comintern, and the result was a failure either to establish an effective vanguard party or to influence a broader reformist one.

CHAPTER 14

Political Violence and Insurrection

> It was characteristic of Connolly that on that occasion he should declare that it was not a man's death that should be commemorated but the deed he had done or tried to do. A man's death, he said, or the manner of his death, was not ordinarily determined by himself, but it was a man's own will that determined whatever deed he should be remembered for . . . that was the very essence of Connolly's philosophy. His was a philosophy of action and a maxim of his was that what the working-class and Ireland needed was Less philosophising and more fighting , provided of course that it was fighting for a definite and worthy object. Nobody loved fighting or violence for its own sake less than he but few of his generation prepared themselves more thoroughly for such fighting as his ideals called for.
>
> Cathal O'Shannon, 1933.[1]

CATHAL O'SHANNON, who wrote the above lines, was arguably Ireland's most astute and accurate interpreter of Connolly's political legacy. He had worked closely with Connolly for a number of years prior to the Rising, and was not only one of the country's most important labour leaders but had also been a member in good standing of both the Irish Republican Brotherhood and the Irish Republican Army. O'Shannon's understanding of Connolly's thought and practice is not in doubt, his contributions to the labour press, establish him as being, in theoretical terms, the most brilliant and faithful Connolly socialist of his—or any other—generation. And yet even with the benefit of O'Shannon's intellectual leadership and the less dazzling but nonetheless substantial talents of men like William O'Brien and Thomas Foran, both of whom were steeped in Connolly's teachings, Irish labour was unable to follow Connolly's teachings and example in regards to the importance of physical force in the struggle to achieve a revolutionary socialist reconstruction of society and the creation of the Worker's Republic.

As late as 1937 William O'Brien could write an article in the *Tipperary Star* invoking Connolly's critique of nationalists as not having 'sufficient dash and desperation to deal with the matter' (the 'matter' in question being the military guard expected to protect a meeting which Asquith had been scheduled to hold in Dublin in September 1914). O'Brien noted that the letter which Connolly wrote to him on this matter concluded with the words 'I am ready for any call',[2] a statement which in this context could only mean that he himself had the necessary 'dash and desperation' and was willing to lead an attack on the military forces guarding the meeting. Yet despite an almost fanatical devotion to Connolly's writings (as Connolly's literary executor, he held all of Connolly's personal papers) and exalting his memory above all else, O'Brien, like his fellow labour leaders, was unable to replicate Connolly's qualities as a revolutionary socialist leader. Writing in the *Voice of Labour* in July 1918, Maud Eden noted that 'It is not enough to read Connolly or quote Connolly, it is necessary to be like Connolly.' As we proceed to examine labour's role in the violent upheaval which occurred in post-Rising Ireland in the years when the gun held sway, Eden's exhortation should be held in the foreground. Her words ring through the years as a challenge, an accusation, and ultimately an explanation.

Any attempt to understand the role of the labour movement in the armed struggle in Ireland must in the first instance consider the Irish Citizen Army. The ICA, which under Connolly played an important part in the 1916 Rising and which Connolly had invested with such revolutionary import, never regained anything like its former glory. After Connolly's execution it became an organisation which struggled to exist, rather than one which existed to struggle. Odd flashes of its old militancy and vigour cannot disguise the fact that the organisation had stagnated—and this at a time when related organisations such as the IRA, Sinn Fein and the ITGWU underwent massive and dramatic expansion. In studying the ICA's failure to thrive, its relationship with the labour movement in general and the ITGWU in particular is of central importance. Given the ICA's fighting reputation and republican credentials, not the least of which was the link with Connolly, and its historically close relationship with the ITGWU, a rapid expansion of the ICA's strength and influence in line with the huge expansion of the ITGWU should have been within reach. That this expansion did not take place—indeed the reverse occurred—is in large part due to the leadership of the ITGWU's decided lack of enthusiasm for the ICA. The tepid attitude of the ITGWU leaders had its roots in their fear of the consequences which could have arisen through involvement with the ICA.

In an unpublished memoir, William O'Brien noted that by May 1917 'a good deal of friction existed between the officials and committee of the Irish Transport and General Workers Union and members of the reorganised Irish Citizen Army'. He then goes on to state that:

> The cause of this was that the Citizen Army had no suitable premises associated with James Connolly and the individual members of the Citizen Army, most of whom were members of the Irish Transport and General Workers Union, took up an attitude that they could make use of Liberty Hall in any way they liked. Drilling of course had been resumed and this was done in a very open manner calculated, in the view of the Union Officials, to draw the attention of the authorities on what was going on. The Volunteers also had resumed drilling but it was done in a different manner and in less public places than Liberty Hall. This attitude came to a head about May 1917 and as a result on May 15th., an order to close Liberty Hall was served on Thomas Foran, the President of the

Union. The Union had made good headway in reorganising in the previous 8 or 10 months but the closing of Liberty Hall would have been a very severe blow and might have had serious consequences.[4]

O'Brien's statement justifies lengthy quotation because it encapsulates the difference between the old Connolly-led ITGWU and the post-Rising Union. The 'discretion is the better part of valour' attitude, the tendency to protect the Union at all costs—even at the cost of the Union's own goals—would simply not have occurred to Connolly. Any caution on his part, any delay in immediately confronting the enemy, would be purely a temporary logistic expedient in order to gather strength. A tactical pause was part of his armoury, but the type of avoidance of conflict and the dumping of comrades to avoid trouble which underlies O'Brien's statement would have been unthinkable to Connolly. Part of the difference, no doubt, lies in the very growth of the union—it had more to lose—but more fundamentally, there is a profound difference in temper and outlook. In his 'officially endorsed' *History of the Irish Citizen Army*, R.M. Fox examines the first post-Rising meeting of the ITUCLP held in Sligo in August 1916 and notes that he is 'compelled to the conclusion that Connolly's own view of the role of the Citizen Army as the workers fighting force, received no endorsement from the Irish Trade Union Congress'. Fox considers that this was partly due to the 'feeling that the time was not opportune for any defiant declaration' and shrewdly recalls that 'even in Connolly's time, there was strong opposition to the Citizen Army using the hall and to the association of the Army with Union activities'.[5] While Connolly was alive, he had in fact to some extent forced the ICA upon a Union leadership, many of whom were deeply and volubly concerned about the possible ramifications of the ITGWU's relationship with the militant and volatile ICA.[6]

Frank Robbins, an ICA and ITGWU militant, whose record as an activist included participation in the Easter Uprising, a period of imprisonment, and travel to America on an important mission for the ITGWU (he was sent to re-establish contact with James Larkin), found on his return to Ireland early in 1918 that major changes had occurred in the ICA. There was, he writes, 'a new atmosphere, a new outlook, entirely different from that which had been moulded by Connolly and Mallin'. To Robbins, the Army's new recruits 'seemed to lack the spirit, the understanding and the discipline which were so characteristic of the earlier period'. He was disturbed by the fact that the:

> close co-operation which had previously existed officially between the Irish Transport Union and the Citizen Army seemed to have disappeared completely. Relations had indeed deteriorated to such a degree that it would not be an exaggeration to say that but for stalwarts such as I have named, an openly hostile situation would have been inevitable.[7]

Robbins does not however blame the ITGWU leadership for the ICA's problems. In his opinion the ICA's new Commandant, James O'Neill, was 'chiefly responsible for the post-insurrection situation' and the reason for his failure was 'entirely due to his lack of desire or ability to pursue the Connolly philosophy'. In Robbins' view, O'Neill's attitude was to 'procrastinate' rather than to provide leadership by taking 'the line which would have been laid down by Connolly or Mallin', with the result that due to lack of effective leadership new recruits in the ICA 'did not hold or advocate the social and political views that had motivated those who fought in 1916'.[8]

It is possible that Robbins was allowing his loyalty to the ITGWU—a Union he had belonged to since he was fifteen years of age—to cloud his judgement. O'Neill was by all accounts a poor leader, indeed he was eventually stripped of his command and imprisoned on charges of having sold ICA rifles to the Volunteers. But his incompetence and alleged corruption cannot be entirely divorced from the ITGWU leadership. The men who controlled the ITGWU were vastly experienced and highly skilled political operators. There can be little doubt that had O'Brien, O'Shannon and company decided to oust O'Neill and reorganise the ICA into a more effective body, they could have done so with little difficulty. Men who could do battle with James Larkin—a heroic figure who had become a legend in his own time and was worshipped by large sections of the Dublin working class—and ultimately succeed in expelling him from the Union which he had himself founded, could clearly have taken over the ICA more or less at will.

As far as the labour press was concerned, in the years following the Rising the ICA might as well have ceased to exist. The few scattered references which did occur mainly concerned the results of ICA fund-raising lottery draws—creating the impression that the ICA had decided that the drawing of lotteries was more to their taste than the drawing of guns. This lack of publicity for the ICA helps to explain the organisation's difficulty in gaining new members: many militant workers who would have been attracted to the ICA joined the IRA simply because they were unaware that the ICA still existed. Peadar O'Donnell, for example, a left-wing ITGWU organiser who rose through the ranks to become a Commandant-General in the IRA, informed the writer that he 'would much rather have joined the ICA than the IRA. Quite a number of us would have joined if the ICA had been there'.[9] Whilst working for the ITGWU prior to becoming a fulltime IRA man, O'Donnell spent most of his time working for the Union in the North-East and West of Ireland (even in the militant ITGWU, O'Donnell stood out as a firebrand) and thus, reliant on the labour press for much of his information, was simply unaware that the ICA was still 'active'. If the ITGWU had encouraged its organisers and rank-and-file members to join or at least support the ICA, many men who became prominent leaders and/or fighting men in the IRA would have taken their military, organisational and political talents into the ICA—an organisation which, as we have seen, was in desperate need of such talents.

When Connolly took over as acting General Secretary of the ITGWU and Commandant of the ICA in 1914, he turned what had previously been a worker's defence organisation whose members armed themselves with wooden sticks, into an armed, offensively orientated military unit. Despite avowals to the contrary, his successors in the ITGWU basically wanted to turn the clock back. A low profile ICA, non-offensive (in both senses of the word), committed to defending Union meetings, rallies etc. was their ideal. A more positive and constructive, let alone revolutionary, vision of the ICA's role in the working class and republican struggle was, despite Connolly's teachings and example, beyond their level of audacity. The 'dash and desperation' so highly valued and richly displayed by Connolly was lacking. Fox described the conflict between the ITGWU and the ICA well:

> Pictures of Connolly and the Citizen Army decorated the walls of Liberty Hall and about these there was the glamour of the past. But it was quite another thing to have members of that same Army drilling and gathering arms on the premises. Between the cautiousness of those who placed the safety of the hall above everything and the impetuousity of others who thought the struggle was always worth the cost there was a great gap.[10]

Even the singing of 'seditious' songs was perceived—and not without reason—as being a threat to the continued operations at Liberty Hall, and efforts were made to stop rebel songs being sung at the regular Sunday night concerts held in the Hall. This attempted censorship was rejected by many Citizen Army men who felt that 'to keep silent or to force others to keep silent was to foreswear Connolly'.[11] Given that Connolly had written a song entitled 'A Rebel Song', which had as its first line the injunction 'Come workers sing a rebel song') it is hard to find fault with the ICA men's argument.[12] Moreover, in the GPO during the Rising, Connolly had 'burst into the rousing strains of a favourite marching song', namely Peadar Kearney's 'The Soldiers Song' (later to become the Irish national anthem), a song whose lines include the most definitely seditious:

> Soldiers are we, whose lives are pledged to Ireland . . . 'Mid cannon's roar and rifle's peal we'll chant a soldier's song.[13]

Poorly led, with an effective strength of less than 200, and all but ostracized by the labour movement, the ICA played only a minor part in the War of Independence.[14] In an assessment of the reasons behind the ICA's 'Lack of Action' and the long term consequences which he felt emanated from this failure, Robbins noted:

> The failure of the Citizen Army to play a worthwhile role in the fight against the British forces during the period 1918-21 was due in the main to our failure to throw up leaders with dynamic vision of Connolly and Mallin. This failure was indeed a costly one for those of us who accepted the socialist principles of the workers' republic preached by James Connolly, for it meant that we missed a unique opportunity to play our part in the struggle for Irish Freedom and in the subsequent shaping of a free Ireland.[15]

In 1920 a war of words erupted between rival factions of the Socialist Party of Ireland (SPI). The size, organisation and relative importance of the ICA became the subject of controversy when two contradictory reports were sent from the SPI to the Amsterdam Sub-Bureau of the Third International. The first report entitled 'The Political and Working Class Organisation in Ireland' was sent by a group of young radical members of the SPI led by Sean McLoughlin (as a 16-year-old McLoughlin had been promoted by Connolly to the position of Commandant during the Easter Rising), Paddy Stevenson, and Connolly's son Roddy (also a 1916 veteran). In its assessment of the ICA this group noted that:

> This organisation still exists, but it is nearly finished. It has declined since the death of Connolly. It is hostile to Sinn Fein and to the official element in Liberty Hall, but its opposition is very weak. It was a genuine Red Guard with a Socialist Constitution, but it is now in the hands of a very few incompetent men who are very narrow and almost reactionary. Its membership has dwindled down to almost sixty, all of whom are armed, but it counts for nothing as an organisation. An attempt to revive it and work it in conjunction with the Revolutionary Socialist Party failed, but the few who are left would fight for the Socialist Republic.[16]

Connolly's eldest surviving daughter Nora[17] brought the contents of this report to the attention of the old guard O'Brienite leadership of the SPI (largely a mirror image of the leadership of the ITGWU), which then prepared a further report vehemently opposing both the factual content and the analytical assessments of the original correspondence. The old-guard leadership arguing that in respect of the ICA:

> The circulation of statements regarding the numerical strength of a revolutionary fighting force is the work of an enemy spy, even if, as in this case, the figure is so low as to be ridiculous. The other comments are equally untrue. Public reflection upon the capacity of officers who are annually elected is an insult to the rank and file.[18]

This debate on the ICA is rather reminiscent of two doctors arguing over the correct diagnosis and treatment of a patient while he expires at their feet for want of attention.

As early as 1918 the ITGWU, speaking on behalf of organised labour, was at pains to deny that it was in any way a pacifist movement. An article which appeared in April of that year in *Irish Opinion* asserted that 'Irish Labour is anything but pacifist, is indeed as militant a movement as any within the International', and went on to claim that 'deriving from James Connolly, Irish Labour could not be otherwise'.[19] Side by side with the ITGWU's retreat from and eventual disassociation from the ICA, such articles and editorials continued to appear in the Union's newspaper, the *Voice of Labour*. In May 1919, for example, an article was published by Nora Connolly entitled 'James Connolly,

Revolutionist', which stated that her father had believed that 'social revolutionists who did not prepare themselves to be capable of meeting and defeating the
trained and disciplined armies of the capitalist powers were not true to the
people they were urging to fight' and that he had 'believed that there should be
a military arm or wing to the working class'. She then proceeded to pose an
obviously rhetorical question: 'Was Connolly the man to ask his followers to
fight with their bare hands?'[20]

In 1919 the ITGWU had its own internal problems (a foretaste of the later
Larkinite 'disruptions'). During these disputes, which centered upon P.T. Daly,
some of Daly's supporters 'brandished revolvers' at an ITGWU meeting and
made a 'treacherous, unprovoked and blackguardly attack' on William O'Brien.[21]
Commenting on this serious breach of standing orders, the *Voice of Labour*
noted that Daly's friends used their revolvers 'for the purpose of bullying
opponents and preventing free speech' and went on to state that 'We do not
believe those revolvers were purchased for this purpose but they were used for
this purpose'. In an attempt to explain the correct etiquette of revolver usage,
the writer noted that there was 'a time and place for the use of revolvers, and
we should like to see them properly used', but that the time and place was 'not
in the middle of a speech, and the place is not at a Union meeting'.[22] The somewhat cryptic allusion to the purpose for which the revolvers in use at the
meeting were originally purchased, is a reference to the fact that one of the
revolvers was in the hands of a young ICA man named Pat Colgan (he later
married James Larkin's sister Delia).[23]

Less than a fortnight after Ireland's plenipotentiaries signed the Articles
of Agreement with Great Britain,[24] the *Voice of Labour* urged the 'Labour
movement' to remain aloof from the political furore over the Treaty. In this it
claimed that it was 'expressing the general feeling of the organisation of which
it is the organ and the organised Irish Labour movement of which it is the
unofficial mouthpiece'. The *Voice* editorial of 17 December 1921 advised its
readers that 'whatever the provocation, whatever the depth of feeling, let no
Union, Branch or Council as such, take sides, by resolution or otherwise, with
either party in the division of opinion in the Dáil'. While accepting that trade
unionists as individuals had the 'right and duty' to express 'their opinions and
give force and effect to them', they should, the editorial argued, 'keep such
speech and action out of the Unions as organisations'. Coming from an ordinary trade union, such advice might be seen as consistent and sensible. But
emanating from the ITGWU, with its militant nationalist, indeed socialist
republican, background, the request for organisational neutrality appears to be
a retreat from—perhaps even a negation of—leadership, especially when combined with an exhortation that members actively engage, at a personal level, in
what is described as 'the most terrible trial in our modern history'. The writer
of the editorial noted that it was with 'no great willingness but with much
reluctance and deep pain' that the editorial was written.[25] This inner turmoil is
certainly reflected in the conclusion of the article which presented a tortuous

and rather confusing argument, which in the greater part consisted of an extremely dubious paraphrase of one of Connolly's most famous dicta. Possibly feeling rather guilty over his somewhat cavalier use of Connolly's words, the writer avoided using Connolly's name, referring to him simply as 'a man greater than any of us'.[26]

An address given by O'Shannon was published in the next issue of the *Voice*, under the title 'Toward the Republic'. O'Shannon was quoted, somewhat incongruously given the contents of the previous issue, thus:

> Your Union is the most effective fighting Union in these islands, but it must be better. Enlarge your branches. There are many ways of attaining your ends. There is a political way, the industrial way, and the physical way, but those who were not afraid of English jails will not be afraid of Irish jails. Political freedom is not all. We still have a very long way to go to reach the goal for which Connolly fought and died—namely the industrial freedom of the Workers Republic.[27]

Compared to the decidedly negative and non-interventionist stance of the week before, this is a fiery statement, although it would perhaps have been stronger and more positively in the Connolly tradition if it had referred to 'not be afraid' of English and Irish guns or bullets rather than the somewhat defeatist 'jails'.

Early in 1922 the *Voice* proclaimed the importance of 'the political, economic and military force, of a people and a class which has a fully developed social consciousness and social idea different from capitalism'.[28] A few weeks later in an 'editorial reply' to a letter from Louie Bennett which had touched upon the overthrow of the Imperial Duma in Russia, O'Shannon noted that 'Other weapons, including the military weapons which we wish Miss Bennett would join us in advocating, were combined to overthrow the Duma. Personally we have always advocated the use of all these weapons industrial, political and military.'[29] A week later the *Voice* again returned to this theme with the unequivocal statement that 'the industrial weapon and the military weapon are more potent for Labour's good than the Parliamentary weapon'.[30]

On 10 April 1922 the National Executive of the ILP issued an anti-militarist Manifesto. The manifesto protested against 'the rise of the gun and the bayonet' and against men on both the Treaty and the anti-Treaty side who 'seek to impose their will upon the people by virtue of their armaments alone'. Claiming to 'speak for the masses of the workers of Ireland', the manifesto went on to threaten that 'If the country is to resume warfare we shall endeavour to ensure that it is for something worthwhile for the workers to enter into the struggle'. The manifesto concluded by asking the 'workers who are members of the several armies to refuse to be drawn into violent actions' and to 'stand ready to take action when the call comes'.[31] In the same issue an editorial entitled 'Irish Labour and Irish Militarism' loyally supported the Labour Party's anti-militarist manifesto. While supporting anti-militarism, the writer was extremely anxious to emphasize the non-pacific nature of Labour's objections to militarism. 'Let this be clearly understood,' he writes:

> Irish Labour's opposition is directed against militarism not against the use of military force. Irish Labour recognises, none better, that under certain circumstances the application of armed forces is both necessary and desirable. Many even in Irish Labour will go as far as to say that under certain circumstances an armed force of the workers is necessary. But there is a vital difference between this and militarism. It is to drive home this distinction that Irish Labour has spoken. [32]

The writer who failed to define what he meant by 'certain circumstances' or to clarify the 'vital distinction' between the militarism of the IRA, and the labour movement's belief in armed force, went on to complain that the two factions of the IRA had become 'a law unto themselves', and that they 'every day commit acts which we who are not at all opposed to the use of arms, never have been, and never shall be, can only describe as the sheerest militarism'.[33]

There is a certain amount of confusion evident in labour's response to the deteriorating situation in Ireland. A cynic might suggest that for labour, militarism is everybody else's guns whilst anti-militarism is the guns that we believe in but don't have. This confusion continued in the next issue of the *Voice* where it was again asserted that 'the Irish Labour movement has not been, is not now, and so long as it remains under the present leadership, will not be pacifist'. And once again it noted that 'Many people in the Labour movement . . . have all along recognised and many more realise now, that an armed force of the workers for the workers defence and in the workers interests is equally necessary'.[34]

The Labour Party issued another 'Anti-militarist Manifesto' on 20 April 1922. This manifesto called for a General Strike on 24 April.[35] In its report of the 'great Workers Demonstration' held in O'Connell Street in Dublin, the *Voice* proudly noted that the strike was held on 'the anniversary date and day of the Insurrection of Easter Week, 1916' and asserted that 'it is not altogether unbecoming that the workers should raise their voices in defence of civil liberty on the anniversary of the noblest declaration of national Liberty ever made in Ireland'. That an anti-militarist meeting should take such pains to so closely identify itself with an armed insurrection is somewhat odd, although perhaps understandable, within the context of Irish politics at the time. That some of the speakers should use an avowedly anti-militarist platform to make inflammatory statements is less accessible to logical political analysis. For example, Tom Irwin, who was an official in the Plasterers Union and one of the speakers on platform one, told his audience that it could come to it that they 'might have to provide the members of their unions with guns', and William O'Brien, Treasurer of both the ILP and the ITGWU, who presided on platform three, informed his fellow anti-militarists that 'Labour was not prepared to tolerate a state of affairs in which the sole right to rule was vested in the possession of a gun' and that 'recent events had shown that Labour required its own armed force to protect it against aggression'.[36] It is also worth noting that each of the three anti-militarist platforms was guarded by a detachment of the ICA under the command of Major Michael Kelly.[37]

The ICA's rather unexpected presence at the O'Connell St. meeting was linked to an attempt by prominent Labour Party and ITGWU leaders to use the ICA as the nucleus of a new all-Ireland Workers Army. Meetings took place between labour leaders and senior ICA officers,[38] but despite some progress the long standing bad feeling which existed between the ICA and the leadership of the labour movement, and the fact that the labour leaders 'wished to detach the Citizen Army from the IRA section, which now stood in militant opposition to the Treaty'[39] ensured that the plans for a Workers Army came to nothing. In fact the whole Workers Army project weakened the ICA as it created a good deal of confusion and disunity within its ranks.[40] Essentially, labour officials had decided that at a time when 'every man with a gun has become a law unto himself, and every man who can get ten men with guns has become a government unto himself',[41] it might be prudent to establish a body which would provide a protective screen, under their control, for the labour movement's normal activities. Far from envisaging a revolutionary role for its new military wing, it appears that O'Brien and his fellow labour leaders intended it to remain in a stance of armed neutrality, to act as a bystander whilst Treatyites and anti-Treatyites fought for control of the country.[42]

The period encompassing the Truce and the Civil War in Ireland was an extremely difficult one for Irish labour. The *Voice of Labour* noted many instances, most commonly in country areas, of Union members and officials threatened and assaulted, of Union property damaged and of picket lines broken by armed members of IRA factions.[43] There is even an instance on record of an employer sending a cheque to the Ministry of Defence in appreciation of 'the protection afforded us during the recent Labour trouble here'.[44] During the Civil War years labour leaders lived under threat of their lives. Whilst Peadar O'Donnell was being held in prison as a hostage, Lile O'Donel (later to become O'Donnell's wife) visited Tom Johnson, who as labour Leader in the Dáil, was, from the perspective of Republicans, guilty of complicity with the Free State Government, with the simple message: 'I came to tell you, Mr. Johnson, that you will be shot if Peadar O'Donnell is murdered in Finner.'[45] For good measure, O'Donnell's aunt contacted William O'Brien regarding O'Donnell's predicament and warned him that 'If Peadar goes the way of other brave men, you share fully the responsibility for his murder.'[46] On another occasion O'Brien received a polite but deeply threatening letter from Ernie O'Malley, the famous IRA leader. One can sympathise with O'Brien—to be singled out for possible retribution by a man of O'Malley's reputation and standing within the IRA, would give even the most courageous of men considerable grounds for disquiet.[47]

As if the problems created by the Civil War were not enough for the Irish labour leaders to contend with, James Larkin returned to Ireland, and within a matter of weeks 'there was a Civil War raging in the Irish Labour Movement'.[48] Fortunately the ill-feeling and violence which arose out of the ITGWU's internal problems stopped short of either side resorting to arms. According to an ITGWU Annual Report 'Bullying, terrorism, physical violence, lying, libelling and intimidation by large bodies of men were the methods adopted.'[49] There can be no doubt that having ITGWU members picketing Liberty Hall—their own Union Headquarters—and on occasion brawling for control of the building,[50] was extremely embarrassing and damaging to the Union. Given that a fair number on both sides of the dispute were no strangers to the gun, the rival factions can perhaps be given some credit for limiting the extent of the violence.

With the retreat of the post-Connolly labour movement from the armed struggle to achieve a 'Workers Republic', or indeed any other form of Republic, Connolly's revolutionary socialist legacy tended to find its most responsive audience within the left-wing of the IRA. In the late 1920s and early 1930s a radical Workers-Republic-oriented wing of the IRA led by O'Donnell, Frank Ryan, George Gilmore, and Michael Price attempted with some temporary success to radicalize the IRA.[51] Most of the leftists within the IRA eventually resigned in order to have more freedom to pursue their political objectives. It is worth noting in this context that in 1934, Price, Seamus MacGowan (1916 ICA man) and Roddy Connolly, concerned about the threat from Ireland's own fascist variant, the Blueshirts, made an unsuccessful and hence shortlived attempt to revive the Irish Citizen Army.

As the 1930s progressed, the threat of fascism both internal and external began to claim much of the revolutionary left's energies and resources. Fierce street battles with the Blueshirts provided a prelude to the left's commitment to supporting Loyalist Spain. A number of important leaders,—notably Frank Ryan,[53] failed to return from service in Spain. In tribute to Connolly, the Irish detachment which went to Spain to fight with the International Brigade chose the title 'James Connolly Unit' and did honour to his name by fighting with great distinction.[54]

One of Connolly's most important legacies to the Irish labour movement lay in the example he had shown of revolutionary vigour and daring. His acceptance of revolutionary violence, of force, was a central aspect of his legacy. The fact that his boldness and almost frantic eagerness to grasp any and every revolutionary possibility, however remote, cost him his life, and in the short term disrupted the labour organisations which he led, is one very understandable explanation of why so many of those who proclaimed his teachings and example, found it impossible to emulate him. In his 'Rebel Song' Connolly wrote that:

The slave who breaks his slavery's chain. A wrathful man must be.[55]

The men who replaced him were excellent men in many respects, but what wrath they felt for the capitalist system was in large part subsumed in the day-to-day struggle to rebuild and administer the labour movement. The success they had—and success it was, at least in quantitative terms—produced its own brake on any remnant of revolutionary fervour. The War of Independence and the Civil War provided a potentially revolutionary situation. Irish labour was unable to grasp this opportunity—an opportunity which Connolly had himself played no small part in creating. The men and women who did have Connolly's aggressive drive and who shared his willingness to test their beliefs through 'the arbitration of the sword' found their home in the Republican movement rather than with organised labour. By the time left-wing, Connolly-inspired Republicans had managed to come to the fore of the republican movement, the revolutionary situation had long since passed. And, as we have seen in the last chapter, they had no organisation with which they could take advantage of any revolutionary possibilities which might have arisen.

CHAPTER 15

Revolution—Conclusions

Yours for the Barricades.   James Connolly, 1906.[1]

The Labour Party is determined that no action of theirs would be such as would precipitate renewed strife, civil war or revolutionary effort.

Tom Johnson, Chairman of Irish Labour Party, 1927.[2]

Across the whole conduct of Ireland's national struggle following Easter '16 is written in giant letters the words 'fear of Social Revolution'.

Sean Murray, 1936.[3]

GIVEN THAT JAMES Connolly was above all else a revolutionary socialist, it is fitting that this chapter on revolution in post-Rising Ireland concludes the study. Socialist revolution was Connolly's undeviating goal and the driving force which inspired and impelled his life. It is only through recognising the depth, the passion and indeed the ruthlessness of his revolutionary commitment that his political career—and the complex nature of his political legacy—can be understood. In previous chapters we have examined the development of Connolly's political thought and practice and have explored the uses, misuses and abuses which his political legacy encountered after his execution in 1916. One very clear conclusion which has emerged from this study is that the left in Ireland failed to sustain the revolutionary momentum which Connolly's political, and military, initiatives had created during the years 1913–16. Connolly's greatest achievement as a revolutionary socialist was that during the last few years of his life he managed to steer the Irish labour movement—or at least its most militant sections—into a position at the vanguard of the national struggle. Connolly's success should not, however, be overstated. Pearse, Clark, MacDonagh and the other Easter Rising leaders constituted a minority movement within the nationalist community; indeed, they were a minority even within the Irish Volunteers, an organisation which was itself supported by a minority of the Irish people. The alliance which Connolly cemented in 1916 was an alliance of extremists, an alliance of the most impatient and aggressive physical force elements in the nationalist camp and men of similar temperament from within the ranks of organised labour.

Through the force of his intellect, selflessness and sheer aggressive drive, Connolly pushed labour into the forefront of physical force republicanism. This was in itself no mean feat given the fact that the militant workers' republican wing of the labour movement had not attracted any really sizeable number of adherents. In 1916 Connolly had at his command around 200 fully armed, well-disciplined ICA men, the more general support of the few thousand members of the ITGWU, and the political support of the handful of socialists in the SPI. Clearly the forces of revolutionary workers Republicanism were not large—Connolly's genius was to ensure that they were significant. He achieved this through his willingness to personify the very 'dash and recklessness' which he had always argued was an essential characteristic of revolutionary leaders and revolutionary movements.[4]

Some six months prior to the Easter Rising, Connolly wrote that 'an epoch to be truly revolutionary must have a dominant number of men with the revolutionary spirit—ready to dare all, and take all risks for the sake of their ideals'.[5] Connolly recognised that his chances of leading a purely socialist revolution in Ireland were remote. His strategy therefore was based upon his belief that militant labour had an opportunity, through sheer militancy and revolutionary drive, of 'taking and keeping the lead' in what he referred to as the 'true nationalist side'.[6] For Connolly, of course, the only 'true nationalists' were the physical force Republicans. Given the fact that in Easter 1916 Connolly was not only General Secretary of the ITGWU and Commander of the ICA but also Vice-President of the Provisional Government of the Irish Republic and Commandant-General of the Dublin Division of the IRA (Patrick Pearse described him during the Rising as 'the guiding brain of our resistance'),[7] Connolly's strategy, although it cost him his life, was perhaps not altogether unsuccessful.

Connolly's legacy—the strategy which he bequeathed to the Irish labour movement—was straightforward and unequivocal. If it was to follow Connolly's teaching and example, labour would have had to maintain and extend its hard won position as the most militant, most uncompromising and most dynamic force involved in Ireland's struggle for national independence. Such a course of action might have given labour some chance of taking a leading, possibly even *the* leading, role in Irish political life. The stakes were high, but the dangers involved in pursuing Connolly's path were daunting. The Rising itself had radicalized the national struggle. Labour's involvement in the Rising had already cost it dearly in terms of lives lost, men and women imprisoned, union property destroyed and general disruption to normal labour activities.

In the wake of the Rising the ICA, the ITGWU, the ITUCLP and the SPI were in dire straits. These organisations had suffered such severe damage as a result of the Rising that their future existence was doubtful. The Irish Left had, for the first time, made a major impact on Irish political life. In that sense Connolly's strategy had been vindicated, but the cost had been devastating. In deciding their future course of action, the surviving labour leaders had to balance not only their own personal viewpoints, their own strengths and weaknesses, but also the all too obvious costs—life, liberty and the pursuit of a strong and secure labour movement—which following Connolly's revolutionary strategy would certainly have entailed.

Connolly was a bold, vibrant, physically courageous man, for whom being an 'Irish Rebel' and a socialist revolutionary were almost second nature. Militancy and revolutionary activities were well suited to his character and personality. Despite his formidable intellectual capacities and attainments, he retained throughout his life a robustly partisan and passionately felt commitment to a total black-and-white, class-based perspective. His aptly titled 'Rebel Song' provides an insight into the type of thought processes which made him the political leader he was:

> Come workers sing a rebel song,
> A song of love and hate,
> Of love unto the lowly
> And of hatred to the great . . .
> The serf who licks the tyrants rod
> May bend forgiving knee;
> The slave who breaks his slavery's chain
> A wrathful man must be.[8]

Connolly, a wrathful man if ever there was one, was still leading the singing amidst the bullets and flames of the GPO in 1916.[9]

There is little doubt that some people active in the labour movement after the Rising had an understanding of the internal forces which drove Connolly. In 1918 an article appeared in *Irish Opinion: Voice of Labour*, which noted that:

> No-one would say that in his supreme sacrifice, Connolly considered the capitalists of his country. Connolly gave his life for the workers, while Pearse suffered death for his countrymen both rich and poor.[10]

The fact that there were influential people in the labour movement like William O'Brien and Cathal O'Shannon who had an understanding of Connolly's political stances and psychological processes did not, even after he had become a near-deified heroic figure, mean that they had the capacity or even the desire to emulate either the style or the content of his political leadership.

In December 1922 the Dublin correspondent of the *Morning Post,* describing a joint meeting of the Dáil and the Seanad, made the perceptive, if somewhat acerbic comment that:

> Irish Labour, however, must have its playboys. Actually Tom Johnson and the other labour leaders that count are staunch conservatives at heart. The real bolshies, like the knife-faced Cathal O'Shannon, count for little but noise.[11]

O'Shannon, who, as it has been previously argued in this book had an excellent understanding of Connolly's political legacy, has been described as an 'intellectual giant' who was 'frustrated by the greater strength of character of the more

humdrum O'Brien'.[12] O'Shannon was essentially a newspaper editor and propagandist. He was a significant figure within the labour movement for many
years but, as the *Morning Post* correspondent suggested, he never achieved a
position of real power or influence. Greaves makes the point that while there
was no question that O'Shannon conducted considerable research into Irish labour
history, he 'lacked the application to make anything of it'.[13] By the rigourous
standards set by Irish labour leaders, O'Shannon appears to have been a somewhat
'bohemian' character; sobriety was not perhaps his greatest strength. This combined with his consistently leftist, Connolly-inspired, stance, seems to have been
enough to ensure that he did indeed 'count for little but noise'. Certainly he never
became a labour leader of the first rank.

The two men who undoubtedly did constitute the first rank of the labour
movement during the period of this study were William O'Brien and Thomas
Johnson. James Larkin, whom one might have expected to be placed alongside
these two men, did not in fact regain his pre-war pre-eminence in the labour
movement after his return to Ireland in 1923. Larkin had all the 'dash and
recklessness' which Connolly had prescribed as being the essential characteristics
of a revolutionary leader, but he did not have sufficient discipline, organisational
skills or theoretical clarity to constructively focus and direct his great energies and
his fiery militancy. Connolly himself, in a letter to O'Brien in 1911, said of Larkin,
'The man is utterly unreliable—and dangerous because unreliable.'[14] Connolly's
words were prophetic, for although Larkin did figure prominently in the labour
movement in the 1920s, his influence was largely disruptive and counter-
productive and his power steadily diminished. Larkin's disruption of the labour
movement was to a large extent based on personal antagonisms rather than on
points of principle or socialist strategy. As such, his contribution to the labour
movement and to revolutionary socialism must be deemed to have been negative.

In the post-Rising period, William O'Brien was in terms of sheer power and
influence the most important labour leader in Ireland. O'Brien's elder brothers had
been founder members of the ISRP and O'Brien himself had joined the Party
when he was little more than a boy. Indeed, for many years Connolly affec-
tionately referred to him as 'the kid'. O'Brien had a long and (in as much as he
could be said to have become close to anyone) a close relationship with Connolly.
O'Brien claimed, and with some justification, that he had been instrumental in
arranging Connolly's return to Ireland in 1910. He was extremely proud of this
service to both Connolly and in retrospect, to the nation as a whole and frequently
cited it later in his career. O'Brien was not 'out' in 1916 although he was arrested
(while in the company of Connolly's son Roddy who was to grow into one of his
most bitter critics) in the general round-up of noted nationalist sympathisers which
took place after the Rising. Given his longstanding record as a militant socialist-
republican, it is perhaps rather surprising that he did not bear arms. Certainly he
was no pacifist and, short of military involvement, appears to have lent his support
to the Rising.[15] The fact that he had been lame since childhood explains his non-
participation to some extent. But being lame did not keep Sean MacDermott out

of the fight and Joseph Plunkett bore arms despite being seriously, probably terminally, ill. Both of these men were executed after the Rising; in fact MacDermott and Connolly, although executed separately, faced the same firing squad at Kilmainham Jail on the morning of the 12th of May.

O'Brien himself claimed that he was following Connolly's orders by not taking part in the Rising, as on Easter Monday, immediately prior to the setting out from Liberty Hall to attack the GPO, Connolly instructed him to 'Go straight home now and stay there, there is nothing that you can do now, but you may be of great service later on.'[16] Connolly's desire to keep O'Brien out of the fighting is verified by a statement made by Nora Connolly, a statement which her mother also signed, recording her last visit to her father before his execution. Nora records that on being informed of O'Brien's arrest Connolly said 'I am very sorry to hear that, I wanted O'Brien to be safe.'[17] Clearly Connolly had a high regard for O'Brien's energy, talents and potential contribution to the labour movement. Equally clearly, Connolly did not consider O'Brien's particular strengths and abilities to be suited to any form of military involvement. O'Brien's physical courage is not in question here. There is no doubt that he was a brave and dedicated man. The fact remains, however, that he was not a man who was suited to, or indeed capable of, following and implementing Connolly's revolutionary strategy.

O'Brien's personality and political priorities were very much in evidence when he gave his Chairman's address to the ILPTUC's 1918 Congress, and it should be noted that at this period O'Brien, and the ILPTUC in general, were still fond of and much given to, revolutionary rhetoric, a trait most evident in the near ecstatic welcome with which they had greeted the Russian Revolution. Delegates to the Congress, which was held in Waterford early in August, were told by O'Brien that he had

> Long been convinced, and every day that passes strengthens that conviction, that . . . Our movement is, in a certain sense, the great business organisation of a great cause . . . Here now is our opportunity, when we are a growing and expanding movement. Let us get our fully equipped offices let us man them with the best men and women either love or money can buy; let our officials be highly skilled, well trained, able, and where necessary, experts and specialists in their particular lines, and let us adopt all the best and most up-to-date methods of conducting business. For the conduct of our movement is, to a certain degree, a great business, and we must have it managed on business lines.[18]

When he gave this speech and for a number of years afterwards, O'Brien was considered by many people in the labour movement to have the potential to become 'the Irish Lenin'[19], to be in fact, 'the embryo President of the Workers Republic of Ireland'.[20]

As his speech at Waterford showed, O'Brien's business was business, labour business—but business nonetheless. His vision was of a secure, financially sound, well-organised labour movement led by the best 'either love or money can buy'. This is in direct contrast to Connolly, who only a few years earlier, had been proud to state, and to state with absolute sincerity 'my business is revolution'.[21] Throughout his long and distinguished career in the labour movement O'Brien never totally abandoned the revolutionary rhetoric of his youth and early manhood. As late as 1935, during the Dublin tram and bus strike, he noted that 'General strike talk is foolish unless you are prepared to put an alternative government forward. If it were a revolutionary situation I'd be for a General Strike. As it is I'm against it.'[22] In truth O'Brien was an organiser; he was a highly skilled bureaucratic functionary, rather than a real labour leader; certainly he was not a leader in the Connolly tradition. For O'Brien the 'revolutionary situation' would never arise, he was so busy organising, so busy developing labour's bureaucratic structures that he failed to recognise that means had become ends and that Connolly's vision had been lost in the process. In the decade which followed the Rising, Tom Johnson, an English socialist who had built his reputation in the labour movement through his work in Belfast, became, at least in terms of official posts, the most important labour-leader in Ireland. In reality O'Brien wielded more actual power than Johnson through his position with the ITGWU. Johnson was no revolutionary. He has been accurately described as 'a brand of English socialist, not an Irish revolutionary'.[23] Johnson never at any time claimed to be a revolutionary socialist. He was a man of peace, moderation and reason who drew his inspiration from the New Testament and Fabianism rather than from Irish revolutionary traditions or the example set by the Soviet system in Russia. In 1925 Johnson set down his political credo in an internal Labour Party communication. In this statement he argued that labour must:

> preach the Gospel of faithful service—for the up-building of the Nation—materially and spiritually. We must ever insist on maintaining the rights won through suffering, but the power to maintain our rights is increased tenfold when we also do our duty faithfully and fulfil our obligations.[24]

Johnson's 'Gospel of faithful service' is of course a very long way from the Gospel of discontent and audacious revolutionism which inspired Connolly and formed the basis of his political legacy.

By the 1930s the Labour Party, by now divorced from the ITUC, had become so far removed from Connolly's political legacy that a number of delegates to the Labour Party Conference in 1932 expressed serious concern that not only Connolly's political teachings but his very name might be forgotten.[25] In response to this note of concern, a delegate stated that in his view 'Connolly would not be so much worried to know that his name was forgotten as he would be to know that his name was being used to promote other political faiths'.[26] While clearly reflecting an accurate assessment of the distaste which Connolly had always displayed towards any suggestion of personality-based or leader-worshipping politics, this comment ignored the rather obvious point that the Labour Party itself was arguably the worst offender with regard to the charge of using Connolly's name to promote political stances and policies which Connolly himself would have rejected out of hand. Over the years the Labour Party became steadily more anti-communist and became increasingly influenced by the hierarchy of the Roman Catholic Church. This right-wing and often reactionary drift in the political complexion of the Party is apparent in the assertion, by a labour member of the Dáil at the 1937 Party Conference, that members of the Labour Party were 'Catholics first and politicians afterwards'.[27] At the 1939 Conference one delegate—a well educated man representing the Irish National Teachers' Organisation—in the course of congratulating the Party on dropping its commitment to establishing a Workers' Republic, made the startlingly understated and ill-informed comment that there was 'a socialistic tinge in the Workers' Republic as envisaged even by Connolly'.[28] Comments such as this prompted Roddy Connolly to enter the fray and he put the case strongly, although perhaps somewhat defensively, that there was:

> No need to apologise in the slightest for James Connolly: his policy and programme would be vindicated in time . . . There should not be any need to hide the fact that James Connolly was a revolutionary socialist.[29]

One major reason why there was no need to 'apologise' for Connolly's policy or programme—and the main explanation why his political legacy proved to be so limited in its political effect—was the fact that even on the Irish left hardly anyone had a real grasp of what Connolly's policy and programme had actually been. As early as 1920, *The Watchword and Voice of Labour*, when announcing the publication (by the SPI) of one of the very few reprints of Connolly's work published during the period of this study, noted that:

> It is of no credit to the Irish Labour Movement as a whole that the literary remains of James Connolly should still be dispersed through the files of forgotten and very scarce journals, and in out of print editions, and that the best of his propaganda writings should only be obtainable in foreign editions nor has any attempt been made to put his works into Irish.[30]

It was of even less credit to the Irish labour movement that in the two decades which followed this admission of neglect, Connolly's writings remained out of print. Left-wing newspapers almost invariably included quotations from his writings and often printed the words of his more popular labour songs, but full length reprints of his articles were relatively rare and substantial non-newspaper based publication of his writings was almost non-existent. Some attempts were made to make Connolly's writings more readily available. In 1933 a Connolly Memorial Committee was established. This Committee avowed

> Our aim and object is to have every man and woman in Ireland a Trades Unionist and every Trades Unionist a follower of Connolly. The basis of our work will be the widespread dissemination of the teachings of James Connolly.[31]

Like a number of other initiatives of a similar nature, this Committee was
unable to find sufficient financial support to achieve its goal. In the mid-1920s
Constance de Markievicz wrote of Connolly that 'the writings that he has left
us are the marching orders of a risen people.'[32] Clearly Markievicz and a few
other republican and labour activists recognised the importance and potential
of Connolly's writings and yet despite the reverence with which his name and
memory had been invested, Connolly's writings remained unpublished and
thus unread and unheeded.

Throughout the 1920s and early 1930s, socialist republicans within the IRA
found that the task of 'reconciling social radicalism and traditional physical-
force methods of freeing Ireland' was beyond them.[33] In reference to the IRA
in the mid 1920s, Bowyer Bell has noted that 'while many members of the
Executive did, in fact, have deep political convictions, often of the Connolly-
Mellows variety, the 1925 IRA remained largely apolitical.'[34]

Commenting on the same period, Coogan has made the point that 'the whole
IRA ethos was antipathetic to politicians' and that the IRA was 'forced' by circumstances rather than by a positive commitment when it indulged in political
debates and political action.[35] Men with strong socialist republican beliefs did
achieve high rank within the IRA, but their influence was based on their outstanding military records rather than their political persuasiveness or credibility.
Over the years noted left-wing republicans within the IRA included men who had
won real standing within the republican movement—Sean MacBride, Michael
Price, Peadar O'Donnell, David Fitzgerald, Michael Fitzpatrick, Frank Ryan and
the Gilmore brothers being perhaps the major figures. In terms of sheer numbers,
however, the left never gained effective control over the IRA. As we have seen,
most left-wing activists, whether voluntarily or by expulsion, left the IRA in the
early 1930s.

In terms of political theory, the socialist republican wing of the IRA failed to
construct a credible and effective left-wing republican model capable of seriously
challenging de Valera and his 'apolitical' Republican Fianna Fail Party. Given that
Paedar O'Donnell, who has been accurately described as having been the 'Chief
theoretician of the Republican Left',[36] was honest enough to publicly state that he
did not think that he had 'a gift of theoretical guidance',[37] the failure of the
republican left is perhaps not very surprising.

With regard to mainstream, publicly-organised Communism in Ireland, the
common denominator which ran through all the various manifestations of the
Communist Party during the years encompassed by this study was their ineffec-
tiveness. Communism did not thrive in Ireland and never at any stage appeared
likely to do so. Being a strongly Roman Catholic country with a small industrial
base, Ireland was not fertile ground for Communism. The tiny communist parties
which did form managed to compound the very real difficulties which faced them
by their susceptibility to both internal divisions and to what often appeared to be a
somewhat slavish acceptance of Comintern directives. Moreover, as we have seen
those instructions were often based on very grave misreadings of the Irish political

situation. Thus despite being able to claim direct descent, through the SPI, from Connolly's political leadership, and to his marxist political doctrine, the Irish communist parties were unable to make any headway. Not even the fact that both Connolly's son and Jim Larkin's son were prominent communist leaders gave the movement popular appeal. Individual communists—Sean Murray and Sean McLoughlin being good examples—enjoyed a large measure of respect and even a certain amount of influence within republican circles, but their acceptance was invariably based on their military prowess rather than on political factors. In 1909, while he was living in America and desperately anxious to return to Ireland, Connolly, in a letter to his friend Matheson, gave an accurate assessment of his political potential and importance. 'I feel,' he informed Matheson that,

> most anyone can do the work I am doing here, but that there is work to be done in Ireland I can do better than most anyone.[38]

Connolly, whose 'business' was revolution, did indeed find or rather create 'work' for himself on his return to Ireland and there can be little doubt that he did do it better than 'most anyone'. With his death, however, the work which he had started, and which he had given his life to advance, fell into the hands of men who lacked the resolve to attempt to bring it to fruition. Connolly's 'work' was revolution, his political legacy could only be implemented through revolution. Halfhearted or partial acceptance of his legacy was inherently contradictory and doomed to failure. If correctly interpreted and seriously applied, Connolly's political legacy demanded totally committed, near suicidal, revolutionary audacity and opportunism. During the War of Independence and the Civil War period, indeed up until the formation of Fianna Fail which effectively institutionalized and democratized Republican aspirations, Ireland underwent a process of violent, often chaotic political transformation. Had he survived, there is little doubt that Connolly would have perceived the immediate post-Rising years as ones which offered great revolutionary potential.

In his dual role as politician cum-military leader, Connolly managed to be both a revolutionary firebrand and a hard-headed realist. Ryan, his earliest biographer, found himself drawn to Keats's phrase 'fire in the heart, and ice in the brain'.[39] Connolly's commitment to socialist revolution was such that he was prepared to run any risk rather than miss the slightest, most fleeting revolutionary opportunity. In the final analysis, there was very little chance of socialist revolution in Ireland. Connolly's uniqueness lay in his willingness to make much of little, to seize any and every opportunity, however remote, however dangerous. His successors in the labour movement, on the other hand, although they were generally men of real ability and high character, were confined by their own pragmatic political 'realism'. Connolly's legacy—the revolutionary spirit which underpinned his political teachings and personal example—was lost to them. In direct contrast to Connolly who made much of little, his successors made little, or nothing, of the revolutionary possibilities which the turbulent post-Rising years presented to them.

APPENDIX: SUMMARY OF POLITICAL AND LABOUR ORGANISATIONS

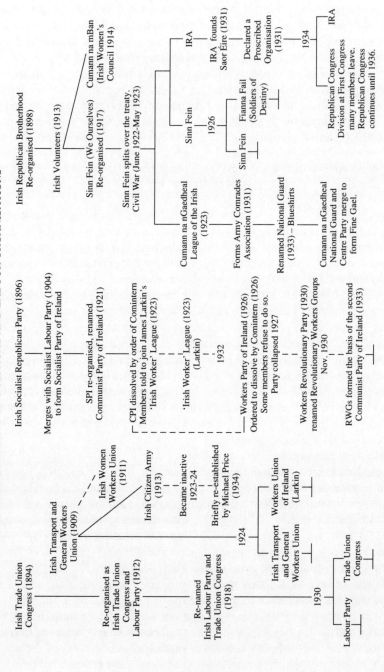

Notes

INTRODUCTION

1 D. Fitzpatrick, *Politics and Irish Life 1913–1921*, Gill and Macmillan, Dublin, 1977, p.146.
2 D. Ryan, *James Connolly His Life Work and Writings*, Talbot Press, Dublin, 1924.
3 R.M. Fox, *James Connolly The Forerunner*, The Kerryman, Tralee, 1946.
4 C.D. Greaves, *The Life and Times of James Connolly*, Lawrence and Wishart, London, 1976.
5 S. Levenson, *James Connolly-Socialist Patriot and Martyr*, Quartet Books, London, 1977.
6 B. Ransom, *Connolly's Marxism*, Pluto Press, London, 1980. See also the same writer's 'James Connolly and the Scottish Left', Ph.D., Edinburgh University, 1975.
7 M. O'Riordan, *James Connolly in America*, Irish Communist Organisation, Belfast, 1971.
8 C. Reeve and A.B. Reeve, *James Connolly and the United States—the Road to the 1916 Irish Rebellion*. Humanities Press, New Jersey, 1978.
9 A. Morgan, *James Connolly: A Political Biography*, Manchester University Press, 1988.
10 K. Allen, *The Politics of James Connolly*, Pluto Press, London, 1990.
11 N. Connolly-O'Brien, *Portrait of a Rebel Father*, Talbot Press, Dublin, 1935.
12 I. Connolly-Heron, 'James Connolly—a biography'. Serialised in *Liberty*, Journal of Irish Transport and General Workers Union, March-October 1916.
13 A. Mitchell, *Labour in Irish Politics 1890–1930*, Irish University Press, Dublin, 1974.
14 M. Milotte, *Communism in Modern Ireland*, Gill and Macmillan, Dublin, 1984.

CHAPTER 1

1 *IW*, Vol. II, No. 31, Christmas, 1912, p.6.
2 *WR*, Vol. I, No. 1, 13 Aug. 1898, p.7.
3 O'Brien, Msl3953.

4 C. Reeve and A.B. Reeve, *James Connolly and the United States*. Humanities Press, N.J.,1978, p.254. See also C. Reeve, *The Life and times of Daniel De Leon*, Humanities Press, New Jersey, 1972, pp.165–175.
5 *H*, Vol. I, No. 12, Dec. 1908, p.4.
6 *H*, Vol. II, No. 3, Mar. 1909, p.4.
7 See *IC*, Vol. I, No. 1, 25 May 1912 article entitled 'Organised Suffragism in Ireland' for an informed and detailed breakdown of the organised suffrage groups in Ireland at this time.
8 I. Connolly-Heron, 'James Connolly', *Liberty*, Mar. 1966, p.18.
9 Ibid., p.4.
10 *IW*, Vol. I, No. 24, 28 Oct. 1911, p.l. Connolly's efforts on behalf of the 'mill girls' was not appreciated by Larkin President of ITGWU. W. O'Brien later described the events thus: 'a number of women and girls employed in the Textile Industry in Belfast approached James Connolly, then Belfast Branch Secretary and Ulster District Organiser of the ITGWU and pressed him to admit them into membership of that Union. He did so, but much to his astonishment and disgust Mr Larkin acting as Executive Committee of the ITGWU laid it down that person' in the rules of that union meant male person, and he (Larkin) ordered Connolly to cancel the admission of the factory women and girls to have their membership cards taken from them, and to make them members of the Irish Women Workers Union! W. O'Brien, '*The ITGWU and the IWWU. A bit of History*', n.d., O'Brien, Ms13970.
11 R.M. Fox, *James Connolly the Forerunner*. The Kerryman, Tralee, 1946, p.103.
12 S. Pankhurst, *The Suffragette Movement*, Virago, London, 1977, p.376.
13 R.M. Fox, *Louie Bennett Her Life and Times*, Talbot Press, Dublin, 1958, p.45. Bennett was no

uncritical admirer of Connolly, she notes that although Connolly was 'A strong suffragist, he valued only the militant movement'. ibid, p.45. She was also of the opinion that he was an autocrat of Liberty Hall and that he meant to dominate the Women's Union there just as he did every other department. Ibid, p.49.

14 J. Van Vorris, *Constance de Markievicz. In the Cause of Ireland,* University of Massachusetts Press, Amherst, 1967, p.101.

15 M. MacCurtain, 'Women the Vote and Revolution', in M. MacCurtain and D. O'Corrain (eds.), *Women in Irish Society,* Arlen House, Dublin, 1978, p.50. MacCurtain also notes that Connolly was 'the darling of the Irish Women's Franchise League', p.57.

16 O'Brien, Ms13906

17 S. Levenson, *James Connolly, Socialist, Patriot and Martyr,* Quartet Books, London, 1977, p.224.

18 *IW,* Vol. III, No.44, 14 Mar. 1914, p.3.

19 J. Connolly, *The Reconquest of Ireland,* 1st edn, 1915, New Book Publications, Dublin, 1972, p.47. The sense of comradeship which Connolly recognised between women in revolt and socialists was one for which he for his own part took very seriously. In 1912 for example whilst resident in Belfast he 'travelled especially to Dublin to speak in Phoenix Park after the attack on Asquith when the women were fiercely attacked. Larkin complained bitterly to me [W. O'Brien] of his action in doing so' *O'Brien,* Ms13942(4). Peader O'Donnell recalled that 'the first time I saw Connolly was in Phoenix Park, he was on a suffragette platform with Sheehy and others—he was pelted off the stage and had to escape into the Zoo'—conversation with the writer, 4 Sept. 1985.

20 Connolly, ibid., p.41.

21 Connolly, loc. cit.

22 *WR,* Vol. I. No. 46, 8 Apr. 1916, p.1.

23 *Forward,* 23 Aug. 1913.

24 Connolly, op. cit., p.45.

25 I. Connolly-Heron, 'James Connolly,' *Liberty,* July 1966, p.46.

26 Pankhurst, op. cit., p.505.

27 *Freeman's Journal,* 14 Nov. 1913, p.8. The antecedents of the ICA are complicated. See Ch. 6 for details.

28 See R.M. Fox, *Rebel Irishwomen,* Talbot Press, Dublin, 1935, p.141. Hannah Sheehy Skeffington's response to the information that the Proclamation was to include 'equal citizenship': 'I know who is responsible for that!' she said meaning Connolly.

29 A. Mitchell and P. O'Snodaigh, *Irish Political Documents, 1916–49,* Irish Academic Press, Dublin, 1985, p.17.

30 N. Connolly O'Brien, *Portrait of a Rebel Father,* Talbot Press, Dublin, 1935, p.326.

31 B. Ransom, 'James Connolly and the Scottish Left', Ph.D. thesis, Edinburgh University, 1975, p.67. Original source, *Labour Leader,* 15 Feb. 1896.

32 M. O'Riordan, *James Connolly in America,* Irish Communist Organisation, Belfast, 1971, p.37. Original source, *Socialist,* June 1904.

33 *Weekly People,* 9 Apr 1904.

34 *O'Brien,* Ms13929. See also Ms13913 and Ms13977 for further information on what has been termed the 'Wages Marriage and the Church' controversy.

35 O'Brien, Ms13913.

36 O'Riordan, op. cit., p.16.

37 *H,* Vol. I, No. 12, Dec. 1908, pp.2–3.

38 *W,* 9 Jan. 1915, p.2.

39 O'Brien, Ms13947. Letter, Lillie Connolly to Thomas Foran, ITGWU, dated 20 Aug. 1920. See also letter from Connolly's daughter Nora to Foran dated 9 Aug. 1920 on the same subject, also contained in Ms13947.

40 See article by Hanna Sheehy-Skeffington, 'Reminiscences of an Irish Suffragette', written in 1941 but first published in *Votes for Women— Irish Women's Struggle for the Vote,* A.D. Sheehy-Skeffington and R. Owens, n.d. H.S-S. writes, p.14: 'James Connolly, who (unlike some other labour leaders) recognised from the first the possibilities latent in the movement and welcomed women rebels wholeheartedly. Connolly never once failed to respond to a call for a Mass Meeting, a Protest demonstration, when he went to Belfast he held meetings here for us . . . (James Connolly came to Dublin specially to speak for us, against the will of James Larkin who did not approve).'

41 See M. Gonne MacBride, *A Servant of the Queen,* Gollancz, London, 1938.

42 See E. Gurley Flynn, *The Rebel Girl. An Autobiography,* International Publishers, New York, 1974.

43 See *Labour News,* 29 Jan. 1938, p.6, article entitled 'Helena Moloney tells of the Appeal of the Labour Movement for Women'. Moloney writes 'It was at James Connolly's personal invitation I came to give all the time I could spare to the organisational side of the movement.'

44 Whilst acting as Connolly's secretary during the Easter Rising, Carney refused to leave his side when almost all of the other women were evacuated. See C. Desmond Greaves, *The Life and Times of James Connolly,* Seven Seas Publishers, Berlin, 1971, p.416.

45 C. Markievicz, 'James Connolly as I knew him', *The Nation,* Vol. I, No. 1, 26 Mar. 1927, p.2.

46 *WR,* Vol. I, No. 30, 18 Dec. 1915, p.8. See also N. Connolly O'Brien, *Portrait of a Rebel Father,* The Talbot Press, Dublin, 1935. pp.298– 299. Nora describes how her father 'gave her a small nickel plated revolver' and 'a box of cartridges'.

47 *IW,* Vol. II, No. 31, Christmas 1912, p.6.

CHAPTER 2

1 *WR,* Vol. 2, No.4, 17 June 1899. p.5.

2 D.W. Miller, *Church State and Nation in Ireland 1898–1921,* Gill and Mcmillan, Dublin p.3. Miller notes that the 'intensity of popular devotion to the Church in Ireland' led in the late nineteenth century to the Roman Catholic Church assuming a 'crucial role in the Irish political system alongside the State and the Nation, both of which needed the Church to reinforce their claims to legitimacy'.

3 O'Brien, Ms15674 (2), Letter from the Bishop of Cork Most Rev. Dr. O'Callaghan. The letter was read at all masses in the Diocese of Cork. The letter warned against the 'dangers' of socialism and stated that socialism was based upon 'False philosophy' and 'False principles of morality'. It quotes the Pope's Encyclical Letter 7 Dec. 1887 which warned of the grave errors of socialistic doctrines and their disastrous influences, not merely on material interests, but also on religion and morality. The letter also quotes Papal Encyclical letter 18 Jan. 1901 which stated that 'Socialists are worming themselves into the heart of the State in secret conclave and in the light of day' and were 'inflaming the mind

of the poor. O'Callaghan's own letter concluded with the admonition that 'Socialistic doctrines are not according to the teaching of the Church, and cannot therefore be from God.'

4 See for example J. Connolly, *Labour, Nationality and Religion,* Harp Library, Dublin, 1910.

5 William O'Brien who had close political links with Connolly for twenty years died in 1968. O'Brien became Connolly's literary executor after Francis Sheehy-Skeffington, Connolly's own choice, was murdered during the Easter Rising. For reasons of his own O'Brien restricted access to Connolly's personal papers, C. Desmond Greaves for example while researching his biography of Connolly was given no assistance by O'Brien. In a letter dated 31 Jan. 1957 (O'Brien Ms13942) O'Brien notes that Greaves was 'writing a book on Connolly and appealed to me for assistance twice but I have ignored him'.

6 O'Brien, Ms13906 (iv), Letter J.C. Matheson to Connolly dated 22 Nov. 1907.

7 O'Brien Ms13906, Letter Connolly to J.C. Matheson dated 30 Jan. 1908.

8 *H,* Vol. I, No.9, Sept. 1908, pp.6–7.

9 J. Minahane, 'Connolly's Catholic Pose', *Irish Communist,* November 1980, p.7.

10 M. O'Riordan, 'Dudley Edwards Connolly and Religion', *Irish Communist,* May,1972, pp.10–11.

11 See J.E. Handley, *The Irish in Scotland,* 1st edn, 1943, J.S. Burns and Sons, Glasgow, 1964, for a well documented account of the position of the Roman Catholic Irish in Scotland.

12 Despite his Roman Catholic pose, Connolly still suffered from hostile comments regarding his religious position. During an election campaign in 1902 he was stated at various times to be 'an Orangeman, a Freethinker, a Jew, and a renegade Catholic, his children were going to a Protestant school, they were going to a Catholic school as a blind'. *WR,* Vol. 4, No. 33, March 1902, p.6.

13 *H,* Vol. 1, No. 9, Sept. 1908, p.3.

14 In private correspondence to a trusted recipient Connolly was much less reticent. Writing to Matheson in 1907 he commented, 'The Jews, you knew, are still looking for a saviour. The rest of us have had our saviour already, and as he made a mess of it we intend to mistrust saviours

in the future.' Connolly to Matheson dated 27
Sept. 1907. O'Brien Msl3906.
15 P.B. Ellis, *James Connolly Selected Political Writings,* Penguin, Harmondsworth, 1973,
pp.58–59.
16 *H,* Vol. 1, No. 9, September 1908, pp.6–7.
17 Ellis, op. cit., p.83.
18 *IW,* Vol. IV, No. 14, 15 Aug. 1914, p.2.
19 S. Cronin, *Young Connolly,* Repsol, Dublin,
1983, p.43.
20 *H,* Vol. 2, No. 4, April 1909, p.l.
21 *WR,* Vol. 1, No. 36, 29 Jan. 1916.
22 V.I. Lenin, *On Socialist Ideology and Culture,* Foreign Languages Publishing House,
Moscow, n.d., p.100.
23 *WR,* Vol. 3, No. 10, 28 July 1900, p.5. See also
A. Marreco, *The Rebel Countess, The Life and
Times of Constance Markievicz,* Corgi Books,
London, 1969, p.180. where Connolly referring
to the need to take an oath on joining the IRB,
responded: 'Never mind about formalities; in
times like these I am willing to take a score of
oaths.'
24 J. Connolly, *Erin's Hope. The End and the
Means,* New Book Publications, Dublin, 1972,
p.20.

CHAPTER 3
1 *H,* Vol. 3, No.12, Feb. 1910, p.3.
2 O'Brien, Msl3911. Letter, n.d., Lillie Reynolds
to Connolly.
3 B. Ransom, *Connolly's Marxism,* Pluto,
London, 1980, p.43.
4 *WR,* Vol. 1, No.1, 13 Aug. 1898, p.8.
5 *WR,* Vol. 1, No.2, 20 Aug. 1898, p.5.
6 *WR,* Vol. 1, No.3, 27 Aug. 1898.
7 K. Marx, *Capital,* Vol. III, Moscow Press
Publishers, Moscow, 1961, p.431.
8 See S. Macintyre, *A Proletarian Science,*
Cambridge University Press, Cambridge, 1980,
pp.91–92. Appendix dealing in detail with
English-Language editions of Marx and Engels.
See also the same author's Ph.D thesis, 'Marxism
in Britain, 1917–1933', Cambridge, 1975, p.346.
9 See C. Reeve, *The Life and Times of Daniel
DeLeon,* Humanities Press, New York, 1972,
p.36, for a comment on De Leon's debt to anarchist sources, notably Albert Parsons, August
Spies and Johann Most. The International Working Peoples Association, formed in Chicago in

1883, clearly influenced De Leon, part of its program read 'The International recognises in the
trade union the Embryonic group of the future
society'.
10 At this early stage in their relationship
Connolly, despite his growing reservations still
held De Leon in high regard. See for example his
letter to Daniel O'Brien, Secretary of the ISRP
dated 9 Dec. 1902, in which he writes. 'I ordered
from the Labor News Co., the other week two
copies each of Marx's portrait and De Leon's, to
be sent on to you at my expense—one of each for
the clubroom, and one of each for my own
house.' O'Brien Ms13932. De Leon, unlike
Marx, was not destined for a lengthy tenure as an
adornment to Connolly's home.
11 See O'Brien, Msl3906 IV. Letters, J. Carstairs
Matheson to Connolly dated 22 Nov. 1908 and
16 Feb. 1908 commenting on Connolly's contribution to establishing the Scottish SLP.
12 C. Reeve and A.B. Reeve, *James Connolly
and the United States,* Humanities Press, New
Jersey, 1978, p.46.
13 *WR,* Vol. 3, No.4, 3 June 1900, p.l.
14 M. Riordan, *James Connolly in America,* Irish
Communist Organisation, Belfast, 1971, p.22.
15 *WR,* Vol. 3, No.9, 15 July 1900, p.1.
16 O'Brien, Ms13929. Paper entitled 'Connolly's attitude towards the SLP Trades Union
resolution' Told by John Lyng, a close friend and
collaborator with Connolly in Ireland and USA .
17 *H,* Vol. 1, No.8, Aug. 1908, p.7.
18 O'Brien, Msl3906. Letter, Connolly to Matheson, dated 30 Jan. 1908.
19 O'Brien, Ms13906. Letter, James Connolly
to T. Carstairs Matheson, dated 22 July 1904.
20 Reeves, op. cit., p.53.
21 *H,* Vol. 1, No.1, January 1908, p.9.
22 Reeves, op. cit., p.62.
23 J. Connolly, *The Axe to the Root,* Irish Transport and General Workers Union, Dublin, 1921,
p.28.
24 Ibid., p.31.
25 *H,* Vol. 3, No.11, Jan. 1910, p.4.
26 O'Brien, Ms13908(i), Letter, James Connolly
to W. O'Brien, dated 5 July 1909.
27 *International Socialist Review,* Feb. 1910.
28 *Free Press,* 28 May 1910, quoted in Reeves,
op.cit., p.203. In an article in *Forward,* May
1914, Connolly developed the military analogy

still further when he called for the formation of a sort of Labour War Cabinet which would be invested with the power to 'call out the members of any union when such action is desirable and explain the reasons for it afterwards'.

29 J. Connolly, *The Axe to the Root*, ITGWU, Dublin, 1921, p.21.

30 *WR*, (series two), Vol. 1, No.1, 29 May 1915, p.4.

31 See for example. P. Thomas, *Karl Marx and the Anarchists*, Routledge and Kegan Paul, London, 1980 for a useful discussion of Marxism's relationship to anarchism.

32 *Justice*, 22 July 1893, quoted in B. Ransom, 'James Connolly and the Scottish Left', Ph.D. thesis, Edinburgh University, 1975, p.41.

33 See B. Holton, *British Syndicalism 1900–1914*, Pluto Press, London, 1976, for a sympathetic and detailed account of British Syndicalism. See also J. Quail, *The Slow Burning Fuse, The Lost History of British Anarchists*, Paladin, London, 1978, for an interesting study of British Anarchism, including links with socialist movement and organised labour.

34 V.I. Lenin, *Collected Works*, Vol. 13, Foreign Languages Publishing House, Moscow, 1962, p.167.

35 George Sorel also attempted to give syndicalist theory a sound Marxist base. See for example his *Reflections* on Violence, Collier Books, London, 1969. L. Portis, *George Sorel*, Pluto Press, 1980 has a very good discussion of Sorel's attitude to syndicalism within a Marxist framework. Connolly and Sorel shared many political attitudes, although any direct contact between them seems unlikely.

36 *H*, Vol. 1, No.8, Aug. 1908, p.8.

CHAPTER 4

1 *WR*, Vol. 3, No.10, 28 July 1900, p.1.

2 *H*, Vol. 2, No.3, Mar. 1909, p.2.

3 S. Levenson, *James Connolly– Socialist, Patriot and Martyr*, Quartet Books, London, 1977, p.56. Original source, *Labour Leader*, Jan. 1898.

4 C. Desmond Greaves, *The Irish Crisis*, Lawrence and Wishart, London, 1972, p.120.

5 *H*, Vol. 1, No.3, Mar. 1908, p.7. First published as a pamphlet in 1896.

6 *WR*, Vol. 1, No.1, 13 Aug. 1898, p.8.

7 *WR*, Vol. 4, No.18, 13 Oct. 1900, p.6. First

appeared in *Shan Van Vocht*, January 1897.

8 *WR*, Vol. 2, No.19, 7 Oct. 1899, p.2.

9 *WR*, Vol. 5, No.10, May 1903, p.5.

10 *WR*, Vol. 4, No.18, 13 Oct. 1900, p.6.

11 Levenson, *James Connolly*, p.137.

12 *H*, Vol. 1, No.8, Aug. 1908, p.3.

13 *WR*, Vol. 1, No.4, 3 Sept. 1898, p.3.

14 *H*, Vol. 1, No.8, Aug. 1908, p.3.

15 *H*, Vol. 2, No.3, Mar. 1909, p.2.

16 *H*, Vol. 3, No.11, Dublin, Jan. 1910, p.4.

17 Ibid.

18 Ibid.

19 V.I. Lenin, *The Right of Nations to Self-Determination*, Progress Publishers, Moscow, 1968, p.54.

20 *IW*, 4 Mar. 1914.

21 *IW*, Vol. 4, No.3, 30 May 1914, p.2.

22 Ibid.

23 Levenson, op. cit., p.167.

24 *WR*, Vol. 1, No.30, 18 Dec. 1915, p.1.

25 *WR*, Vol. 1, No.30, 18 Dec. 1915, p.2.

26 *WR*, Vol. 1, No.23, 30 Oct. 1915, p.4.

27 Ibid.

28 *Rossa Souvenir*, July 1915, O'Brien, Ms13942.

29 *WR*, Vol. 1, No.46, 8 Apr. 1916, p.1.

30 *Forward*, 3 June 1911.

31 *Forward*, 10 June 1911.

32 O'Brien, Ms15674(2). W. O'Brien's account books and address book list these exchanges. Newspapers involved include *La Petite Republique, La Voix du Peuple, The Vorwaerts, The Tocsin, People's Newspaper, Brisbane Worker, Sydney Bulletin, The People, Social Democrat, The Class Struggle, Justice, Il Proletario* and *Labour Leader*.

33 Connolly made no attempt to learn Gaelic although he did use an occasional common phrase in his writing. It is also worth noting that to my knowledge he only once used the gaelic form of his name Seumas O'Conghaille, and this one instance was in fact part of an elaborate apology to J.C. Matheson (letter dated 28 Aug. 1902). 'I wish to say then, that I am ashamed of having used that phrase in true bourgeois fashion towards you, and heartily apologise for doing so. When Celt meets Celt words, like blows, are sometimes exchanged in very reckless fashion.' *Shean leat a charadh, Mise,* Seumas O'Conghaille. *O'Brien*, Ms13906(ii).

CHAPTER 5
1 O'Brien, Msl3906(ii), Letter, James Connolly to C. Matheson, 28 Aug. 1902.
2 B. Ransom, 'James Connolly and the Scottish Left', Ph.D., Edinburgh University, 1975, p.42.
3 Ibid., p.44.
4 Ibid.
5 *WR,* Vol. 1, No.4, 3 Sept. 1898, p.l.
6 *WR,* Vol. 2, No.10, 5 Aug. 1899, p.2.
7 *WR,* Vol. 5, No.9, Apr. 1903, p.l.
8 *WR,* Vol. 2, No.19, 7 Oct. 1899, pp.5–6.
9 Ransom, op. cit., p.l43.
10 S. Levenson, *James Connolly– Socialist Patriot and Martyr,* Quartet, London, 1977, p.44.
11 W. O'Brien, *Forth the Banners Go*, Three Candles, Dublin, 1969, p.5.
12 O'Brien, Msl5668. Letter, J.Connolly to Murtha Lyng, Sec. of ISRP,dated 17 Sept. 1901.
13 O'Brien, Msl3932. Letter, J. Connolly to Daniel O'Brien, Sec. of ISRP, dated 3 Nov. 1902.
14 R.D. Edwards, *James Connolly*, Gill and MacMillan, Dublin 1981, p.45.
15 M. O'Riordan, *James Connolly in America,* Irish Communist Organisation, Belfast, 1971, p.10.
16 C. Reeve, *The Life and Times of Daniel De Leon,* Humanities Press, New York, 1972, p.37.
17 Ibid.
18 Ibid.
19 Ibid., p.64.
20 Ibid., p.65.
21 O'Brien, Msl3906. Letter, James Connolly to J.C. Matheson, dated 1 Mar. 1908.
22 *H*, Vol. l, No.l, Jan. 1908, p.9.
23 C.D. Greaves, *The Life and Times of James Connolly*, Lawrence and Wishart, London, 1976, p.215.
24 *H*, Vol. 1, No.7, July 1908, p.7.
25 Ibid., p.6.
26 O'Brien, Ms13906, Letter, J. Connolly to J.C. Matheson, dated 10 June 1909.
27 Levenson, op. cit., p.272.
28 O.D. Edwards and B. Ransom (eds), *James Connolly: Selected Political Writings,* Jonathan Cape, London, 1973, p.28.
29 *WR*, Vol. 1, No.20, 9 Oct. 1915, p.4.

CHAPTER 6
1 *WR,* Vol. 1, No.l, 24 Sept. 1898, p.l. My underlining.

2 *H*, Vol. 1, No.3, Mar. 1908, p.8. Reprinted from article 'Patriotism and Labour', which first appeared in *Shan Van Vocht*, August 1897. This article was also issued as an ISRP manifesto. My underlining.
3 *IW,* Vol. 1, No.35, 22 Jan. 1916, p.l. My underlining.
4 *IW,* Vol. 2, No.45, 29 Mar. 1913, p.2.
5 O'Brien, Ms13942. Letter from John Leslie in Edinburgh, dated 1 Nov. 1916, responding to a request for details of Connolly's early life.
6 See K.R.M. Short, *The Dynamite War, Irish-American Bombers in Victorian Britain*, Gill and Macmillan, Dublin,1979, p.212.
7 Ibid, for details of Fenian activities in Britain. See also P. Quinlan and P. Rose, *The Fenians in England 1865–1872,* John Calder, London 1982. It is worth noting that John Leslie, Connolly's major early political influence, is said to have gravitated towards socialism 'via a sympathy with Fenian revolutionism'. B. Ransom 'James Connolly and the Scottish Left', Ph.D. thesis, Edinburgh University, 1975, p.9
8 See M. Keating and D. Bleiman, *Labour and Scottish Nationalism*, Macmillan, Dublin, 1979, for details of Scottish radical and nationalist traditions.
9 O'Brien, Ms13942. John J. Lyng (an early ISRP member) claims in a letter to O'Brien, dated 29 Apr. 1951, that 'Here in the U.S.A. in the Irish Socialist Federation clubroom Jim said of his military service: I was carried away by the John Boyle O'Reilly propaganda to infiltrate the British Army and found myself in India. Like most of the other Irishmen who enlisted for the same reason.' I would not place too much reliance on the accuracy of Lyng's recall.
10 Connolly was not the only member of his family to 'take the Queens Shilling'. His brother John was in the Army (on his death he received a military funeral) and his uncle, Robert Connolly, serving under the name Peter McBride, was a Sergeant-Major. Military service— under false name—was, it appears, something of a family tradition. See O'Brien, Ms13942 (4). These details were given to O'Brien by Lillie Connolly on 27 July 1934.
11 See S. Edwards, *The Paris Commune 1871*, Eyre and Spottiswoode, London, 1971, for

details of Melliet's activities as a Communard. Melliet's political biography is briefly recounted on p.386: 'Republican Lawyer, and close to Blanquists. Member of Central Committee of National Guard;of Commune for 13th arrondissement; of the Committee of Public Safety. Deputy in Radical Party from 1898 to 1902.'

12 C.U. Greaves, *The Life and Times of James Connolly,* Lawrence and Wishart, London, 1976, p.37. See also Ransom 'James Connolly', p.8, quoting unpublished J. Gilray Ms. Reminiscences, p.3. 'Fresh from his experiences of the commune, he would emphatically insist . . . that without the shedding of blood, there could be no salvation.'

13 *WR,* Vol. 1, No.37, 15 Fe.b 1916, p.l.

14 Greaves, Ibid.

15 *WR,* Vol. 2, No.l, May 1899, p.l.

16 See, for example, *WR,* Vol. 4, No.27, June 1901, p.l, and the IW, Vol. 2, No.41, 1 Mar. 1913, p.3. 'The annual celebration of the Commune of Paris will be held on Monday, 17 of March (St. Patrick's Day) . . . *Vive La Commune .'*

17 *WR,* Vol. 1, No.l, 13 Aug. 1898, p.8.

18 *WR,* Vol. 2, No.9, 22 July 1899.

19 D. Ryan (ed.), *Labour and Easter Week,* Sign of the Three Candles, Dublin, 1949, p.31.

20 K.B. Knowlan, *The Making of 1916 – Studies in the History of the Rising,* Stationery Office, Dublin, 1969, p.190, note 15.

21 *WR,* Vol. 2, No.23, 18 Nov. 1899, p.2.

22 *WR,* Vol. 2, No.22, 4 Nov. 1899, p.5.

23 See *Irish Times,* 3 Jan. 1936, where Cathal O'Shannon, who worked closely with Connolly prior to 1916, states that, 'Connolly was not a pacifist in 1914 any more than in 1916 or 1899.'

24 See Greaves, op.cit., p.136. Defending the platform and flag at a political meeting in Oxford, Connolly who had the flag, 'broke the pole across his knees, as if it were a match, and set about the nearest hoodlums, four of whom he laid out'. Connolly was not always so successful. Greaves in his richly detailed study *The Irish Transport and General Workers' Union. The Formative Years,* Gill and Macmillan, Dublin, 1982, p.118., records that in January 1914 he was kicked in the stomach by a drunken man and quite seriously hurt.

25 See S. Levenson, *James Connolly, Socialist, Patriot and Martyr,* Quartet, London, 1977, p.69,

where he reports that at a Transvaal Committee torchlight demonstration in 1900 'the police charged with batons. Dispersing the mob, they picked out three editors—Connolly, Griffith and O'Leary Curtis of the Weekly Independent—and 'knocked them to the ground'.

26 Charged with inciting to riot and disorderly conduct during the 1913 Lockout, Connolly was imprisoned, not for the first nor the last time. Commenting on his incarceration in MountJoy, Connolly dryly noted: 'It was somewhat mortifying to me to know that I was the only person apparently in goal who had really committed the crime for which I was arrested. It gave me a sort of feeling that I was lowering the moral tone of the prison by coming amongst such a crowd of blameless citizens.' See R.M. Fox, *James Connolly The Forerunner,* The Kerryman, Tralee, 1946, p.145.

27 *WR,* Vol. 1, No.23, 30 Oct. 1915, p.4.

28 Ibid.

29 *IW,* Vol. 4, No.11, 25 July 1914, p.4.

30 *IW,* Vol. 2, No.4, 15 June 1912, p.3.

31 S. Pankhurst, *The Suffragette Movement,* Virago, London, 1977, p.376.

32 It has been argued that the ICA itself developed from an organisation called the Cork Workers Militia founded in 1909 by James Fearon during a dispute between the ITGWU and the Workers Union (founded by Tom Mann in 1898). For details of this argument, see Greaves *ITGWU,* pp.41, 110; B. McCamley, 'The Third James—The story of Irish Labour Pioneer, James Fearon', *Labour History Workshop,* Feb. 1984, pp.11–12, and T. Darragh (pseudonym for Roddy Connolly), in *Communist International,* No. 11–12, June-July 1920, pp.2282–2294.

33 *IW,* Vol. 3, No.44, 14 Mar. 1914.

34 F.S. Lyons, *Ireland since the Famine,* Fontana/ Collins, Glasgow, 1978, p.286.

35 See Cathal O'Shannon's review of Greaves. 'Life and Times of James Connolly', *Evening Press,* 17 Feb. 1961, p.11, for details.

36 See N. Connolly—O'Brien. *Portrait of a Rebel Father,* The Talbot Press, Dublin, 1935, pp.209–214. See also Levenson, *op.cit.,* p.263.

37 O.D. Edwards, *The Mind of an Activist— James Connolly,* Gill and Macmillan, Dublin, 1971, p.78.

38 Greaves, op.cit., p.375. Speech to Trade Council Meeting.
39 Ibid., p.358.
40 D. Ryan, *James Connolly. His Life Work and Writings,* Talbot Press, Dublin, 1924, p.116.
41 *Forward,* 22 Aug. 1914.
42 Greaves, *op.cit.,* p.358.
43 R.M. Fox, *James Connolly, 'The Forerunner',* The Kerryman, Tralee, 1946, p.181. See also Fox's history of *The Irish Citizen Army,* p.110, where he notes that John MacLean, the great Scottish revolutionary socialist, referring to the armed picketing in Dublin, told a meeting in Glasgow that 'the way to do peaceful picketing is to march down with Lee Enfield rifles and not a scab on the horizon. Take a line from the revolutionary dockers in Dublin!'
44 P.B. Ellis, *James Connolly, Selected Writings,* Penguin, Harmondsworth. 1973, p.213.
45 *WR,* Vol. 1, No.27, 27 Nov. 1915, p.2.
46 O.D. Edwards and B. Ransom (eds.), *James Connolly—Selected Political Writings,* Jonathan Cape, London, 1973, p.16.
47 K. Marx and F. Engels, *Manifesto of the Communist Party,* Progress Publishers, Moscow, 1969, p.96.
48 D. McLellan, *Karl Marx. His Life and Thought,* Granada, St. Albans, 1973, p.229.
49 W.Z. Foster, *History of the Three Internationals,* Greenwood Press, Westport, 1968, p.153.
50 Ibid., p.203.
51 G.D.H. Cole, *The Second International 1889–1914,* Macmillan, London, 1960, p.69.
52 V.I. Lenin, *Selected Works,* Vol. 2, Foreign Languages Publishing House, Moscow, 1952, p.365.
53 A. Raftery, *Lenin on Ireland,* New Books, Dublin, 1974, p.32.
54 V.I. Lenin, *Collected Works,* Vol. 41, Foreign Languages Publishing House, Moscow, p.337.

CHAPTER 7
1 *WR,* Vol. 1, No.1, 13 Aug. 1898, p.2.
2 *IW,* Vol. 4, No.22, 10 Oct. 1914, p.1.
3 K. Marx and F. Engels, *Selected Works,* (2 vols). Moscow, Foreign Languages Publishing House, 1951, Vol.2, p.154.
4 D. Ryan, *James Connolly. His Life Work and Writings,* Talbot Press, Dublin, 1924, p.111.

5 E. Aarons, *Lenin's Theories on Revolution,* D.B. Young (for the Communist Party of Australia), Sydney, 1970, p.72.
6 Ryan, *op.cit.,* p.105. Source, *Socialist,* Edinburgh, 17 Apr. 1919.
7 *WR,* Vol. 3, No.5, 16 June 1900, p.2.
8 S. Levenson, *James Connolly, Socialist, Patriot and Martyr,* Quartet, London, 1977, p.271.
9 *WR,* Vol. 1, No.25, 13 Nov. 1913, p.1.
10 *WR,* Vol. 1, No.39, 19 Feb. 1916, p.1.
11 *IW,* Vol. 4, No.14, 15 Aug. 1914, p.2.
12 *H,* Vol. 2, No.5, May 1909, p.1.
13 P.B. Ellis, *James Connolly–Selected Writings,* Penguin, Harmondsworth, 1973, p.45. Source, *Forward,* 14 March 1914.
14 Levenson. op.cit., p.247.
15 *WR,* Vol. 1, No.28, 4 Dec. 1914, p.1.
16 D. Ryan (ed.), *Labour and Easter Week,* Sign of the Three Candles, Dublin, 1949, p.31.
17 Beresford Ellis, op.cit., p.112.18. *WR,* Vol. 1, No.27, 27 Nov. 1915, p.2.
18 WR Vol 1 No.27 Nov. 1915 p.21
19 See, for example, *WR,* Vol. 1, No.1, 29 May 1915, p.1.
20 N. Connolly-O'Brien, *We Shall Rise Again,* Mosquito Press, London, 1981, p.33.
21 Ryan, op.cit., p.81.
22 *WR,* Vol. 1, No.25, 13 Nov. 1915, p.1.
23 B. Ransom, *Connolly's Marxism,* Pluto Press, London, 1980, p.79, Source, *Forward,* 22 Aug. 1914.
24 C. Reeve and A.B. Reeve, *James Connolly and the United States—the Road to the 1916 Irish Rebellion* Humanities Press, New Jersey, 1978, p.36.
25 *IW,* Vol. 4, No.21, 3 Oct. 1914, p.1.
26 *H,* Vol. 2, No.8, Sept. 1909, p.4.
27 *IW,* Vol. 4, No.16, 29 Aug. 1914, p.3
28 *H,* Vol. 3, No.14, Apr. 1910, p.5.
29 *WR,* Vol. 1, No.27, 27 Nov. 1915, p.8.
30 Levenson, op.cit., p.282.
31 J. Connolly, *Erin's Hope: The End and the Means,* New Book Publications, Dublin, 1972, p.23.
32 Levenson, op.cit., p.264.
33 *WR,* Vol. 2, No.20, 21 Oct. 1899, p.2.

CHAPTER 8
1 M. Goldring, *Faith of our Fathers,* Repsol Publishing, Dublin, 1982, pp.89 –90.

2 See S.V. Larsen and O. Snoddy, '1916—A Workingman's Revolution?' *Social Studies,* Vol. 2, No.4, 1973, pp.377–98.
3 D. Ryan (ed.), *Labour and Easter Week,* Sign of the Three Candles, Dublin, 1949, p.21.

CHAPTER 9

1 *An Phoblacht,* Vol. 7, No. 20, June 1932, p.6.
2 *Labour News,* 8 May 1937, Moloney as Chairman of the ITUC addressing the 1937 'James Connolly Commemoration' held on 2 May 1937.
3 L. Levenson, *With Wooden Sword. A Portrait of Francis Sheehy-Skeffington, Militant Pacifist,* Gill and Macmillan, Dublin, 1983, p.212.
4 *IC,* Vol. 4, No.39, Sept. 1916.
5 See B. Farrell article 'Markievicz and the Women of the Revolution', in F.X. Martin (ed.), *Leaders and Men of the Easter Rising,* Ithaca, Cornell University Press, 1967, p.235, where he notes the 'implacable remembrance crusade' which developed out of the Rising.
6 J.L. McCracken, *Representative Government in Ireland,* London, 1958, p. 90.
7 See R.K. Carty, 'Women in Irish Politics', *Canadian Journal of Irish Studies,* Vol. 6, No . 1, June 1980, p . 91 .
8 Ward, op.cit., p.137.
9 Carty, op . cit ., p. 9 3 .
10 See L. Conlin, *Cumann na mBan and the Women of Ireland, 1913–25,* Kilkenny People, 1969, p.50. Conlin notes that on 11 Aug. 1917 Markievicz, addressing a meeting in Cork, hailed them as 'Fellow Soldiers and Friends'. Markievicz privileged background may have played some, albeit minor, role in her political advancement.
11 J. Van Voris, *Constance Markievicz in the Cause of Ireland,* University of Massachusetts Press, Boston, 1967, p. 132.
12 *Freeman's Journal,* 6 May 1914.
13 Ward, op.cit ., pp. 109–110.
14 *IC,* Vol. 4, No.53, Nov. 1917.
15 F. Pakenham (Lord Longford), *Peace by Ordeal,* 1st edn., 1935, Sidgwick and Jackson, London, 1977, pp.83–84.
16 Ward, op.cit., p.165.
17 Ibid., pp . 17 1–17 3 .
18 *An Phoblacht,* 16 July 1933.
19 Ward, op.cit., p.252.
20 N. Cardoza, *Maude Gonne—Lucky Eyes and a High Heart,* Victor Gollancz, London, 1979,

p.359. Original source, J. Hone, *W.B. Yeats 1865–1939,* Macmillan, London, 1943.
21 F. Robbins, *Under The Starry Plough: Recollections of the Irish Citizen Army,* Academy Press, Dublin, 1977.
22 O'Brien, Ms13970, 'The I.T. & G.W.U. and the I.W.W.U. A bit of History'.
23 Ibid.
24 *Irish Times,* 2 May 1955. Letter by W.O'Brien headed 'Women and Unions.'
25 Figures taken from Irish Labour Party and Trades Union Congress Official Reports of proceedings for annual meetings 1919–1930.
26 *IC,* Vol. 7, No.1, May 1919.
27 *IC,* Vol. 7, No.2–3, June-July 1919.
28 *IC,* Vol. 7, No.9, Jan. 1920.
29 *VL,* Vol.9, No.7, 12 Feb. 1927.
30 *An Bhean Oibre,* Feb. 1927.
31 The Commission of Inquiry was set up at the Special Trade Union Conference in April 1936.
32 O'Brien, Ms13971, 'Interim Report Commission of Inquiry into the position of the Irish Trade Union Movement' dated 28 Jan. 1937, addressed to the National Executive ITUC marked 'Private'.
33 James Connolly Souvenir, Dublin Labour Year Book, *May Day Celebration,* 1930, Dublin Trades Union and Labour Council, Dublin, 1930, pp.31–33.
34 Ibid., p.49.

CHAPTER 10

1 O'Brien, Msl3942. *The Gaelic American,* 17 June 1939.
2 J. Newsinger, 'I Bring not Peace but a Sword. The Religious Motif in the Irish War of Independence', *Journal of Contemporary History,* Vol. 13 (1978), p.609.
3 E. Roper (ed.), *Prison Letters of Constance Markievicz,* Longman Green, London, 1934, p.21.
4 Ibid.
5 A. Linklater, *An Unhusbanded Life—Charlotte Despard: Suffragette Socialist and Sinn Feiner,* Hutchinson, London, 1980, p.63.
6 R MacColl, *Roger Casement,* Four Square, London, 1965, p.233.
7 P.F. MacLochlainn, *Last Words,* Kilmainham Jail Restoration Society, Kilmainham, 1971, pp.121–122.
8 *WL,* Vol. 1, No.58, 4 Jan. 1919, p.549.
9 Ibid.

10 *IVOL*, Vol. 4, No.8, 10 Dec. 1921, p.4.

11 The Catholic Truth Society of Ireland produced a whole series of pamphlets dealing with socialism and social reform, notable titles being: Rev. J.E. Canavan S.J., *How far may a Catholic agree with Socialists?* Dublin 1919, Rev. M. Phelan S.J., *The Pillar of Socialism*, Dublin 1922, and Rev. W. Moran D.D., *Social Reconstruction in an Irish State*, Dublin n.d.

12 C. de Markievicz, *James Connolly's Policy and Catholic Doctrine*, place and date of publication not noted on pamphlet, *c*.1925.

13 Rev. L. McKenna S.J., 'The Teachings of James Connolly', *Irish Monthly*, Vol. 47, Aug. 1919, p.431.

14 Ibid.

15 Ibid, p.440.

16 Ibid, p.438.

17 Ibid, pp.433–434–

18 *Irish Monthly*, Vol. 47, Oct. 1919, p.541.

19 *Irish Monthly*, Vol. 47, Aug. 1919, p.434.

20 Ibid.

21 *Irish Monthly*, Vol. 47, Oct. 1919, p.542.

22 Rev. P. Coffey, 'James Connolly's Campaign Against Capitalism in the Light of Catholic Teaching', *Catholic Bulletin*, Vol. 10, 1920, p.212.

23 Ibid, p.217.

24 Ibid, p.220.

25 Ibid, p221 Father Coffey was also in direct communication with Labour leaders; see O'Brien, Msl3961. Letter, Coffey to O'Brien, dated 29 April 1921. In his letter Coffey states that 'Connolly was a master thinker. But he had not time to think out all the implications of any solution of such a vast problem as that of ending a world-wide economic system and finding a desirable substitute' and later notes in reference to Irish priests that 'we can understand and excuse, even if we have to deprecate as ultimately mischievous, the tone of bitterness and revenge and the glorification of class hatred and revolution which run through the writings of such really sincere and noble and single-minded men as James Connolly.'

26 Markievicz, op.cit., p.33.

27 O'Brien, Ms13951. Letter from Thomas Johnson to members of the National Executive of Labour Party dated 5 July 1925. It is worth noting that Johnson being English-born and having an Anglican-Unitarian Church background, clearly felt himself to be in a rather delicate position when dealing with the Roman Catholic Church; see J.A. Gaughan, *Thomas Johnson*, Kingdom Books, Dublin, 1980, p.16 for details of Johnson's religious background.

28 *Irish Rosary*, April 1928, p.365.

29 Ibid.

30 *Irish Rosary*, July 1928, pp.542–43.

31 *Anti State Activities Papers*, Cabinet file S5864B, Public Record Office, (Dublin Castle) Letter L.T. MacCosgair to Joseph Cardinal McRory dated 10 Sept. 1931. Cabinet minutes Cab5/75/30/7/31 item No.7 notes decision to enlist assistance of Catholic hierarchy.

32 Ibid.

33 *Anti State Activities*, S5864B, Cabinet file 'Memorandum' attached to letter to Cardinal McRory. Copies of this 'Memorandum' were sent to all the Archbishops and Bishops in Ireland.

34 *Catholic Bulletin*, Vol. 21, No.11, Nov. 1931, pp.1021–22.

35 See P.Feely, 'The Siege of 64 Great Strand Street', *Old Limerick Journal*, Winter 1981, No. 9, pp.22–24. and Spring 1982, No. 10, pp.33–36, gives details of this incident.

36 See M. Manning, *The Blueshirts*, Gill and Macmillan, Dublin, 1970. M. Manning 'The Irish Experience: The Blueshirts', in S.V. Larsen et al. (eds.), *Social Roots of European Fascism*, Bergen, 1970, and J. Bowyer Bell, 'Ireland and the Spanish Civil War', *Studia Hibernica*, Vol. 9, 1969, pp.137–63, for information on the Blueshirt movement and Irish reaction to the Spanish Civil War.

37 M. O'Riordan, *Connolly Column: The Story of the Irishmen who fought for the Spanish Republic 1936–39*. New Book Publications, James Connolly House, Dublin, 1979.

38 Irish Labour Party, Report of the Proceedings of the *Fourth Annual Conference*, Oct. 1934, Administrative Council of the Irish Labour Party, Dublin, 1934, p.113.

39 Ibid, p.114.

40 O'Brien, Msl5674(4). Letter W. Norton to Cardinal Pacelli dated 23 Feb. 1937

41 ILP Report of the Proceedings Annual Conference, Apr. 1939, p.161.

42 Ibid, p.163.

43 Ibid, p. 171.

CHAPTER 11

1 ITGWU, *Annual Report for 1918,* ITGWU, Dublin, 1919, p.6.
2 ITGWU, *The Attempt to Smash the Irish Transport and General* Workers *Union,* National Executive ITGWU, Dublin, 1924, p.xxi.
3 ITGWU, *Annual Report 1918,* p.6. See also C. Desmond Greaves, *The Irish Transport and General Workers Union The Formative Years,* Gill and Macmillan, Dublin, 1982, ch.9.
4 Ibid., pp.7–8.
5 ITGWU, *Attempt to Smash,* p.xxiii.
6 See B. Holton, *British Syndicalism 1900–1914: Myths and Realities,* Pluto, London, 1976. p.206.
7 See A. Mitchel, *Labour in Irish Politics 1890–1930,* Irish University Press, Dublin, 1974, p.70.
8 T. Johnson, *The Future of Labour in Ireland,* Irish Trades Union Congress and Labour Party, Dublin, 1916, p.3.
9 See J.A. Gaughan, *Thomas Johnson,* Kingdom, Mount Merrion, County Dublin, 1980. For a detailed and sympathetic biography of this thoroughly decent and dedicated, moderate labour leader.
10 ITGWU, *The Lines of Progress,* ITGWU Liberty Hall Library No.l, Dublin, 1918, p.2.
11 J. Connolly, *The Axe to the Root,* ITGWU, Dublin, 1921, p.3.
12 Ibid., p.5.
13 *IOVL,* Vol. 1, No.1, 1 Dec. 1917.
14 *IOVL,* Vol. 1, No.8, 19 Jan. 1918.
15 *IOVL,* Vol. 1, No.9, 26 Jan. 1918.
16 *VL,* Vol. 4, No.8, 10 Dec. 1921.
17 *IOVL,* Vol. 1, No.37, 10 Aug. 1918.
18 *IOVL,* Vol. 1, No.41, 7 Sept. 1918.
19 *The Bottom Dog,* Vol. 1, No.29, 4 May 1918.
20 See *WL,* Vol. 1, No.8, 15 Nov. 1919 and same paper Vol. 1, No.50, 11 Sept. 1 1920.
21 *WL,* Vol. 1, No.51, 18 Sept. 1920.
22 See for example *IOVL,* Vol. 1, No.13, 23 Feb. 1918. p.145. 'Was Connolly a Bolshevik?', by Cathal O'Shannon and 'If the Bolsheviks came to Ireland' in the same issue, by T. Johnson.
23 Madame Markievicz and Dr. Kathleen Lynn also spoke at the meeting, both women having strong connections with the ITGWU and more particularly the ICA.
24 See *Irish Times,* 5 Feb. 1918 and *IOVL,* Vol. 1, No.11, 9 Feb. 1918, p.132.

25 See D.R. O'Connor Lysaght's studies, *The Story of the Limerick Soviet, April 1919,* People's Democracy, Limerick, 2nd ed., 1981. 'The Month of the Soviets', Vol. 1, No.1, *The Plough,* 'The Munster Soviet Creameries', *Irish History Workshop Journal,* No. 1, 1981. See also M. McCarthy, The Broadford Soviet', *The Old Limerick Journal,* No. 4, Sept. 1980, and J. Kemmy, 'The Limerick Soviet', *Saothar,* 2, 1976.
26 See for example *The Bottom Dog,* Vol. 1, No.5, 17 Nov. 1917, Vol. 1, No.15, 26 Jan. 1918 and Vol. 1, No.30, 11 May 1918. 48 issues of this lively little paper were published.
27 *IOVL,* Vol. 1, No.11, 9 Feb. 1918.
28 *VL,* Vol. 1, No.73, 12 Apr. 1919.
29 *Workers Bulletin,* Vol. 1, No.6, 21 Apr. 1919.
30 *Irish Times,* 25 Apr. 1919
31 VL, Vol. 1, No.77, 10 May 1919.
32 *ILP of TUC Annual Report 1919,* p.106.
33 Ibid., p.104.
34 *Workers Voice,* 13 Apr. 1935.
35 See E. Larkin, *James Larkin Irish Labour Leader 1876–1947,* New English Library, London, 1968, for a fine biography of Larkin.
36 *Irish Labour Journal,* June 19 1909.
37 *VL,* Vol. 1, No.88, 26 July 1919.
38 Larkin op.cit., p.227.
39 See for example *Some Pages from Union History The Facts Concerning Larkin's Departure to America,* ITGWU, Dublin, 1927, reprinted from *VL,* 12 Apr. 1924, and The Attempt to Smash the Irish Transport and General *Workers Union,* National Executive of ITGWU, Dublin, 1921.
40 See *Attempt to Smash,* pp.77–79.
41 *ITGWU, Annual Report 1923,* p.6.
42 *Some Pages from Union History,* op.cit., p.6.
43 Ibid., p.1.
44 ILPTUC, *Report of Proceedings,* Special Congress, Dublin, 28 Feb—1Mar 1930, p.4.
45 ILPTUC, *Report of Proceedings,* 1929, p.106.
46 ILPTUC, *Special Congress,* 1930, p.7.
47 Ibid., p.8. Miss Chenevix moved the amendment, Mrs. Dowling formally seconded and Miss Louie Bennett spoke in favour of the amendment. All three were IWWU members.
48 O'Brien, Ms13971. Interim Report Commission of Inquiry into the position of the Irish

Trade Union Movement, dated 28 Jan. 1937, addressed to the 'National Executive ITUC' marked 'Private', p.1.

49 Ibid., p.10. Helena Moloney supported the O'Brien position but wanted a separate organisation of Women Workers to continue within the new framework.

50 Ibid., p.10.

51 Ibid., p.11.

52 Ibid., p.11.

53 See C. McCarthy, *Trade Unions in Ireland 1894–1960*, Institute of Public Administration, Dublin, 1977, pp.142–163, for a detailed description of the Inquiry and Conference.

54 *WVL*, Vol. 1, No.57, 30 Oct. 1920, p.7.

CHAPTER 12

1 *ITUC LP Annual Report*, 1918, p.2. Chairman's address by William O'Brien, 6 Aug. 1918.

2 N. Connolly, 'James Connolly Revolutionist', *VL*, Vol. 1, No.79, 10 May 1919, p.3.

3 Leslie was a prominent Scottish socialist. A member of the SDF, he had also been the first secretary of the Scottish Socialist Federation. His book, *The Present Position of the Irish Question*, London 1894, is claimed by one biographer to have 'Laid the basis for much of Connolly's thinking'; S. Levenson, *James Connolly*. Quartet, London, 1973, p.31.

4 J. Leslie, 'James Connolly an Appreciation', *Justice* 18 May 1919, p.3. See also H.M. Hyndman 'The Sinn Fein Revolt in Dublin', *Justice* 4 Dec. 1916. In this article Hyndman wrote of Connolly that: 'Like many another genuine revolutionist, he lashed himself up to the conviction that unorganised force could hasten on economic and social development. He has given his life for his ill-balanced opinions without our being able to canonise him as the reckless hero of the Commune of Dublin. There can be no sadder criticism on our society of to-day than that fine able fellows should have seen so little hope for their class and their country that they deliberately threw themselves away on this mad endeavour; and that the national soldiers of the same social stratum as themselves should feel impelled to shoot them down as men afflicted with criminal insanity'.

5 See J.A. Gaughan, *Thomas Johnson*, Kingdom, County Dublin, 1980. For a detailed and sympathetic biography of Johnson.

6 See Gaughan ibid., p.399. For details of Johnson's Fabian influences.

7 C. Desmond Greaves, *The Irish Transport and General Workers Union*, Gill and Macmillan, Dublin, 1982, p.173.

8 *ITUCLP 1916 Report*, p.22.

9 T. Johnson, *The Future of Labour in Ireland*, ITUCLP, Dublin, 1916.

10 *ITUCLP* 1916 Report, pp.22–23.

11 Loc.cit.

12 Loc.cit.

13 Greaves, op.cit., p.174.

14 See W. O'Brien, *Forth the Banners Go*, Three Candles, Dublin 1949, for a fairly candid description of the assistance O'Brien gave to Sinn Fein—in a private capacity.

15 O'Brien, Ms13962. See particularly pp.48–49.

16 *Dublin Saturday Post*, 21 Apr. 1917.

17 P. O'Donnell, *There Will be another day*, Dolmen, Dublin, 1963, pp.1–5.

18 *Irish Opinion: a weekly Journal of industrial and political democracy*, Vol. 1, No.1, Dec. 1 1917, p.6. A rather bland politically vague title for a newspaper which claimed to descend (albeit somewhat indirectly) from Connolly's *Workers Republic* and Larkin's *Irish Worker*. The title was in fact changed to *Irish Opinion: The Voice of Labour* in January 1918 and the *Irish Opinion* component of the title was relegated in importance from this time. Thus although officially entitled *IOVL* the paper began to refer to itself by the title *Voice of Labour*—the paper's content reflected this change of emphasis.

19 *IOVL*, op.cit., p.3.

20 Gaughan, op.cit., p.82.

21 Gaughan, ibid. Johnson accepted 500 pounds—with another 500 pounds to follow—from Lyon on behalf of the ITUC. He purchased the title *Irish Opinion* from its previous owner for 100 pounds in Nov. 1917.

22 Gaughan, op.cit., p.83.

23 D. Ryan, *James Connolly*, Talbot, Dublin, 1924, p.17. There is of course a very great difference between accepting money from a comrade of long standing and high repute, and accepting money from a wealthy non-socialist of dubious intent. In Johnson's favour it is worth noting that the appointment of O'Shannon to replace Byrne as editor was—in the light of O'Shannon's well known socialist Republican stance—bound to exacerbate rather than alleviate Lyon's dissatisfaction with the paper's political content.

24 *Daily Bulletin*, 4 Jan. 1923.

25 *IW*, 14 June 1924.

26 *IW*, 7 June 1924.

27 *IW*, 7 March 1925. It is worth noting in the light of Larkin's abuse of Johnson, particularly with regard to Johnson's English nationality, that Larkin and Johnson were both Liverpool-born, and in fact were born in houses within 500 yards of each other.

28 A. Mitchell, *Labour in Irish Politics*, Irish University Press, Dublin, 1974, p.89.

29 *IOVL*, Vol. 1, No.45, 5 Oct. 1918.

30 Ibid.

31 *IOVL*, Vol. 1, No.46, 12 Oct. 1918.

32 *IOVL*, Vol. 1, No.47, 19 Oct. 1918.

33 ILPTUC Report 1918, See also *IOVL*, Vol. l, No.50, 9 Nov. 1918.

34 *Loc.cit.*

35 ILPTUC Report 1918.

36 Gaughan, ibid., p.119.

37 Mitchell, ibid. p.98. Original source Sinn Fein Standing Committee Minutes, 7 and 10 Oct. 1918.

38 *IOVL*, Vol. 1, No.56, 21 Dec. 1918.

39 *IOVL*, Vol. 1, No.20, 13 Apr. 1918.

40 *IOVL*, Vol. 1, No.21, 20 Apr. 1918.

41 *WL*, Vol. 1, No.1, 27 Sept. 1919.

42 *WL*, Vol. 1, No.2, 4 Oct. 1919.

43 See author unknown, 'Sean McKeon One of Ours', *VL*, Vol.4, No.17, 11 Feb. 1922, p.6. The article notes that 'It is not generally known that Commdt. Sean McKeon T.D. was and is a member of the ITGWU and many of the men in his commando are also OBU members. We rather reckon that, if a record were prepared showing the services to Ireland of each class in the community in the Anglo-Irish Wars, from 1916 onwards, the workers record would, as in the previous struggles, be one to be proud of, and one far ahead of that of any other section of the Irish people'. McKeon—often spelt MacEoin—later became a General, was a pro-Treaty deputy and Free State Army Chief of Staff 1928–29. He had a long political career including a period as Minister for Defence 1954–57. Sometimes referred to as 'the blacksmith of Ballinalee'. See also S.V. Larsen and

0. Snoddy, '1916—A Workingmen's Revolution'. *Social Studies*, Vol.2, No.4, 1973, pp. 377–98.

44 See *VL*, Vol. 1, No.78, 17 May 1919, p.6. and *WL*, Vol. 1, No.2, 4 Oct. 1919 for examples.

45 *WL*, Vol. 1, No.44, 31 July 1920, p.7.

46 *WVL*, Vol. 1, No.56, 23 Oct. 1920.

47 *WVL*, Vol. 1, No.62, 4 Dec. 1920, p.3

48 O'Brien, Ms13955. Correspondence dated 30 Sept. 1921 and 1 Nov. 1921.

49 *VL*, Vol.4, No.5, 19 Nov. 1921, p.8.

50 *VL*, Vol.4, No.15, 28 Jan. 1922, p.4.

51 *VL*, Vol.4, No.15, 28 Jan. 1922, p.4.

52 O'Brien, Ms13955.

53 ILPTUC, 1924 Report, p.120.

54 E. O'Malley, *On Another Man's Wound*, 1st edn. 1936, Anvil, Dublin 1979, p.59. See also *The Singing Flame*, Anvil, Dublin 1979, by the same author. O'Malley by 1921 was in Command of the Southern Division of the IRA. He was also a major figure in the anti-Treaty IRA during the Civil War.

55 *VL*, Vol.4, No.40, 22 July 1922, p.l.

56 *VL*, Vol.4, No.10, 24 Dec. 1921, p.3.

57 J. Connolly, 'Coronation fiasco', *WR*, Vol. 5, No. 1, July 1902, p.3. In this article Connolly writes that 'we offer to King Edward in the name of ourselves and our class the only homage we owe him, viz, OUR HATRED''.

58 *WR*, Vol. 3, No.10, 28 July 1900, p.5.

59 *Evening Press,* 17 Feb. 1961, Review article by Cathal O'Shannon. Connolly was speaking to O'Shannon when he made this remark. It is of interest to note that Patrick Pearse is also recorded as stating that 'At the most such an oath would only bind me while there'. See D. Ryan, *Remembering Sion,* London, Arthur Barker, 1934, pp.138–139.

60 See Dáil Eireann. *Official Report: Debate on the Treaty between Great Britain and Ireland Signed in London on the 6th December* 1921. Stationery Office, Dublin, 1922, pp.180–186.

61 *VL,* Vol.4, No.52, 14 Oct. 1922, p.8.

62 *VL,* Vol.4, No.37, 1 July 1922, p.3.

63 *Daily Bulletin*, 2 Dec. 1922.

64 *Daily Bulletin*, 4 Jan. 1923.

65 *IOVL*, Vol. 1, No.38, 17 Aug. 1918, p.382.

66 G. Gilmore, The *Irish Republican Congress,* Cork Workers Club, Cork, 1978, p.34.

67 Gilmore, ibid., pp.37–38.

68 Gilmore, ibid., p.44.

CHAPTER 13

1 Quoted in *WR*, Vol. 1, No.3, 22 Oct. 1921, p.3.

2 *IOVL*, Vol. 1, No.22, 27 Apr. 1918, p.239.

3 E. Cullingford, *Yeats Ireland and Fascism,* Macmillan, London,1981, p.6.

4 E. Roper (ed.), *Prison Letters of Countess Markievicz,* Longman and Green, London, 1934, p.101.

5 *Sinn Fein,* 31 Oct. 1923, p.1.

6 E. O'Malley, *On Another Man's Wound,* 1st edn. 1936, Anvil, Dublin, 1979, p.45. Cathal Brugha (IRA Chief of Staff 1917–1919 and then Minister of Defence until January 1922), speaking at the treaty debate, presented an example which gave an insight into the absolute nature of his own Republican commitment when he said, 'Why, if instead of being so strong, our last cartridge had been fired, our last shilling had been spent and our last man were lying on the ground and his enemies howling round him and their bayonets raised, ready to plunge them into his body, that man should say—true to the traditions handed down—if they said to him; Now will you come into the Empire?—he should say, and he would say: 'No I will not.' *Dail Eireann Official Report Debate on the Treaty,* Dublin, 1922, p.330.

7 *VL,* Vol.1, No.48, 26 Oct. 1918, p.458. Almost any issue of this and indeed almost any other Irish labour paper would contain a similar statement regarding the centrality and importance of Connolly's teaching and example.

8 See J. Molyneux, *Marxism and the Party,* Pluto, London, 1978. Molyneux, argues (p.22) that 'Because of Marx's vagueness on this point it is not possible to construct or reconstruct any single or systematic theory of the party . . . Marx's lack of clear definition of the political party is neither accidental nor a product of laziness of thought. Rather it reflects the fact that for a large part of Marx's career political parties in the modern sense of the term did not exist, either for the bourgeois or for the proletariat.' He later asserts that 'Marx never made a fetish of any particular organisational form or indeed of any particular party. As conditions changed so did his attitude.' p.18.

9 J. Hinton, *The First Shop Steward's Movement,* George Allen and Unwin, London, 1973. p.276.

10 See *IOVL*, Vol. 1, No.10 and 11, 2 and 9 Feb. 1918, for details of this meeting. *Irish*

Independent also published a very full account of the meeting.

11 I.L.P.T.U.C. *Annual Report* 1918, pp48–49. See also A. Cornwell, 'A Bolshevik in Belfast: An Episode in the Biography of Maxim Litvinov', *Irish Slavonic Studies,* No.5, Belfast 1984, p.46.

12 *IOVL*, Vol. 1, No.10, 2 Feb. 1918, p.117.

13 *IOVL*, Vol. 1, No.11, 9 Feb. 1918. In a short advertisement in the same issue the SPI note not only that the party was 'founded by James Connolly' but also that it had a 'Statement of Principles drawn up by James Connolly'.

14 O'Brien Ms15674 (4). 'Ireland and the International'.

15 O'Brien Ms15674.(3). Communication of the Amsterdam Sub-Bureau of the IIIrd International 'The Political and Working Class Organisation in Ireland'. At the ILPTUC 26th Annual Meeting in Cork in August 1920 O'Brien was, at least publicly, inclined to treat the whole thing as a Joke and commented at one stage, 'Mr. Chairman, I can produce documentary evidence that I am not a Socialist, that I have never been a Socialist (laughter)' p.107. O'Brien's comment certainly suggests that the report and its contents were well known in Labour circles.

16 O'Brien Ms15674 (3). An untitled reply to the Amsterdam Sub-Bureau Report. The Sub-Bureau did tend at this time to take what can be termed as an ultra leftist position. See J. Braunthal, *History of the International 1914–43,* trans. J. Clark, Thomas Nelson, 1967.

17 *WR,* Vol. 1, No.3, 22 Oct. 1921, p.4.

18 Ibid., p.5.

19 *The Communist,* 8 Oct. 1921.

20 *WR,* Vol. 1, No.24, 25 Mar. 1922, p.1.

21 *WR,* Vol. 1, No.9, 3 Dec. 1921, p.4.

22 M. Milotte, *Communism in Modern Ireland. The Pursuit of the Workers Republic, since 1916,* Gill and Macmillan, Dublin, 1984, p.48.

23 *WR,* Vol. 1, No.9, 3 Dec. 1921, p.4.

24 *WR,* Vol. 1, No.10, 10 Dec. 1921, p.4.

25 *WR,* Vol. 1, No.11, 17 Dec. 1921, p.3. The European Socialist parties nearly all went through a disciplinary process of Bolshevization in 1921–1922. See H. Gruber, *International Communism in the Era of Lenin. A Documentary History,* Anchor, New York, 1972.

26 Ibid.

27 W. Gallacher, *Ireland: Can it remain neutral?* CPGB, London, nd. (*c.* early 1930s), p.ll.

28 See M. Caulfield, *The Easter Rebellion*, Four Square, London, 1965, p.333. McLoughlin and De Valera were the two highest ranking 1916 survivors.

29 See R.M. Fox, *The History of the Irish Citizen Army,* James Duffy, Dublin, 1944. pp.227–228.

30 Milotte, ibid., pp.60–61. Basically Connolly and McLoughlin were urging the IRA to establish a Civilian Government in Cork.

31 R. Connolly, 'Republican Struggle', *WR,* No.56, 25 Nov, No.57, 2 Dec, No.58, 9 Dec, No.59, 16 Dec, and No.60, 23 Dec. 1922.

32 R. Connolly, 'Past and Future Policy', *W.R,* No.62, 6 Jan. No.63, 13 Jan, and No.64, 20 Jan. 1923.

33 Milotte, ibid., p.65.

34 See Cowan Papers, University College Dublin, Archives Department, p34/D/20. Seamus McGowan, ICA veteran and early member of CPI made this statement after his release from internment in December 1923 'I came away with high hopes of the future. But when I got home I found the Party Dying and heavy in Death. No Paper. No Unity and was wound up on the 26/1/24.'

35 Milotte, ibid., p.69.

36 E. Larkin, *James Larkin Irish Labour Leader 1876–1947,* New English Library, London, 1965, p.251.

37 R.M. Fox, *Jim Larkin, Irish Labour Leader*, International, New York, 1957, p.23.

38 Larkin, ibid., p.269.

39 Ibid., p.260.

40 Milotte, ibid., p.74. See Ch. 5, for an instructive comparison of Connolly's attitude to attending meetings and working within a disciplined party structure.

41 See O'Brien Ms13958. A Report made by D. O'Connor & Co. Chartered Accountants giving details of their examination of WUI Annual Returns 1924–1936. This report instigated by W. O'Brien was extremely critical of WUI accounting practices—practices which included 'the conversion of (a) Deficiency into a Balance to credit without explanation'. The report noted that the Union's membership claims did not correspond to subscriptions. In 1930 for example the Union claimed 16,909 members but only 5,269 subscriptions. The report also noted that 'Loans to members throughout the Returns have been considerable, in some years reaching as high as 25% of the Income'. Larkin was not in any sense financially corrupt but his Union's finances were chaotic and his union was clearly having difficulty in maintaining membership levels.

42 State Paper Office, S5864A, Revolutionary Organisations, 4 Apr. 1930, p.11.

43 State Paper Office, S5074B, Workers Revolutionary Party, 16/630, p.1.

44 Ibid., p.2.

45 Communist Party of Ireland, *Communist Party of Ireland Outline History,* New Books, Dublin, n.d. p.8. In all, twelve students went to the school in 1928 but only four stayed to complete the course.

46 State Paper Office, S5074B, 'Draft Letter to the Comrades in Ireland'. The Department of Justice circulated copies of this letter to the Free State Executive Council on 1 Aug. 1930.

47 J. Bowyer Bell, *The Secret Army*, Sphere, London, 1972, pp.98–99.

48 T.P. Coogan, *The IRA,* Fontana Collins, London, 1971, p.83.

49 Saor Eire, *Draft Constitution and Rules,* Dublin, 1931. See A. Mitchell and P. O'Snodaigh, *Irish Political Documents 1916–1949,* Irish Academic Press, Dublin, 1985, pp.182–185, for complete reprint of this Constitution.

50 S. Cronin, *Irish Nationalism, A History of its Roots and Ideology,* Pluto, London, 1983, p.156.

51 *Irish Independent*, 19 Oct. 1931.

52 Mitchell, *Irish Political Documents,* pp.190–191. The other ten organisations were: Fianna Eireann, Cumann na mBan, Friends of Soviet Russia, Irish Labour Defence League, Worker's Defence Corps, Women Prisoners Defence League, Workers Revolutionary Party, Irish Tribune League, Irish Working Farmers Committee and the Worker's Research Bureau.

53 Peadar O'Donnell, personal conversation, 4 Sept. 1985, stated that he believed that as far as the IRA Executive was concerned Saor Eire was 'a dishonest sort of thing' and was in effect 'an avoidance of concrete action'.

54 G. Gilmore, *The Irish Republican Congress*, Cork Workers Club, Cork, n.d. p.33. This pamphlet is an important source of information about Republican Congress, see also M. Mc-Inerney, *Irish Social Rebel*, O'Brien, Dublin, 1974, Ch. 8.

55 S. Cronin, Frank Ryan. *The Search for the Republic*, Repsol, Dublin, 1980, p.52.

56 *RC*, Vol. 1, No.l, 5 May 1934, p.2.

57 Loc cit. Connolly's daughter Nora was the first signatory of the Manifesto.

58 *RC*, Vol. 1, No.1, 5 May 1934, p.l.

59 *RC*, Vol. 1, No.24, 13 Oct. 1934, p.2.

60 *RC*, Vol. 1, No.7, 16 June 1934, p.1.

60 *RC*, Vol. 1, No.l, 5 May 1934, p.3.

62 *RC*, Vol. 1, No.23, 6 Oct. 1934, p.1.

63 Loc cit.

64 Ibid., On the First vote by 'show of hands' a certain amount of creative voting and/or counting seems to have taken place as the voting was first announced as '110 for, 91 against, giving a total of 201 votes when only 186 delegates were present.

65 Milotte, op.cit., p.167, states that *RC*, survived until February 1936, but I have been unable to trace any issues after December 1935.

66 M. 0'Riordan, *Connolly Column*, New Books, Dublin, 1979. See also, by the same author, 'Connolly's power of conversion,' *New Hibernia*, Vol. 11, No.10, Oct. 1985, p.20, wherein he relates the influence that Connolly, and more particularly his book *Labour and Irish History*, exerted on his personal political development.

67 Milotte, op.cit., p.180.

68 0'Brien Ms13951, Letter dated 5 July 1925.

69 ILPTUC, Special Congress on Re-Organisation Report, 1930, p.18.

70 Ibid., p.19.

71 Labour Party, Tenth Annual Report (1940) and Report of Proceedings Annual Conference, 1941.

72 C. O'Leary, *Irish Elections 1918–1977*, Gill and Macmillan, Dublin, 1979, pp.101–102.

CHAPTER 14

1 C. O'Shannon, 'James Connolly and the People', *Irish Press*, 12 May 1933 (pub. on the 17th anniversary of Connolly's execution.)

2 *Tipperary Star*, 29 May 1937, Original from a letter James Connolly to Wm O'Brien undated but received by O'Brien 23 Sept. 1914.

3 M. Eden, 'The Connolly Ideal', *VL*, Vol. 1, No. 33, 13 July 1918.

4 O'Brien Ms13962. Undated typescript statement by Wm O'Brien.

5 R.M. Fox, *The History of the Irish Citizen Army*, James Duffy, Dublin 1944, p.189.

6 See for example C.D. Greaves, *The Life and Times of James Connolly*, Seven Seas, Berlin, 1971, p.402.

7 F. Robbins, *Under the Starry Plough— Recollections of the Irish Citizen Army*, Academy Press, Dublin, p.201.

8 Robbins, ibid., p.202.

9 Peadar O'Donnell, personal conversation, Dublin 4 Sept. 1985. See also M. McInerney, *Peadar O'Donnell. Irish Social Rebel*, O'Brien, Dublin, 1974, p.38, where O'Donnell is quoted as saying 'I was a bit disappointed however that I was not encouraged to join the Irish Citizen Army and that, in fact, the Citizen Army did not seem to have a place within the Union'.

10 Fox, op.cit., p.200.

11 Fox, ibid., p.199.

12 P. Beresford Ellis, *James Connolly Selected Writings*, Penguin, Harmondsworth, 1973, p.294.

13 S. Levenson, *James Connolly Socialist Patriot and Martyr*, Quartet, London, 1977, p.310. See also M. Caulfield, *The Easter Rebellion*, Four Square, London, 1965, p.271.

14 Fox, ibid., pp.227–241, gives details of ICA membership during Easter Rising and War of Independence. On page 218 he notes that 'Army records show that 125 men and 18 women took the field in the Civil War.

15 Robbins, *op. cit.* pp.206–207.

16 O'Brien Ms15674. The Political and Working Class Organisation in Ireland, p.3.

17 Connolly's eldest daughter, Mona, died as a result of an accident in Dublin in 1904 while Connolly was working in America.

18 O'Brien Ms15674.

19 *IO*, Vol. 1, No.16, 16 Mar. 1918, p.188.

20 *VL*, Vol.l, No.77, 10 May 1919, p.3.

21 *VL*, Vol.l, No.89, 2 Aug. 1919, p.4.

22 *VL*, Vol.l, No.88, 26 July 1919, p.2.

23 See C. Desmond Greaves, *The Irish Transport and General Workers Union: The Formative Years*, Gill and Macmillan, Dublin, 1982, p.245. Greaves only gives Colgan's surname. E. Larkin, *James Larkin*, New English Library, London, 1968, gives his Christian name, p.295. See also Fox, op.cit., p.233.

24 See F. Pakenham (Lord Longford), *Peace by Ordeal,* (lst edn., 1935), Sidgwick and Jackson, London, 1972. and C. Younger, *Ireland's Civil War,* Fontana-Collins, Glasgow, 1979, for details regarding Treaty negotiations.

25 Author unknown, 'The Political Crisis', *VL,* Vol. 4, No.9, 17 Dec. 1921, p.4. This article was probably written by the *Voice's* editor Cathal O'Shannon, although the writing is of not his usual standard, suggesting either that he was unhappy with the article's contents or that the article may have been written by someone else.

26 The quotation in question was Connolly's April 1916 statement that 'The Cause of Labour is the Cause of Ireland. The Cause of Ireland is the Cause of Labour. They cannot be dissevered.' *WR,* Vol.l, No. 46, 8 April 1916, p.1. In the *VL's* editorial this is paraphrased as 'We believe that not only is the cause of Ireland the cause of Labour, but equally that the cause of Labour is the cause of Ireland.' Connolly's: They cannot be dissevered' sentence is dropped in favour of a comment that 'Too many, even among our fellow workers, are apt to ignore that latter great truth'—a comment which clearly undermines the meaning and objective of Connolly's statement.

27 *VL,* Vol.4, No.10, 24 Dec. 1921, p.6.

28 *VL,* Vol.4, No.13, 14 Jan. 1922, p.4.

29 *VL,* Vol.4, No.21, 11 Mar. 1922, p.4.

30 *VL,* Vol.4, No.22, 18 Mar. 1922, p.3.

31 *VL,* Vol.4, No.26, 15 Apr. 1922, p.1.

32 Ibid., p.4.

33 *Loc cit.*

34 *VL,* Vol.4, No.27, 22 Apr. 1922, p.4.

35 *VL,* Vol.4, No.28, 29 Apr. 1922, p.8.

36 *Loc cit.*

37 Robbins, op.cit., p.232.

38 O'Brien Ms15673 (1) and Msl5705.

39 Fox, ibid., p.217.

40 Despite the disruptive effect herein noted, almost 150 ICA men and women took part in the Civil War on the Republican side. It is also worth noting that Connolly's son Roddy and about 12 members of the recently established Communist Party of Ireland (trained by Liam O'Flaherty) fought with the anti-treaty IRA. See M. Milotte, *Communism in Modern Ireland: The pursuit of the Workers' Republic since 1916,* Gill and Macmillan, Dublin, 1984, pp.59–63 for details.

41 *VL*, Vol.4, No.28, 29 Apr. 1922, p.4.

42 Cathal O'Shannon, speaking at Drogheda in early May, uttered perhaps the most extreme example of Labour's aggressive neutrality when he 'asked the young men of both sections of the IRA both Beggars Bush and Four Courts to turn their guns rather on the officers who ordered them to shoot their fellow workers than upon their fellow-workers and late comrades-in-arms' *VL,* Vol.4, No.30, p.3. This advice echoes Connolly's advice to soldiers at the start of World War One.

43. See for example *VL,* Vol.4, No.22, 18 Mar. 1922, p.l.: 'eight fully armed IRA guarding the Blacklegs'; Vol.4, No.23, 25 Mar. 1922, p.3.: 'IRA Captain threatens to arrest Knockbridge branch Sec.'; Vol.4, No.30, 13 May 1922, p.2.: 'an armed guard of IRA men was put on Conroy's shop to prevent the scabs being arrested'; Vol.4, No.33, 3 June 1922, p.3.: IRA Officer in Clashmore 'struck and threatened to pull a gun on to Branch Sec.'; Vol.4, No.35, 24 June 1922, p.8.: in Cork 'revolver shots' are fired and the Transport Hall (ITGWU) was broken into and damaged by a 'section of the Local Military Party'.

44 O'Brien Ms13955. Letter dated 24 Feb. 1922. One wonders how O'Brien managed to add this letter to his collection.

45 Peadar O'Donnell, personal conversation, 4 Sept. 1985 See also P. O'Donnell, *The Gates Flew Open,* (1st edn. 1932) Mercier, Cork,1965, p.68.

46 O'Brien Ms. 13961, 7 Apr. 1922. Later in the year Liam Mellows, a senior IRA man, who had been deeply influenced by Connolly's political ideas and who had in turn made an excellent impression on Connolly, was murdered in a just such a hostage-reprisal execution whilst a prisoner in Mountjoy Jail. Mellows was not only a man of action but also a gifted political theorist and he, more than any other figure in either the labour or republican movements had appeared capable of providing the type of leadership that the left had lacked since Connolly's death. Mellows death was a great blow to 'Connolly socialists' in the IRA. See C. Desmond Greaves fine biography—*Liam Mellows and the Irish Revolution,* Lawrence and Wishart, London, 1971, for details of

Mellows relationship with Connolly and his role in the IRA.

47 O'Brien Ms. 13957 O'Malley wrote two of the best accounts of the revolutionary period in his books *On Another Man's Wound*, (1st edn 1936) Anvil, Dublin 1979 and the *Singing Flame* Anvil, Dublin, 1979.

48 L. Larkin, James Larkin: *Irish Labour Leaders 1876–1947*. New English Library-Mentor, London 1968 p.241. Larkin returned on 30 Apr. 1923.

49 ITGWU, *Annual Report*, 1924 p.6

50 Ibid., pp.5–6.

51 See J. Bowyer Bell, *The Secret Army: A History of the IRA 1916–70*. Sphere, London, 1972, pp.93–121, for details of internal politics of IRA during these years.

52 Milotte, op.cit., p.150.

53 See S. Cronin. *Frank Ryan the search for the Republic* Repsol, Dublin 1980.

54 A. Bessie. *Men in Battle* (Ist edn., 1939) Pinnacle, New York, 1977, notes on p.28 that Connolly's 'Rebel Song' was a popular marching song in the International Brigade.

55 Beresford Ellis, op.cit., p.295.

CHAPTER 15

1 O'Brien Ms13906. Letter, Connolly to J.C. Matheson, 13 Dec. 1906.

2 *Irish Independent*, 16 May 1927. See also letter signed by 'A Trade Unionist' under the title 'The Irish Labour Party and Revolution', *The Nation*, Vol. 1, No.11, 4 July,1927, p.6.

3 S. Murray, *The Irish Revolt—1916 and after*, Communist Party of Great Britain, London, 1936, p.11.

4 *WR*, Vol. 1, No.25, 13 Nov. 1915, p.1.

5 Ibid.

6 O'Brien Ms13908 (i). Letter, James Connolly to W. O'Brien dated 7 Oct. 1914.

7 D. Macardle, *The Irish Republic* (1st edn., 1937), Corgi, London, 1968, p.163.

8 P.B. Ellis, *James Connolly Selected Writings*, Penguin, Harmondsworth, 1973, pp.294– 295.

9 S. Levenson, *James Connolly Socialist Patriot and Martyr*, Quartet, London, 1973, p.310. Levenson writes that on the Wednesday of Easter Week Connolly: 'went around talking to the men. They were becoming exhausted and frightened and could think only of the imminent assault against them. After looking into their

unshaven faces, Connolly suddenly burst into the rousing strains of a favourite marching song, the song that would one day become the Irish national anthem. The men listened, dumbfounded at first, then slowly joined in until the building was filled with the strains of 'The Soldier's Song'. 'Soldiers are we, whose lives are pledged to Ireland . . . 'Mid Cannon's roar and rifle's peal We'll chant a soldier's song.'

10 *IOVL*, Vol. 1, No.15, 9 Mar. 1918, p.179.

11 *Morning Post,* 13 Dec. 1922.

12 C. Desmond Greaves, *The Irish Transport and General Worker's Union,* Gill and Macmillan, Dublin, 1982, p.349. Statement made by Peadar O'Donnell to the author.

13 Ibid.

14 O'Brien Ms13908 (i), letter dated 24 May 1911, James Connolly to William O'Brien. Connolly's relationship with Larkin was a stormy one and he regularly expressed fears regarding Larkin's effect on the Labour movement, see O'Brien Ms13908 (i), letter dated 13 Sept. 1912 wherein Connolly stated: 'I begin to fear that our friend Jim has arrived at his highest elevation, and that he will pull us all down with him in his fall.' Connolly was even more forthright in a letter to O'Brien dated 29 July 1913 when he wrote: 'I don't think that I can stand Larkin as a boss much longer . . . He is consumed with jealousy and hatred of anyone who will not cringe to him and beslaver him all over . . . Larkin seems to think that he can use Socialists as he pleases, and then when his end is served throw them out, if they will not bow down to his majesty. He will never get me to bow to him.'

15 O'Brien appears to have been a member of the Irish Republican Brotherhood, the secret oath bound organisation which was the organising force behind the Rising. See O'Brien Ms13961 (2), letter Diarmuid Lynch to W. O'Brien dated 1 Mar. 1946 in which Lynch writes 'Incidentally, I may remark when I first met you (at the NDU in pre 1916 times) when Sean MacDermott recommended you as an IRB man whose co-operation in the job on hand would be most useful . . .'

16 O'Brien reports this conversation in his introduction to D. Ryan (ed.), *Labour and Easter Week*, Sign of the Three Candles, Dublin, 1949, p.21.

17 O'Brien Ms13947, 'Statement by Nora Connolly' n.d.

18 ILPTUC, 1918 Report, pp.15–16.

19 P. O'Donnell, conversation with the author 4 Sept. 1985. See also M. McInerney, *Peadar O'Donnell Irish Social Rebel,* O'Brien, Dublin, 1974, p.39, where O'Donnell, referring to the ITGWU in 1918, when he was employed by the Union as an organiser, notes that 'Bill O'Brien, a close friend of James Connolly, was general secretary. We did not like him, but we admired him and he won confidence and some respect from us all; he would be our Connolly when the time came, we felt.'

20 *IOVL,* Vol. 1, No.20, 7 Feb. 1920, p.1.

21 D. Ryan, *James Connolly. His Life, Work and Writings,* Talbot, Dublin, 1924, pp.111–112. Responding to a question which at a meeting of Irish Volunteer officers at which he was giving a lecture on street fighting, Connolly said: 'How do I know so much of military and revolutionary matters? You forget that my business is Revolution.'

22 *Workers Voice,* 13 Apr. 1935. See also B. McCamley, The Role of the Rank and file in the 1935 Dublin tram and bus strike, *Labour History Workshop,* Dublin, 1981, for a detailed analysis of O'Brien's involvement in this strike.

23 P. O'Donnell, conversation with the author, 4 Sept. 1985.

24 O'Brien Ms13951. Letter, T. Johnson to National Executive of Labour Party dated 5 July 1925. The letter tendered Johnson resignation as official leader of the Labour Party.

25 LP, *Report of the Proceedings Second Annual Conference,* Dublin, 1932, p. 8. E.J. O'Flaherty (Post Office Workers Union) noted that it was 'not outside the bounds of possibility that the memory of a man (Connolly) who had done more to bring about the success of the Labour Movement would be forgotten'. Frank Robbins ex-ICA agreed with O'Flaherty that it 'was within the realms of possibility that he might be forgotten'. Robbins went on to qualify his statement when he said that 'Connolly would never be forgotten by the present generation, but there was a danger that he might be forgotten by the rising generation.'

26 Ibid. This statement was made by T. McPartlin, his father had been an associate of Connolly, and had been President of the ITUCLP in 1917,

27 LP, *Report of Proceedings Seventh Annual Conference,* Dublin, 1938, p.193.

28 LP, *Report of Proceedings Eighth Annual Conference,* Dublin, 1939, p.166.

29 Ibid., p.171. When speakers were being selected during this debate Roddy Connolly told Conference that 'he thought he had some title to speak', p.170.

30 *WVL,* Vol. 1, No.49, 4 Sept. 1920, p.3. The reprint in question was *Labour Nationality and Religion.*

31 O'Brien Ms13913, Circular with date stamp 'Rec'd 15 May 1933'. The circular notes a Conference to be held on 20 May 1933 and is signed by Roddy Connolly and Michael Donnolly, both of whom appear to have been secretaries for the Committee.

32 C. de Markievicz, *James Connolly's Policy and Catholic Doctrine,* no publication details given (*c*.1925).

33 S. Cronin, *Irish Nationalism,* Pluto, London 1983, p.159.

34 J. Bowyer Bell, *The Secret Army,* Sphere, London, 1972, p.70.

35 T.P. Coogan, *The IRA,* Fontana-Collins, London, 1971, p.68.

36 Cronin, op.cit., p.158.

37 *Gaelic American,* 17 June 1939. In this article O'Donnell notes that 'it is because I see how a knowledge of Connolly would resolve confusion in the awakening people that I am eager to talk of the things he did and said'.

38 O'Brien Ms13906. Letter, Connolly to Matheson dated 10 June 1909. It is worth noting that the long running correspondence between Connolly and Matheson appears to have ended in 1914. Matheson fought in France during the War and it appears likely that this created a breach in their friendship. See undated letter *circa* 1917–18. From Matheson's wife, Jane Carstairs Matheson to W. O'Brien, O'Brien Ms13906, wherein she notes that her husband is 'in the trenches in France'.

39 D. Ryan, *James Connolly: His Life Work and Writings,* Talbot, Dublin, 1924, p.81.

Bibliography

I. UNPUBLISHED MATERIAL

Desmond Barry, T.D., Papers, University College Dublin, Archives Department (St Stephens Green).
Communist Party Records, Public Records Office of Northern Ireland (Sean Murray Papers).
Cowan and McGowan Papers, University College Dublin, Archives Department.
Eugene Downing Papers, University College Dublin, Archives Department.
Thomas Johnson Papers, National Library of Ireland, Dublin.
Thomas McPartlin Papers, University College Dublin, Archives Department.
William O'Brien Papers, National Library of Ireland, Dublin.
Cathal O'Shannon Papers, National Library of Ireland, Dublin.
Desmond Ryan Papers, University College Dublin, Archives Department.
Saorstat Eireann (1930), Revolutionary Organisations, 5 Apr (S5864), State Paper Office Dublin (Dublin Castle).
Saorstat Eireann (1929–30), Communist Activities in Saorstat Eireann, Cabinet File S5074, State Paper Office (Dublin Castle).
Saorstat Eireann (1931), Cabinet Minutes / Executive Council Decisions, State Paper Office, (Dublin Castle).

1. PERIODICALS

An Bhean Oibre, 1927.
An Phoblacht, 1925–36.
Bottom Dog, 1917–18.
Catholic Bulletin, occasionally.
Communist, 1920–23.
Communist International, occasionally.
Communist Review, occasionally.
Dalcassian, 1919.
Daily Bulletin, 1926.
Dublin Saturday Post, occasionally.
Dublin Strike News, 1929.
Dublin Trades Journal / Irish Trades and Labour Journal
Eire: The Irish Nation, 1923–24.
Evening Press, occasionally.
Forward, occasionally.
Freemans Journal, occasionally.
Free Press, occasionally.
Gaelic American, occasionally.
Harp, 1908–1910.
Industrial Syndicalist, 1910–11.
Irish Citizen, 1912–20.

Irish Citizen Army Bulletin, 1934–35.
Irish Communist, occasionally.
Irish Democrat, 1937.
Irish Front, 1935.
Irish Hammer and Plough, 1926.
Irish Independent, occasionally.
Irish Labour Journal, 1909.
Irish Opinion: Voice of Labour, 1917–19.
Irish Press, occasionally.
Irish Rosary, occasionally.
Irish Times, occasionally.
Irish Work, 1914.
Irish Worker, 1911–1914: 1923–25: 1930–32.
Irish Workers Voice, 1930–36.
Irish Workers Weekly, 1939–40.
Irishman, 1927–30.
Justice, occasionally.
Labour News, 1936–38.
Liberator and Irish Trade Unionist, 1913.
Morning Post, occasionally.
Nation, 1924–25, 1927–31, 1935.

New Statesman, 1918–22.
New Way, 1917.
Pioneer, 1924–25.
Red Flag, 1919.
Republican Congress, 1934–35.
Shan Van Vocht, occasionally.
Sligo–Leitrim Liberator, 1927.
Sunday Independent, occasionally.
Tipperary Star, occasionally.
Toiler, 1913–14.
Truth That Is News, 1932.

Voice of Labour, 1921–27.
Watchword, 1930–32.
Watchdog of Labour, 1919–20.
Watchword of Labour, 1919
Weekly People, occasionally.
Woman Worker, 1928.
Worker, 1914–15: 1936–37.
Workers Bulletin, 1919.
Workers Republic, 1898–1903: 1915–1916:
    1921–23: 1927–29: 1938.
Workers Voice, occasionally.

3. THESES

Boyle, J.W. 'The Rise of the Irish Labour Movement 1888–1907'. PhD thesis, University of
    Dublin. Trinity College,1961.
Brewer, K.P. 'The American Career of James Connolly Irish Agitator'. MA thesis,
    University of the Pacific. California, 1972.
Harbinson, J.F. 'A History of the Northern Ireland Labour Party, 1891–1949'. MSc. thesis,
    Queen's University Belfast, 1966.
O'Riordan, M. 'James Connolly in America: The Political Development of An Irish Marxist
    as Seen from his Writings and his Involvement with the American Socialist Movement,
    1902–1910'. MA thesis, University of New Hampshire, 1971.
Ransom, B. 'James Connolly and the Scottish Left'. PhD thesis, University of Edinburgh,
    1975.

4. ARTICLES

Allum, P., 'The Irish Question', *Crane Bag,* No. 15, Mar 1985, pp.6–14.
Bell, T., 'James Connolly: Some Reminiscences', *Labour Monthly,* Vol. 19, No. 4, Apr 1937,
    pp.241–247.
Bell, T.J., 'The Situation in Ireland', *Labour Monthly,* Vol. 12, No. 2, Feb 1930, pp.90–96.
Bowyer-Bell, J., 'Ireland and the Spanish Civil War, 1936–1939', *Studia Hibernica,* No. 9,
    1969, pp.137–163.
Boyle, J.W., 'Irish Labor and the Rising', *Eire-Ireland,* Vol. 2, No. 3, 1967, pp.122–131.
Brown, K.D., 'Trade Unionism in Ireland', *Saothar,* 5, pp.56–60.
Brown, T., 'Internationalism and International Politics The External Links of the Labour
    Party', *Irish Studies in International Affairs,* Vol. 1, No. 2, 1980. pp.74–94.
Burns, E., 'Class issues in the Irish Free State', *Communist Review,* Vol. 5, No. 2, Feb 1933,
    pp.75–77.
Carty, R.K., 'Women in Irish Politics', *Canadian Journal of Irish Studies,* Vol. 6. No. 1, June
    1980, pp.90–104.
Coady, S., 'The Remarkable Patrick Daly', *Obair,* 2, Jan 1985, pp. 10–11.
Cody, S., 'May Day in Dublin, 1890 to the Present', *Saothar,* 5, pp.73–79.
Coffey, Rev., P., 'James Connolly's Campaign against Capitalism, in the Light of Catholic
    Teaching', *Catholic Bulletin,* Vol. 10, 1920, in five parts: pp.275–279, 346–354,
    407–412, 489–492, 212–224.
Communist Party of Ireland. 'Documents of the Class Struggle Irish Communist Party
    Statutes', *Communist Review,* Vol. 6, No. 9, Sept 1933, pp.373–4.
——. 'Documents of the Class Struggle The First Congress of the Irish Communists',
    Communist Review, Vol. 6, No. 8, Aug 1933, pp.354–356.
Connolly, M. (S.J.)., 'James Connolly, Socialist and Patriot'. *Studies,* Vol. 12, 1952,
    pp.293–308.
Conway, T.G., 'Women's Work in Ireland', *Eire-Ireland,* Vol. 7, No. 1, 1972, pp.10–27.

Cowe, W., 'The Belfast Railway Strike', *Labour Monthly*, Vol. 15, No. 4, Apr 1933, pp.244–251.

Cronin, F., 'Connolly and Lenin', *Retrospect*, 1974, pp.l2–23.

Cronin, S., 'Connolly's Leap in the Dark', *Capuchin Annual*, 1977, pp.309–324.

——. 'The Rise and Fall of the Socialist Labour Party of North America', *Saothar*, 3, 1977, pp.21–33.

Cronin S., 'The Transport Workers Union of America—the Irish Connection', *Labour History Workshop*, Dublin, 1984.

Curd, T.W.C. (Capt.), 'The Coming Conflict. Catholicism v. Communism', *Irish Monthly*, Vol. 60, June 1932, pp.353–358.

Deasy, J., 'Connolly and Socialism', *Socialist Quarterly*, Vol. 1, No. 3, 1977, pp.10–12.

Deighan, J., 'James Connolly and the British Labour Movement', *Labour Monthly*, Vol. 50, No. 6, June 1968, p.276.

Devine, F., 'Sources: The Irish Labour History Society Archive', *Saothar*, 8, 1982, pp.86–93.

Devine, P., 'Easter Week, 1916', *Labour Monthly*, Vol. 18, No. 4, Apr 1936, pp.227–236.

Edwards, O.D., 'Connolly and the Irish Tradition', *The Furrow*, Vol. 30, No. 7, July 1979, pp.411–424.

——. 'Divided Treasons and Divided Loyalties: Roger Casement and others', *Royal Historical Society Transactions*, Vol. 32, 1982, pp.l53–174.

Farrell, B., 'Labour in Irish Politics', *Saothar*, 2, 1976, pp.61–62.

Feeley, P., 'The Castlecomer Mine and Quarry Union', *Old Limerick Journal*, Part 1, No. 6, Spring 1981, pp.33–36,   Part 2, No. 7, Summer 1981, pp.37–40, Part 3, No. 8, Autumn 1981, pp.32–35.

——. 'The Siege of 64 Great Strand Street', *Old Limerick Journal*, Part 1. No. 9, Winter 1981, pp.22–24, Part 2, No. 10, Spring 1982, pp.33–36.

——. 'The Concept of Republicanism in Ireland', *Exchange*, Vol. 2, No. 1, May 1973, pp.11–13.

Fennell, D., 'James Connolly and George Russell', *Crane Bag*, Vol. 9, No.l, 1985, pp.56–62.

Fleay, C. and Sanders, M.L., 'The Labour Spain Committee: Labour Party Policy and the Spanish Civil War', *Historical Journal*, Vol. 28, No. 1, 1985, pp.l87–197.

Foster, R.F., 'History and the Irish Question', *Royal Historical Society Transactions*, Vol. 33, 1983, pp.169–192.

Fox, R.M., 'Ireland To-day', *Labour Monthly*, May 1924, pp.305–309.

Gallagher, M., 'The Pact General Election of 1922', *Irish Historical Studies*, Vol. 21, No. 84, 1979, pp.404–421.

——. 'Socialism and the Nationalist Tradition in Ireland, 1798–1918', *Eire-Ireland*, Vol. 12, No. 2, 1977. pp.63–102.

Gannon, J., 'The Long March of Irish Republicanism', *New Edinburgh Review*, No. 17, 1972, pp.11–15.

Garvin, T., 'The Discreet Charm of the National Bourgeoisie', *Third Degree*, Vol. 1, No. 1, Spring 1977, pp. 16–20.

Gillan, P., 'Pasture, Pastorals and Politics', *Teoiric*, No.9, Spring 1980, pp.8–10.

Gilmore, G., 'The Failure of Republicanism: Why Commemorate 1916', *Ripening of Time*, No. 5, Oct–Dec 1976, pp.29–40.

Glandon, V.E., 'The Irish Press and Revolutionary Nationalism', *Eire-Ireland*, Vol. 14, No. 1, 1981, pp.21–33.

Goldring, M., 'Essays in Review—Connolly Reassessed', *Saothar*, 7, May 1981, pp.50–53.

Gore-Booth, E., 'For God and Kathleen Ni Houlihan', *Catholic Bulletin*, Vol. 8, May 1918, pp.230–234.

Greaves, C.D., 'James Connolly (1868–1916) Marxist', *Marxism Today*, June 1968, p.173.

Greene, S., 'The Plough and the Stars', *New Statesman and Nation*, Vol. 33, No. 840, 12 Apr 1947, p. 256.

Hazelkorn, E., 'Marx, Engels and Ireland', *Teoiric,* No.10, Autumn 1980, pp.13–16.

Heron, I.C., 'James Connolly—a biography', *Liberty,* (Journal cf the ITGWU), Serialised, Mar-Oct 1966.

Hoffman, J., 'James Connolly and the theory of Historical Materialism', *Saothar,* 2, 1976, pp.53–61.

Howorth, J., 'French Workers and German Workers: The Impossibility of Internationalism, 1900–1914', *European History Quarterly,* Vol. 15, No. 1, 1985, pp.71–97.

Irish Workers League, 'Ireland: The Programme of the Worker's League', *Labour Monthly,* Vol. 10, Feb 1928, pp.124–125.

Kemmy, J., 'The General Strike—1919', *Old Limerick Journal,* No. 2, Mar 1980, pp.26–31.

——. 'The Limerick Soviet', *Saothar,* 2, 1976, pp.45–53.

Keogh, D., 'William Martin Murphy and the Origins of the 1913 Lock out', *Saothar,* 4, 1978, pp.15–34.

Lane, J., 'Connolly', *Irish Communist,* Part 1, Nov 1973, p.6, Part 2, Dec 1973, p.16, Part 3, Feb 1974, p.12.

Larkin, E., 'Socialism and Catholicism in Ireland', *Church History,* Vol. 33, 1964, pp.462–493.

Larson, S.V. and Snoddy, O., '1916—A Workingmen's Revolution? An Analysis of those who made the 1916 Revolution in Ireland', *Social Studies,* Vol. 2, No. 4, 1973, pp.377–398.

Lawlor, S.M., 'Ireland From Truce to Treaty: War or Peace? July to October 1921', *Irish Historical Studies,* Vol. 22, No. 1, 1980, pp.49–64.

Lee, J., 'Irish Nationalism and Socialism: Rumpf Reconsidered', *Saothar,* 6, May 1980, pp.59–64.

Levenson, S., 'A History of the Irish Working Class P.B. Ellis', *Studies,* Vol. 64, Autumn 1972, pp.286–289.

——. 'James Connolly, Unquiet Spirit', *Eire-Ireland,* Vol. 6, No. 4, Winter 1971, pp.110–117.

McCamley, B., 'The Third James', *Liberty,* Vol. 36, No. 6, Jan 82, pp.8–10.

McCarthy, C., 'From Division to Dissension: Irish Trade Unions in the Nineteen Thirties', *Economic and Social Review,* Part 1, Vol. 5, No. 3, 1974, pp.353–384, Part 2, Vol.5, No. 4, 1974, pp.469–490.

——. 'The Impact of Larkinism on the Irish Working Class, *Saothar,* 4, 1978, pp.54–56.

McCarthy, M., 'The Broadford Soviet', *Old Limerick Journal,* No. 4, Sept 1980, pp. 37–40.

MacEoin, G., 'The Irish Republican Army', *Eire–Ireland,* Vol. 9, No. 2, 1974, pp.3–29.

McGrath, R., 'The Irish Communist Congress', *Communist Revlew,* Vol. 6, No. 7, July 1933, pp.307–310.

McHugh, R., " Always Complainin : The Politics of Young Sean', *Irish University Review,* Vol. 10, No. 1, 1980, pp.91–97.

McInerney, M., 'The Enigma of Frank Ryan', *Old Limerick Journal,* Part 1, No. 1, Dec 1979, pp.25–28, Part 2, No.2, Mar 1980, pp.32–34.

MacKee, S., 'The Constituent Congress of the Irish Communist Party', *Communist Review,* Vol. 6, No. 6, June 1933, pp.283–291.

McKenna, L.(Rev.)., 'The Teachings of James Connolly', *Irish Monthly,* Part 1, Vol. 47, Aug 1919, pp.431–440, Part 2, Vol.47, Sept 1919, pp.479–490, Part 3, Vol. 47, Oct 1919, pp.523–90.

McKevitt, P.(Rev.)., 'James Connolly and the Irish Labour Movement', *Irish Ecclesiastical Record,* 5th series, Vol. 57, Feb 1941, pp.128–138.

McKillen, B., 'Irish Feminism and Nationalist Separatism, 1914–23', *Eire-Ireland,* Part 1, Vol. 17, No. 3, pp.52–57, Part 2, Vol. 17, No. 4, pp.72–90.

McLernon, D.S., 'Trade Union Organisation in the South of Ireland in the XIXth Century', *Journal of European Economic History,* Vol. 10, No. 1, Spring 1981.

MacMahon, J.A., 'The Catholic Clergy and the Social Question in Ireland 1891–1916', *Studies,* 70, Winter 1981, pp.263–288.

MacRory, J. (Cardinal) and others., 'Joint Pastoral Letter', (includes a copy of 'Constitution Amendment Bill 1931')., *Catholic Bulletin and Book Review*, Vol. 21, No. 11, Nov 1931, pp.l009–1040.

Mair, P., 'Labour and the Irish System Revisited: Party Competition in the 1920s', *Economic and Social Review*, Vol. 9, No. 1, 1977–78, pp.59–70.

Martin, F,X. (O.S.A.)., '1916 Myth Fact and Mystery', *Studia Hibernica*, No. 7, 1967, pp.7–124.

——. 'The 1916 Rising—a Coup de Etat or a Bloody Protest ?', *Studia Hibernica*, No. 8, 1968.

Miller, D.W., 'The Roman Catholic Church in Ireland 1898–1918', *Eire-Ireland*, Autumn 1968, pp.75–91.

Minahane, J., 'Connolly's Catholic Pose', *Irish Communist*, Nov 1980, p.4.

——. 'Fenian Marxism', *Irish Communist*, Oct 1980, p.7.

Mitchell, A., 'Labour and the National Struggle 1919–21', *Capuchin Annual*, Vol. 38, 1971, pp.261–88.

——. 'William O'Brien, 1881–1968, And the Irish Labour Movement', *Studies*, Autumn-Winter 1971, pp.311–331.

Mitchell, R.H.S., 'Connolly's Politics', *Society for the Study of Labour History Bulletin*, No. 28, 1974, pp.72–76.

Mooney, Mairin., 'Women in Ireland', *Labour Monthly*, Vol. 61, No. 2, pp.75–81.

Moran, B., '1913, Jim Larkin and the British Labour Movement, *Saothar*, 4, 1978, pp.35–49.

Morgan, A., 'A British Labourist in Catholic Ireland', *Saothar*, 7, May 1981, pp.54–61.

——. 'James Connolly in Belfast, 1910–1914', *Society for the Study of Labour History Bulletin*, No. 35, Autumn 1977, pp.9–11.

Morrissey, H., 'Working Class Unity in the 1930s', *Irish Socialist Review*, Winter 1984, pp.1–5.

Munck, R;, 'At the Very Doorstep: Irish Labor and the National Question , *Eire-Ireland*, Vol. 18, No. 2, 1983, pp.36–51.

——. 'Class and Religion in Belfast—A Historical Perspective', *Journal of Contemporary History*, Vol. 20, 1985, pp.241–259.

Murphy, J.T., 'Ireland and the International Working Class', *Labour Monthly*, May 1923, pp.161–171.

Murray, S., 'From Cosgrave to De Valera', *Labour Monthly*, Apr 1932, pp.235–239.

Nevin, D., 'Bibliography of Writings about James Larkin', *Saothar*, 4, 1978, pp.57–60.

Newbold, J.T.W., 'Ireland and the Illusion of Macdonaldism', *Labour Monthly*, Sept 1924.

Newsinger, J., I Bring Not Peace But a Sword. The Religious Motif in the Irish War of Independence', *Journal of Contemporary History*, Vol. 13, 1978, pp.609–628.

——. 'Old Chartists, Fenians, And New Socialists', *Eire-Ireland*, Vol. 17, No. 2, pp.19–45.

——. 'Revolution and Catholicism in Ireland, *European Studies Review*, Vol. 9, 1979, pp.457–480.

O'Brien, C.C., 'Nationalism and the reconquest of Ireland', *Crane Bag*, Vol. 1, No. 2, 1981, pp.8–13.

O'Connor Lysaght, D.R., 'Aug-Sept 1921 Month of the Soviets', *The Plough*, Vol. 1, No. 1.

——. 'The Munster Soviet Creameries', *Irish History Workshop Journal*, No. 1, 1981, pp.37–49.

——. The Rake's Progress of a Syndicalist: The Political Career of William O'Brien, Irish Labour Leader', *Saothar*, 9, pp.48–62.

——. 'The Unorthodoxy of James Connolly', *International*, Vol. 1, No. 3, Jan-Feb 1971, pp.5–24.

O'Connor, E., 'Agrarian Unrest and the Labour Movement in County Waterford 1917–23', *Decies*, Vol. 14, 1980, pp.5–23.

O'Connor, E. 'An Age of Agitation', *Saothar*, 9, pp.64–70.
——. 'The Labour Movement in Waterford City 1913–1923', *Decies*, Vol. 18, 1981, pp.17–32.
——. 'The Reformation of the Labour Movement inWaterford: From New Model Unionism to Larkinism', *Decies*, Vol. 12, Sept 1979, pp. 32–42.
O'Connor, P., 'Labour After Connolly 1916–23', *Irish Communist*, Dec 1980, p.10.
——. 'Socialism and Religion, Preview for a Debate',*Democratic Socialist*, No. 7, Spring 1985, pp.13–15.
O'Fiaich, T., 'The Catholic Clergy and the Independence Movement, *Capuchin Annual*, 1970, pp.480–502.
O'Muraile, N., 'The Socialism of James Connolly', *Zenith*, Vol. 1, 1971, pp.66–73.
O'Murchu, E., 'The State in Northern Ireland', *Marxism Today*, Vol. 24, No. 4, Apr 1980, p.26.
O'Neill, B., 'The Irish Labour Party and Fascism', *Labour Monthly*, Jan 1934, pp.48–52.
O'Neill, T.P., 'In Search of A Political Path: Irish Republicanism, 1922 to 1927', *Historical Studies*, Vol. 10, 1977, pp.147–171.
O'Riordan, M., 'Communism and Nationalism: A Complex History', *Democratic Socialist*, No. 7, Spring 1985, pp.16–20.
——. 'Dudley Edwards, Connolly and Religion', *Irish Communist*, May 1972, p.5.
——. 'From Greaves to Reeves: A New Look at Connolly and De Leon', *Irish Communist*, July 1979, p.7.
——. 'From Reeves back to Greaves', *Irish Communist*, Sept 1979, p.11.
——. 'Greaves, Reeves and The Plough and the Stars', *Irish Communist*, Oct 1979, p.13.
——. 'Labour and Nationalism in Southern Ireland 1913–21', Part 1, 'Sean O'Casey and the Irish Volunteers', *Irish Communist*, Dec 1972, p.18. Part 2, 'Sean O'Casey on James Connolly', *Irish Communist*, Jan 1973, p.13.
——. 'Larkin in America', *Saothar*, 4, 1978, pp.50–53.
——. 'Leninism and the Connolly—Walker Controversy', *Irish Communist*, Nov 1975, p.7.
——. 'Ireland's International Heroes', *OBAIR*, 2, Jan 1985, pp.4–6.
Orlova, M., 'Ireland the First British Colony', *Irish Socialist Review*, Winter 1984, pp.9–10.
Owens, R., " Votes for Ladies. Votes for Women Organised Labour and the Suffrage Movement, 1876–1922', *Saothar*, 9 May 1983, pp.32–47.
Patterson, H., 'James Larkin and the Belfast Dockers and Carters Strike of 1907', *Saothar*, 4, 1978, pp.8–14.
——. 'Reassessing Marxism on Ulster', *Saothar*, 5, 1979, pp.50–55.
Paul, W.M., 'The Irish Situation', *Communist Review*, Vol. 1, No. 4, Aug 1921, pp.15–22.
Power, C., 'The 1918 Congress of the Irish T.U.C. and Labour Party', *Decies*, 19, 1982, pp.33–38.
Probert, B., 'Marxism and the Irish Question', *Saothar*, 6, 1980, pp.65–71.
Pyne, P., 'The New Irish State and the Decline of the Republican Sinn Fein Party, 1923–26', *Eire-Ireland*, Vol. 11, No. 3, 1976, pp.33–65.
Raftery, A., 'Connolly the Marxist', *Irish Socialist Review*, No. 2, 1975, pp.3–8.
Reade, H., (Major)., 'Socialists Grip on Ireland', *Saturday Review*, Vol. 158, No. 4113, pp.11–12.
Reed, D., 'The Communist Tradition in Ireland', *Fight Racism, Fight Imperialism*, Part 1, No. 7, Nov-Dec 1980, Part 2, No. 8, Jan-Feb 1981, Part 3, No. 9, Mar-Apr 1981, Part 4, No. 10, May-June 1981.
Revolutionary Workers Groups., 'Ireland's Fight Against British Imperialist Aggression', *Communist Review*, Vol. 6, No. 8, Aug 1932, pp.387–390.
Rigney, P., 'Some Records of the I.T.G.W.U. in the National Library of Ireland', *Saothar*, 3, 1977, pp.14–15.
Rust, W., 'The War on Ireland', *Labour Monthly*, Aug 1932, pp.491–496.
Ryan, F., 'Sinn Fein and Reaction', *Labour History Workshop*, 1984.
——. 'Socialism Democracy and the Church', *Labour History Workshop*, 1984.

Schneider, F.D., 'British Labour and Ireland, 1918–1921: The Retreat to Houndsditch', *Review of Politics,* Vol. 40, No. 3, July 1978, pp.368–91.

Shields, J., 'The Republican Congress and Ireland's Fight', *Labour Monthly,* Nov 1934, pp.686–691.

Snoddy, O., 'Sean O'Casey as Troublemaker', *Eire-Ireland,* Vol. 1, No. 4, 1965–66, pp.33–38.

Sweeney, G., 'Emmet Larkin, James Larkin, 1876–1947, Irish Labour Leader', *Saothar,* 4, 1978, p.61.

——. 'Labour Politics 1927–1932', *Civil Service Review,* Vol. 35, No. 17, Nov-Dec 1979, pp.14–16.

Taplin, E., 'James Larkin, Liverpool and the National Union of Dock Labourers: The Apprenticeship of a Revolutionary', *Saothar,* 4, 1978, pp.1–7.

Thornley, D., 'The Development of the Irish Labour Movement', *Christus Rex,* Vol. 18, 1964, pp.7–21.

Tierney, W., 'Irish Writers and the Spanish Civil War', *Eire-Ireland,* Vol. 7, No. 3, 1977. pp.36–55.

Townshend, C., 'The Irish railway strike of 1920: industrial action and civil resistance in the struggle for independence', *Irish Historical Studies,* Vol. 22, No. 83, Mar 1979, pp.265–282.

——. 'The Irish Republican Army and the development of guerilla warfare, 1916–21', *English Historical Review,* Vol. 94, No. 371, Apr 1979, pp.318–345.

——. 'Modernization and Nationalism: Perspectives in Recent Irish History', *History,* Vol. 66, No. 217, 1981, pp.233–243.

Trench, W., 'The Plough and the Stars', *New Statesman and Nation,* Vol. 33, No. 837, 22 Mar 1947, pp.192–193.

Walker, W.M., 'Irish Immigrants in Scotland: Their Priests, Politics and Parochial Life', *Historical Journal,* Vol. 15, No. 4, 1972, pp.649–667.

Ward, M., " Suffrage First—Above All Else! An Account of the Irish Suffrage Movement', *Feminist Review,* No. 10, 1982, pp.21–36.

——. and McGivern, M.T., 'Images of Women in Northern Ireland', *Crane Bag,* Vol. 4, No. 1, 1980.

Willis, F., 'Ireland and the Social Revolution', *Communist Review,* Vol. 1, No. 1, May 1921, pp.7–9.

Wood, I.S., 'Irish Nationalism and Radical Politics in Scotland 1880–1906 ', *Scottish Labour History Society Journal,* 9 June 1975, pp.21–38.

——. 'John Wheatley, The Irish, and the Labour Movement in Scotland', *Innes Review,* Vol. 31, No. 2, Autumn 1980, pp.71–85.

5. PRINTED BOOKS AND PAMPHLETS

Aarons, E. *Lenin's Theories on Revolution.* D.B. Young for the Communist Party of Australia, Sydney, 1970.

Adams, G. *Falls Memories.* Brandon, Kerry, 1982.

Allen, K. *The Politics of James Connolly.* Pluto Press, London, 1990.

Athol Books. *Connolly: The Polish Aspect.* Athol, Belfast, 1985.

Barltrop, R. *The Monument: The Story of the Socialist Party of Great Britain.* Pluto, London, 1975.

Beale, J. *Women in Ireland: Voices of Change.* Macmillan, London, 1986.

Beckett, J.C. *The Making of Modern Ireland 1603–1923.* Faber and Faber, London, 1978.

Bell, G. *The Protestants of Ulster.* Pluto, London, 1976.

Bell, T. *The Struggle of the Unemployed in Belfast, Oct 1932.* The Cork Workers Club, Cork, n.d., *c.*1970.

Bennett, R. *The Black and Tans.* Four Square, London, 1986.

Berresford Ellis, P. *James Connolly: Selected Writings.* Penguin, Harmondsworth, 1973.

Bessie, A. *Men in Battle.* Pinnacle, New York, 1977.

Bew, P. Gibbon, P. and Patterson, H. *The State in Northern Ireland 1921–72*. Manchester University Press, Manchester, 1979.
Blanshard, P. *The Irish and Catholic Power*. Derek Verschoyle, London, 1954.
Bourke, M. *The O'Rahilly*. Anvil, Tralee, 1967.
Bowman, J. *De Valera and the Ulster Question 1917–23*. Clarendon, Oxford, 1982.
Bowyer-Bell, J. *The Secret Army: A History of the IRA. 1916–1970*. Sphere, London, 1972.
Boyce, D.G. *Englishmen and Irish Troubles*. MIT, Massachusetts, 1972.
——. *Nationalism in Ireland*. Croom Helm, London, 1982.
Boyd, A. *The Rise of the Irish Trade Unions 1729–1970*. Anvil, Dublin, 1976.
Boyle, J.W. (ed.) *Leaders and Workers*. Mercier, Dublin, 1978.
Brady, T. *The Historical Basis of Socialism in Ireland*. Cork Workers Club, Cork, n.d.
Braunthal, J. *History of the International 1914–43*. (tr. Clark, J.) Nelson, New Jersey, 1967.
Breen, D. *My Fight for Irish Freedom*. Anvil, Tralee, 1974.
British and Irish Communist Organisation. *The American Trial of Big Jim Larkin*. Athol, Belfast, 1976.
——. *Aspects of Nationalism*. Athol, Belfast, 1977.
——. *Communism in Ireland*. Athol, Belfast, 1977.
——. *Connolly and Partition*. Athol, Belfast, 1972.
——. *The Home Rule Crisis 1912–14*. Athol, Belfast, 1972.
British and Irish Communist Organisation. *The Road to Partition*. Athol, Belfast, 1978.
Broom, J. *John MacLean*. MacDonald, Loanhead, 1973.
Brown, M. *The Politics of Irish Literature*. George Allen and Unwin, London, 1972.
Buckland, P. *A History of Northern Ireland*. Gill and Macmillan, Dublin, 1981.
Burns, E. *British Imperialism in Ireland—A Marxist Historical Analysis*. Cork Workers Club, Cork, 1976.
Butler, E. *Barry's Flying Column*. Tandem, London, 1972.
Cahm, E. and Fisera, V.C. (eds.). *Socialism and Nationalism*. Vol. 2. Spokesman, Nottingham, 1979.
Canavan, Rev. J.E. *How far May a Catholic Agree with Socialists?* Catholic Truth Society of Ireland, Dublin, 1919.
Cantor, N.F. *The Age of Protest*. George Allen and Unwin, London, 1964.
Cardoza, N. *Maud Gonne—Lucky Eyes and a High Heart*. Gollancz, London, 1979.
Carney, J. Larkin, P. Ryan, W.P. and Larkin, J. *Convict No.50945, Jim Larkin Irish Labour Leader*. Cork Workers Club, Cork, n.d.
Carr, A. *The Belfast Labour Movement 1885–93*. Athol, Belfast,
Carty, F.X. *In Bloody Protest: The Tragedy of Patrick Pearse*. Able, Dublin, 1978.
Caulfield, M. *The Easter Rebellion*. Four Square, London,
Challinor, R. *The Origins of British Bolshevism*. Croom Helm-Rowman and Littlefield, London, 1977.
Chubb, B. *Government and Politics of Ireland*. Stanford University Press, California, 1970.
Clarkson, J.D. *Labour and Nationalism of Ireland*. Columbia University Press, New York, 1925.
Coffey, Rev. P. *Between Capitalism and Socialism*. Catholic Truth Society, Dublin, 1919.
Coffey, T.M. *Agony at Easter—The 1916 Uprising*. Penguin, Harmondsworth, 1971.
Cole, G.D.H. *The Second International 1889–1914*. Macmillan, London, 1960.
Comerford, M. *The First Dail*. Joe Clarke, Dublin, 1969.
Communist Party of Ireland. *Communist Party of Ireland: Outline History*. New Books, Dublin, 1975.
——. *Breaking the Chains: Selected Writings of James Connolly on Women*. Northern Area Committee, Communist Party of Ireland, Belfast (?), 1981.
——. *Ireland in Crisis*. New Books, Dublin, 1975.
——. *Ireland's Path to Freedom: Manifesto of the C.P. of I. Adopted at the Inaugural Congress June 3–4, 1933*. Labour Monthly Pamhlets. London Sphinx, Dublin, 1933.

Conlin, L. *Cumann na mBan and the Women of Ireland 1913–25*. Kilkenny People, Kilkenny, 1969.
Connolly, J. *The Axe to the Root*. Irish Transport and General Workers Union, Dublin, 1921.
———. *Erin's Hope and the New Evangel*. New Books Dublin, 1972.
———. *Ireland upon the Dissecting Table*. Cork Workers Club, Cork, 1975.
———. *Labour in Irish History*. New Books, Dublin, 1973
———. *Labour Nationality and Religion*. The Harp Library, Dublin, 1910.
———. *Press Poisoners in Ireland*. British and Irish Communist Organisation, Belfast, 1972.
———. *The Reconquest of Ireland*. New Books, Dublin, 1972.
———. *Yellow Unions in Ireland*. British and Irish Communist Organisation, Befast, 1972.
Coogan, O. *Politics and War in Meath, 1913–23*. Oliver Coogan (self-published), Dublin, 1983.
Coogan, T.P. *The I.R.A.* Fontana-Collins, London, 1971.
Cork Workers Club. *The Connolly Worker Controversy*. Cork Workers Club, Cork, n.d.
Cronin, J.F. and Flannery, H.W. *Labour and the Church*. Burns and Oates, London, 1965.
Cronin, S. *Frank Ryan*. Repsol, Dublin, 1980.
———. *Irish Nationalism*. Pluto, London, 1983.
———. *Kevin Barry*. National Publications Committee, Cork, n.d.
———. *Marx and the Irish Question*. Repsol, Dublin, 1977.
———. *The McGarrity Papers*. Anvil, Tralee, 1972.
———. *The Revolutionaries: The Story of 12 Great Irishmen*. Republican Publications, Dublin, 1971.
———. *Young Connolly*. Repsol, Dublin, 1983.
Cullingford, E. *Yeats, Ireland and Fascism*. Macmillan, London, 1981.
Curriculum Development Unit Dublin. *Divided City: Portrait of Dublin 1913*. O'Brien Educational, Dublin, 1978.
Czira, S.G. *The Years Flew By*. Gifford and Craven, Dublin, 1974.
Dangerfield, G. *The Damnable Question*. Little and Brown, Boston, 1976.
Dawson, R. *Red Terror and Green*. New English Library, London, 1972.
Deasy, J. *Fiery Cross—The Story of Jim Larkin*. New Books, Dublin, 1963.
———. *The Teachings of James Connolly*. New Books, Dublin, n.d., c. 1966.
De Courcy Ireland, J. *Revolutionary Movements of the Past*. Repsol, Dublin, 1974.
De Leon, D. *What Means This Strike*. Socialist Labour Press, Glasgow, n.d.
De Paor, L. *Divided Ulster*. Penguin, Harmondsworth, 1971.
de Vere White, T. *Kevin O'Higgins—strong man in the Free State Government 1922–27*. Anvil, Tralee, 1966.
Devlin, P. *Yes we have no Bananas: Outdoor Relief in Belfast 1920–39*. Blackstaff, Belfast, 1981.
Dewar, H. *Communist Politics in Britain: The CPGB from its Origins to the Second World War*. Pluto, London, 1976.
Diggins, J.P. *The American Left in the Twentieth Century*. Harcourt and Brace Jovanovich, New York, 1973.
Dooley, P. *Under the Banner of Connolly*. Irish Freedom Pamphlet, London (?), n.d.
Downing, T. (ed). *The Troubles*. Thames-MacDonald Futura, London, 1981.
Dublin Trade's Union and Labour Council. *James Connolly Celebration May 11th 1930: Dublin Labour Year Book*. Dublin Trade's Union and Labour Council, Dublin, 1930.
———. *May Day Celebration May 12 1929: James Connolly Commemoration Souvenir*. McParland and Hall, Dublin, 1929.
Duff, C. *Six Days to Shake an Empire*. J.M. Dent, London, 1966.
Duncan, B. *James Leatham 1865–1945: Portrait of a Socialist Pioneer*. Aberdeen Peoples Press.Aberdeen, 1978.
Dutt, R.P. *Ireland—Battleground for Democracy*. New Book Publications, Dublin, n.d., c. 1974.

Edmonds, S. *The Gun Law and the Irish People*. Anvil, Tralee,

Edwards, O.D. *et al. Celtic Nationalism*. Routledge and Keegan Paul, London, 1968.

Edwards, O.D. and Ransom, B. *James Connolly: Selected Political Writings*. Jonathan Cape, London, 1968.

Edwards, O.D. *The Mind of an Activist: James Connolly*. Gill and Macmillan, Dublin, 1971.

——. and Pyle, F. (eds.). *1916 The Easter Uprising*. MacGibbon and Kee, London, 1968.

Edwards, R.D. *James Connolly*. Gill and Macmillan, Dublin, 1981.

——. *Patrick Pearse: The Triumph of Failure*. Gollancz, London, 1977.

Edwards, S. *The Paris Commune*. Eire and Spottiswoode, London, 1971.

Engels, F. *Peaceful Revolution vs. Violence: Can Socialism be Achieved Peacefully?* New York Labour News, New York, 1970.

Fahey, Rev. D. *The Tragedy of James Connolly*. Forum, Cork, 1947.

Farrell, B; *The Founding of Dail Eireann*. Gill and Macmillan, Dublin, 1971.

Farrell, M. *Northern Ireland: The Orange State*. Pluto, London, 1980.

Farrington, Prof. B. *The Challenge of Socialism*. Editorial Board of *Review*. Dublin, n.d. *c*.1946.

Fennell, D. *Irish Catholics and Freedom*. Dominican Publications, Dublin, 1984.

Fisk, R. *In time of War: Ireland, Ulster and the Price of Neutrality 1939–45*. Granada, London, 1983

Fitzpatrick, D. *Politics and Irish Life: Provincial Experience of War and Revolution*. Gill and Macmillan, Dublin, 1977.

Flynn, E.G. *The Rebel Girl: An Autobiography*. International, New York, 1974.

Forester, M. *Michael Collins: The Lost Leader*. Sphere London, 1972.

Foster, W.Z. *History of the Three Internationals*. Greenwood Westport, 1968.

Fox, R. *Marx, Engels and Lenin on the Irish Revolution*. 1st edn 1932. Cork Workers Club, Cork n.d.

Fox, R.M. *The History of the Irish Citizen Army*. James Duffy, Dublin, 1945.

——. *James Connolly: The Forerunner*. Kerryman, Tralee, 1966.

——. *Jim Larkin Irish Labour Leader*. International, New

——. *Labour in the National Struggle*. Harpers, Dublin,

——. *Louie Bennett. Her Life and Times*. Talbot, Dublin,1958.

——. *Rebel Irishwomen*. Talbot, Dublin, 1935.

——. *Smokey Crusade*. Hogarth, London, 1938.

——. *Years of Freedom: The Story of Ireland 1921–48*. Trumpet, Cork, 1948.

Freyer, G. *Peader O'Donnell*. Bucknell University Press, New Jersey, 1973.

Gale, J. *Oppression and Revolt in Ireland*. Workers Revolutionary Party, London, 1975.

Gallacher, W. *Catholics and Communism*. Current, Sydney, n.d.

——. *Ireland: Can it remain neutral*. CPGB, London, n.d., c. 1939–40.

——. *Revolt on the Clyde*. Lawrence and Wishart, London, 1978.

Gallagher, F. *The Indivisible Island*. Gollancz, London,

Garvin, T. *The Evolution of Irish Nationalist Politics*. Gill and Macmillan, Dublin, 1981.

Gaughan, J.A. *Thomas Johnson 1877–1963: First Leader of the Labour Party in Dail Eireann*. Kingdom, County Dublin, 1980.

'Gerhard'. (pseudonym). *The Irish Free State and British Imperialism*. 1st edn 1932. Cork Workers Club, Cork, 1976.

Gilmore, G. *The Irish Republican Congress*. Cork Workers Club, Cork, 1978.

Gilmore, G. *Labour and the Republican Movement*. 1st edn 1966. Repsol, n.d., *c*.1970.

Gilmore, G. *The Relevance of James Connolly*. (self-published?), n.p., n.d., *c*.1970.

Gleeson, J. *Bloody Sunday*. Four Square, London, 1965.

Goldring, M. *Faith of our Fathers: The Formation of Irish Nationalist Ideology 1890–1920*. Repsol, Dublin, 1982.

Gonne-MacBride, M. *A Servant of the Queen*. Gollancz, London, 1938.

Gray, J. *City in Revolt: James Larkin and the Belfast Dock Strike of 1907*. Blackstaff, Belfast, 1985.

Greaves, C.D. *The Irish Crisis*. Lawrence and Wishart, London, 1972.

——. *The Irish Transport and General Workers Union: The Formative Years*. Gill and Macmillan, Dublin, 1982.

——. *Liam Mellows and the Irish Revolution*. Lawrence and Wishart, London, 1971.

——. *The Life and Times of James Connolly*. Lawrence and Wishart, London, 1976.

——. *Reminiscences of the Connolly Association: An Emerald Jubilee Pamphlet 1938–78*. Connolly Association, London, 1978.

——. *Sean O'Casey: Poltics and Art*. Lawrence and Wishart, London, 1979.

Griffith, K. and O'Grady, T.E. *Curious Journey: An Oral History of Ireland's Unfinished Revolution*. Hutchinson, London, 1982.

Gruber, H. *International Communism in the Era of Lenin: A Documentary History*. Anchor, New York, 1972.

Gruber, H. *Soviet Russia Masters of the Comintern: International Communism in the Era of Stalin's Ascendancy*. Anchor, New York, 1974.

Hadden, P. *Divide and Rule*. M.I.M Dublin 1980.

Handley, J.E. *The Irish in Scotland*. Cork University Press, Cork, 1945.

Hepburn, A.C. *The Conflict of Nationality in Modern Ireland*. Edward Arnold, London, 1980.

Hinton, J. *The First Shop Stewards Movement*. George Allen and Unwin, London, 1973.

——. *Labour and Socialism*. Wheatsheaf, Sussex, 1983.

——. and Hyman, R. *Trade Unions and Revolution: The Industrial Politics of the Early British Communist Party*. Pluto, London, 1975.

HMSO. *Communist Papers. Documents selected from those obtained at the arrest of the Communist Leaders on 14 and 21 Oct 1925*. HMSO. CmnD 2682. London, 1926.

——. *Intercourse between Bolshevism and Sinn Fein*. HMSO. CmnD 1326. London, 1921.

Hobsbawn, E.G. *Nationalism: Programme, Myth and Reality*. Cambridge University Press. Cambridge 1991

Hogan, J. *Could Ireland Become Communist: The Facts of the Case*. Cahill, Dublin, 1935.

Holton, B. *British Syndicalism 1900–1914*. Pluto, London. 1976.

Howell, D. *A Lost Left: Three Studies in Socialism and Nationalism*. Manchester University Press, Manchester, 1986.

International Committee of the Irish Labour Party. *Irish Labour and its International Relations in the Era of the Second International and the Bolshevik Revolution*. Cork Workers Club, Cork, n.d.

Irish Feminist Information. *Missing Pieces, Women in Irish History*. Irish Feminist Information and Women's Community Press, Dublin, 1983.

Irish Labour Party and Trade Union Congress. *Annual Report*. 1918–29.

Irish Trade Union Congress. *Annual Report*. 1930–40.

——. and Labour Party. *Annual Report*. 1912–17.

Irish Transport and General Workers Union. *Annual Report*. 1918–40.

——. *The Attempt to Smash the Irish Transport and General Workers Union*. National Executive ITGWU, Dublin, 1924.

——. *The Lines of Progress*. ITGWU, Dublin, 1918.

——. *Some Pages from Union History: The Facts Concerning Larkin's Departure to America*. ITGWU, Dublin, 1927.

Jackson, T.A. *Ireland Her Own: An Outline History of the Irish National Struggle*. Lawrence and Wishart, London, 1971.

Johnson, T. *The Future of Labour*. Irish Trade Union Congress and Labour Party, Dublin, 1916.

Jones, M., *These Obstreperous Lassies*. Gill and Macmillan, Dublin, 1988.

Kautsky, K. *Ireland*. tr. Clifford, A. British and Irish Communist Organisation, Belfast, 1979.

Keating, M. and Bleiman, D. *Labour and Scottish Nationalism*. Macmillan, Dublin, 1979.

Kee, R. *The Green Flag*. Delacotte, New York, 1972.

Kelley, K. *The Longest War: Northern Ireland and the IRA*. Lawrence Hill, Westport, 1982.

Kendall, W. *The Revolutionary Movement in Britain 1900–1921*. Weidenfeld and Nicolson, London, 1969.

Keogh, D. *The Rise of the Irish Working Class*. Appletree, Belfast,1982.

Kim, G. *Leninism and the National Liberation Movement*. Novosti, Moscow, 1970.

Knox, W. *Scottish Labour Leaders 1918–1939*. Mainstream, Edinburgh, 1984.

Koss, S. *The Anatomy of an Anti-War Movement: The Pro-Boers*. University of Chicago Press, Chicago, 1973.

Kynaston, D. *King Labour: The British Working Class 1850–1914*. George Allen and Unwin, London, 1976.

Laffan, M. *The Partition of Ireland 1911–1925*. Dundalgan, Dundalk, 1983.

Lalor, F. *Readings From Fintan Lalor*. Belfast Republican Press, Belfast, 1975.

Lane, T. *The Union Makes Us Strong*. Arrow, London, 1974.

Larkin, E. *James Larkin*. Mentor, London, 1965.

Lenin, V.I. *The Collapse of the Second International*. Progress Publishers, Moscow, 1975.

———. *Collected Works*. Vol. 13 and Vol. 41. Foreign Languages Publishing House, Moscow, 1962.

———. *Left-Wing Communism an infantile disorder*. Foreign Languages Press, Peking, 1965.

———. *Lenin on the National and Colonial Questions*. Foreign Languages Press, Peking, 1967.

———. *Marxism and Insurrection*. Progress Publishers, Moscow, 1980.

———. *On Socialist Ideology and Culture*. Foreign Languages Publishing House, Moscow, n.d.

———. *On the Emancipation of Women*. Progress Publishers, Moscow, 1977.

———. *On Trade Unions*. Progress Publishers, Moscow, 1978.

———. *The Rights of Nations to Self-Determination*. Progress Publishers, Moscow, 1968.

———. *Selected Works*. Vol. 2. Foreign Languages Publishing House, Moscow, 1952.

———. *Socialism and Rellgion*. Foreign Languages Publishing House, Moscow, 1955.

Levenson, L. *With Wooden Sword: A Portrait of Francis Sheehy-Skeffington, Militant Pacifist*. Gill and Macmillan, Dublin, 1983.

———. *A Biography of Yeats Beloved, Maud Gonne*. Cassell, London, 1976.

———. *James Connolly: Socialist Patriot and Martyr.* Quartet, London, 1973.

Liddington, J. and Norris, J. *One Hand Tied Behind Us: The Rise of the Women's Suffrage Movement*. Virago, London, 1978.

Linklater, A. *An Unhusbanded Life: Charlotte Despard. Suffragette, Socialist and Sinn Feiner.* Hutchinson, London, 1980.

Lyons, F.S. *Culture and Anarchy in Ireland 1890–1939*. Clarendon, Oxford, 1979.

———. *Ireland Since the Famine*. Fontana-Collins, Glasgow, 1978.

McCamley, B. *The Role of the Rank and File in the 1935 Dublin Tram and Bus Strike*. Bill McCamley, Dublin, 1981.

Mac an Bheatha, P. *James Connolly and the Workers Repulic*. Foilseachain Naisiunta Teoranta, Co. Mayo, 1978.

MacAonghusa, P. *The Best of Connolly*. Mercier, Cork, 1967.

———. and O'Reagain, L. *The Best of Pearse*. Mercier, Cork, 1967.

McCann, J. *War By The Irish*. Kerryman, Tralee, 1946.

Macardle, D. *The Irish Republic*. Corgi, London, 1968.

McCarthy, C. *Trade Unions in Ireland 1894–1960*. Institute of Public Administration, Dublin, 1977.

MacColl, R. *Roger Casement*. Four Square, London, 1965.

McCracken, J.L. *Representative Government in Ireland*. Oxford University Press, London, 1958.

MacCurtain, M. and O'Corrain (eds.). *Women in Irish Society.* Arlen House: The Women's Press, Dublin, 1978.

MacDonnell, J.M. *The Story of Irish Labour.* 1st edn. *c.*1921. Cork Workers Club, Cork, n.d.

MacEoin, V. *Survivors.* Argenta, Dublin, 1980.

McInerney, M. *Peadar O'Donnell: Irish Social Rebel.* O'Brien, Dublin, 1974.

Macintyre, S. *A Proletarian Science: Marxism in Britain 1917–1933.* Cambridge University Press, Cambridge, 1980.

McLellan, D. *Karl Marx: His Life and Thought.* Granada, St. Albans, 1973.

MacLochlainn, P.F. *Last Words, Letters and Statements of the Leaders executed after the Rising at Easter 1916.* Kilmainham Jail Restoration Society, Dublin, 1971.

MacLysaght, E. *Changing Times: Ireland Since 1898.* Colin Smythe, Gerrards Cross, 1978.

McMullen, W. *With James Connolly in Belfast.* Self-Published(?), n.p., n.d. c. 1951.

McShane, H. and Smith, J. *Harry McShane: No Mean Fighter.* Pluto, London, 1978.

Manning, M. *The Blueshirts.* Gill and Macmillan, Dublin, 1970.

——. *Irish Political Parties.* Gill and Macmillan, Dublin, 1972.

Markievicz, C.D. *James Connolly and Catholic Doctrine.* Self-Published(?), n.p., n.d. c. 1925.

——. *Prison Letters of Countess Markievicz.* Longman Green, London, 1934.

——. *What Irish Republicans Stand For.* Colm O'Lochlainn, Dublin, n.d.

——. *Women Ideals and the Nation.* Inghinidhe na h-Eireann, Dublin, 1909.

Marreco, A. *The Rebel Countess: The Life and Times of Constance Markievicz.* Corgi, London, 1969.

Martin, F.X. (ed.) *Leaders and Men of the Easter Rising: Dublin 1916.* Methuen, London, 1967.

Marx, K. Engels, F. and Lenin, V.I. *Anarchism and Anarcho Syndicalism.* Progress Publishers, Moscow, 1974.

Marx, K. and Engels, F. *Ireland and the Irish Question.* Progress Publishers, Moscow, 1971.

Marx, K. and Engels, F. *Manifesto of the Communist Party.* Progress Publishers, Moscow, 1969.

Marx, K. and Engels, F. *On Religion.* Progress Publishers, Moscow, 1971.

Marx, K. Engels, F. and Lenin, V.I. *On Women and the Family.* Repsol, Dublin, 1983.

Marx, K. and Engels, F. *Selected Works.* 2 Vols., Foreign Languages Publishing House, Moscow, 1951.

Marx, K. *Wages, Price and Profit.* Foreign Languages Press, Peking, 1970.

Mescal, J. *Religion and the Irish System of Education.* Clonmore and Reynolds, London, 1957.

Metscher, P. *Republicanism and Socialism in Ireland*, P. Lang, New York, 1986.

Miller, D.W. *Church State and Nation in Ireland 1898–1921.* Gill and Macmillan, Dublin, 1973.

Milotte, M. *Communism in Modern Ireland: The Pursuit of the Workers Repubiic since 1916.* Gill and Macmillan, Dublin, 1984.

Milton, N. *John MacLean.* Pluto, London, 1978.

Milton, N.(ed). *John MacLean: In the Rapids of Revolution.* Allison and Busby, London, 1978.

Mitchell, A. and O'Snodaigh, P. *Irish Political Documents 1916–49.* Irish Academic Press, Dublin, 1985.

Mitchell, A. *Labour in Irish Politics 1890–1930.* Irish University Press, Dublin, 1974.

Mitchell, J. *The Essential O'Casey.* International, New York,

Moran, Rev. W. *Social Reconstruction in An Irish State.* Catholic Truth Society of Ireland, Dublin, n.d.

Morgan, A. and Purdie, B.(eds.) *Ireland Divided Nation Divided Class.* Ink Links, London, 1980.

Molyneux, J. *Marxism and the Party.* Pluto, London, 1978.

Morgan, A. *James Connolly: A Political Biography.* Manchester University Press, Manchester, 1988.

Murray, S. and others. *The Irish Case for Communism.* 1st edn. 1933. Sphinx, Dublin, 1933.

Murray, S. *The Irish Revolt—1916 and After.* Communist Party of Great Britain, London, 1936.

Nevin, D. *Trade Unions and Change in Irish Society.* Mercier, Dublin, 1980.

Ní Eireamhoin, E. *Two Great Irishwomen: Maud Gonne MacBride and Constance Markievicz.* C.J. Fallon, Dublin, 1971.

Norman, E. *A History of Modern Ireland.* Penguin, London, 1971.

Novack, G. Frankel, D. and Feldman, F. *The First Three Internationals: Their History and Lessons.* Pathfinder, New York, 1974.

Nowlan, K.B. (ed.). *Karl Marx: The Materialist Messiah.* Mercier, Dublin, 1984.

Nowlan, K.B. *The Making of 1916: Studies in the History of the Rising.* Stationery Office, Dublin, 1969.

O'Ballance, E. *Terror in Ireland: The Heritage of Hate.* Presidio, California, 1981.

O'Brien, C.C. *States of Ireland.* Granada, London, 1974.

O'Brien, N.C. *James Connolly: Portrait of a Rebel Father.* Talbot, Dublin, 1935.

——. *The Unbroken Tradition.* Boni and Liveright, New York, 1918.

——. *We Shall Rise Again.* Mosquito, London, 1981.

O'Brien, W. *Forth The Banners Go.* Three Candles, Dublin,

——. *The Irish Revolution and How it Came About.* Allen and Unwin, London, 1923.

O'Broin, L. *Dublin Castle and the 1916 Rising.* Helicon Dublin, 1966.

——. *Revolutionary Underground: The Story of the I.R.B. 1858–1924.* Gill and Macmillan, Dublin, 1976.

O'Casey, S. *The Story of the Irish Citizen Army.* Journeyman, London, 1980.

O'Connor Lysaght, D.R. *The Republic of Ireland.* Mercier, Cork, 1970.

——. *The Story of the Limerick Soviet.* People's Democracy, Limerick, 1981.

O'Connor, E. *Syndicalism in Ireland,* Cork University, Cork, 1988.

O'Connor, G. *James Connolly: A Study of his Work and Worth.* n.p., n.d.

O'Connor, K. *The Irish in Britain.* Torc, Dublin, 1974.

O'Connor, V. *A Terrible Beauty is Born.* Granada, St. Albans,

O'Donnell, P. *The Gates Flew Open.* Mercier, Cork, 1965.

——. *Not Yet Emmet: A Wreath on the Grave of Sean Murray.* New Books, Dublin, n.d.

——. *The Role of Industrial Workers in the Problems of the West.* Kerryman, Tralee, n.d.

——. *There Will be Another Day.* Dolmen, Dublin, 1 963.

O'Donoghue, F. *Tomas MacCurtain: Soldier and Patriot.* Anvil, Tralee, 1977.

O'Dubhghaill, M. *Insurrection Fires at Eastertide.* Mercier, Cork, 1966.

O 'Faolain, S . *Constance Markievicz .* Sphere, London, 1967.

——. *De Valera.* Penguin, Harmondsworth, 1939.

O'Farrell, P. *Ireland's English Question: Anglo Irish Relations 1534–1970.* Schacken, New York, 1971.

O'Flaherty, L. *The Assassin.* Four Square, London, n.d.

——. *The Informer.* New English Library, London, 1980.

——. *Insurrection.* New English Library, London, 1966.

——. *Shame the Devil.* Grayson and Grayson, London, 1934 .

O'Leary, C. *Irish Elections 1918–1977 .* Gill and Macmillan, Dublin, 1979.

O'Luing, S. *I Die in a Good Cause: A Study of Thomas Ashe.* Anvil, Tralee, 1970.

O'Malley, E. *On Another Man's Wound.* Anvil, Dublin, 1979.

——. *The Singing Flame.* Anvil, Dublin, 1979.

O'Riordan, M. *James Connolly in America.* Irish Communist Organisation, Befast, 1971.

——. *Larkinism in Perspective:- From Communism to Evolutionary Socialism.* Labour History Workshop, Dublin, 1983.

——. *Portrait of an Irish Anti-Fascist: Frank Edwards 1907–1983*. Labour History Workshop, Dublin, 1984.
——. *Connolly Column*. New Books, Dublin, 1979.
O'Shannon, C. (ed.) . *Fifty Years at Liberty Hall 1909–59*. Irish Transport and General Workers Union, Dublin, 1959.
——. *The Planting of the Seed*. Irish Transport and General Workers Union, Dublin, n.d.
Pakenham, F. (Lord Longford). *Peace by Ordeal*. Sidgwick and Jackson, London, 1972.
——. *Eamon de Valera*. Arrow, London,
Pankhurst, S. *The Suffragette Movement* Virago London, 1977
Patterson, H. *Class Conflict and Sectarianism*. Blackstaff, Belfast, 1980.
Pearse, P. *The Sovereign People*. Pobal Teoranta, Ath Cliath, 1974.
Pelling, H. *A History of British Trade Unionism*. Penguin, Harmondsworth, 1963.
——. *Origins of the Labour Party*. Oxford University Press, Oxford, 1976.
Phelan, Rev. M. *The Pillars of Socialism*. Office of the Irish Messenger, Dublin, 1922.
Piratin, P. *Our Flag Stays Red*. Lawrence and Wishart, London, 1980.
Pollock, S. *Mutiny for the Cause*. Sphere, London, 1971.
Portis, L. *Georges Sorel*. Pluto, London, 1980.
Probert, B. *Beyond Orange and Green*. Zed, London, 1978.
Quail, J. *The Slow Burning Fuse: The Lost History of British Anarchism*. Paladin-Granada, London, 1978.
Raftery, A. *Lenin on Ireland*. New Books, Dublin, 1974.
Ransom, B. *Connolly's Marxism*. Pluto, London, 1980.
Redmond, S. *Irish Municipal Employees Trade Union 1883–1983*. Irish Municipal Employees Trade Union, Dublin, 1983.
Reed, D. Ireland: *The Key to the British Revolution*. Larkin, London, 1984.
Reeve, C. and Reeve, A.B. *James Connolly and the United States: The Road to the 1916 Irish Rebellion*. Humanities, New Jersey, 1978.
Reeve, C, *The Life and Times of Daniel De Leon*. Humanities, New York, 1972.
Renshaw, P. *The Wobblies: The Story of Syndicalism in the United States*. Eyre and Spottiswoode, London, 1967.
Revolutionary Communist Group. *Ireland, British Labour and British Imperialism*. Revolutionary Communist Group, London, 1976.
Robbins, F. *Under The Starry Plough: Recollections of the Irish Citizen Army*. Academy, Dublin, 1977.
'Ronald'. (pseudonym). *Freedom's Road For Irish Workers*. 1st edn 1917. Cork Workers Club, Cork, 1975.
Rose, C. *The Female Experience: The Story of the Women Movement*. Arlen House, Galway, 1975.
Rose, P. *The Fenians in England 1865–1872*. John Calder, London, 1982.
Ryan, D. *James Connolly: His Life Work and Writings*. Talbot, Dublin, 1924.
——. (ed.). *Labour and Easter Week*. Sign of the Three Candles, Dublin, 1949.
——. *Michael Collins*. 1st edn., 1932. Anvil, Tralee, 1979.
——. (ed.). *The 1916 Poets*. Greenwood, Westport, 1979.
——. *Remembering Sion: A Chronicle of Storm and Quiet*. Arthur Baker, London, 1934.
——. (ed) *Socialism and Nationalism*. Sign of the Three Candles, Dublin, 1948.
——. *The Workers Republic*. Sign of the Three Candles, Dublin, 1951.
Ryan, W.P. *The Irish Labour Movement: From the Twenties to our own Day*. Talbot, Dublin, n.d.
Rumpf, E. and Hepburn, A.C. *Nationalism in Twentieth Century Ireland*. Liverpool University Press, Liverpool, 1977.
Schuller, G. *James Connolly and Irish Freedom: A Marxist Analysis*. 1st edn., 1926. Cork Workers Club, Cork, 1976.

Sheehan, H, *Communism and the Emancipation of Women*. Communist Party of Ireland, Dublin, 1977.

Sheehy-Skeffington, A. and Owens, R. *Votes for Women: Irish Women's Struggle for the Vote*. Self-published, Dublin,

Sheehy-Skeffington, H. *British Militarism As I have Known it*. 1st edn., 1917. Kerryman, Tralee, 1946.

Short, K.R.M. *The Dynamite War: Irish-American Bombers in Victorian Britain*. Gill and Macmillan, Dublin, 1979.

Soldon, N.C. *Women in British Trade Unions 1874–1976*. Gill and Macmillan, Rowman and Littlefield, Dublin, 1978.

Sorel, G. *Reflections on Violence*. Collier, London, 1969.

Spartacist League. *Lenin and the Vanguard Party*. Spartacist, New York, 1978.

Stearns, P. *Revolutionary Syndicalism and French Labour*. Rutgers University Press, New Jersey, 1971.

Stephan, E. *Spies in Ireland*. Four Square, London, 1965.

Stephens, J. *The Insurrection in Dublin*. 1st edn., 1916. Scepter, Dublin, 1966.

Strauss, E. *Irish Nationalism and British Democracy*. Methuen, London, 1951.

Taylor, R. *Assassination*. Hutchinson, London, 1961.

——. *Michael Collins*. Hutchinson, London, 1958.

Thomas, P. *Karl Marx and the Anarchists*. Routledge and Keegan Paul, London, 1980.

Thomson, W.I. *The Imagination of an Insurrection: Dublin Easter 1916—A Study of an Ideological Movement*. Oxford University Press, New York, 1967.

Townshend, C. *Political Violence in Ireland: Government and Resistance since 1848*. Clarendon, Oxford, 1983.

Trotsky, L. *The First Five Years of the Communist International*, New Park, London, 1973.

Valiuilis, M.G. *Almost a Rebellion: The Irish Army Mutiny of 1924*. Tower, Cork, 1985.

Van Voris, J. *Constance de Markievicz: In the Cause of Ireland*. University of Massachusetts Press, Massachusetts, 1967.

Ward, A.J. *The Easter Uprising Revolution and Irish Nationalism*. AHM, Arlington Heights, 1980.

Ward, M. *Unmanageable Revolutionaries*. Pluto, London, 1983.

White, Capt. J.R. *Misifit: An Autobiography*. Jonathan Cape, London, 1930.

Williams, D. (ed.). *The Irish Struggle 1916–26*. Routledge and Keegan Paul, London, 1966.

Wright, A. *Disturbed Dublin: The Story of the Great Strike*. Longmans Green, London, 1914.

Young, J.D, *The Rousing of the Scottish Working Class*. Croom Helm, London, 1979.

Young, T. *Incitement to Disaffection*. Cobden Trust, London, 1976.

Younger, C. *A State of Disunion*. Fontana-Collins, London, 1972.

Younger, C. *Ireland's Civil War*. Fontana-Collins, London, 1979.

Zneimer, J. *The Literary Vision of Liam O'Flaherty*. Syracuse University Press, New York, 1970.

Index

America, Connolly's emigration to,17, Connolly's tour in 1902, 34, return to in 1903, 35

American Socialist Labor Party (SLP): *see* Socialist Labor Party (America).

An Bhean Oibre, and IWWU convention, 83

anarchism, Connolly's views on, 39

Anglo-Irish Treaty: *see* Treaty.

Asquith, Herbert Henry, Earl of Oxford and Asquith, 137

Aston, Edward, 112

Bean na hÉireann , 17

Bebel, Ferdinand, August, 65

Belfast Independent Labour Party (ILP), 47

Belfast mill girls strike, 18

Bennett, Louie, 18, 82, 83,144

Bernstein, Eduard, 68

Blanqui, Louis, 68

Blueshirts, failure to thrive, 94, opposition to by CPI, 135, and ICA, 147

Boer War, 60,61,69

Brugha, Cathal,117

Byrne, L.P. 112

Cahalan, C., 84, 85

Campbell, D.R., 125

Camiez de Arellano, 94

capitalism, 32, 44, Connolly's opinion of, 66,70,71, 91

capitalists, 44, 69

Carney, Winifred, 23,76

Carpenter, Walter, 127, 128

Casement, Roger, 87

Catholicism: *see* Roman Catholicism.

Cavanagh, Maeve,121

Christian socialism, 29

civil war in Ireland, and Irish labour, 144, 147, and political transformation, 157

class war, 38,40, 68: *see* also working class

Clarke, Thomas 79, 149

Coates, W. P., 100

Coffey, Rev. P., 90, 91

Colgan, Pat, 143

Comhairle na Poblachta, and IRA, 133

Comintern, report on political and working class organisation in Ireland, 126, and dissolution of CPI, 129, 130, support for IWL, 130–132, approach to IRA, 133, and effect on Irish left, 136

Commune (of Paris), 60

Communism, opposition to, by the Roman Catholic Church, 93 anti-communist resolution of ILP, 94, failure to thrive in Ireland, 156, 157

Communist Party of Ireland (CPI) 125, establishment of, and objective, 127, membership of, internal divisions,128, opposition to Treaty, 128, commitment to Republic, 129, dissolution of, 129, 130, opposition to Blueshirts, 135,

Communist party of Great Britain (CPGB), interest in Irish affairs, 128

Connolly, Ina, 21, 79

Connolly, Lillie, 23, 87, 104, 107, 153

Connolly Memorial Committee, aims of, 155

Connolly, Nora, 63, 79, 107, 126–128, 134, 142, 153

Connolly, Roderick (Roddy), 94, 95, 125, 126, 127, 131, 134, 142, 147, 152, 155, 157

Connolly Workers Educational Club, 131

Constitution Amendment Act, 93

Cosgrave, William, 81, 93

'Crusade to Spain', 94: *see also* Spanish Civil War.

Cumann na mBan, 76,78, constitution of,79, relationship to IV, 79, allegiance to Republic, 80, conspiracy accusation, 93

Cumann na nGaedheal, 81

Cumann na Savirse, formation of, 81

Daly, Patrick T., 105, 108, 143

Dáil Éireann, 78, women deputies and the Treaty, 80, split, 81, desire of IWWU for

Dáil Éireann (*contd.*)
representative, 84, advertisement for
nation loan 116, election of president, 116,
and ILP, 120, meeting with Seanad, 151
Daily Bulletin, on Thomas Johnson, 120
de Blacam, Aodh, 88
De Leon, Daniel,17, influence on Connolly,
34, 52, criticism of by Connolly, 35, 36,
54, 56, influence on IWW, 37, theories
of party organisation, 53, as leader of
SLP, 53
de Valera, Eamon, 81, 111, speech on
Connolly, 116,117, 156
Desmoulin, Camille, 69
Despard, Charlotte, 87
dual unionism, 34
Dublin lockout of 1913, 21,61,62
Dublin Socialist Club, 33
Dublin Trades Council, 111
Dublin tram and bus strike of 1935, 102, 154
Duffy, Lawrence J., 118

Easter Rising, Connolly's role in, 64,
72–75, 149, and Roman Catholicism,
86, labour's involvement in, 73, 74, 150,
and Irish Red Guard, 86, John Leslie's
views,107, 108 and W. O'Brien, 152,
153, and executions following, 153
Eden, Maud, 138
Engels, Friedrich, views on insurrection,
64, 65, description of Marx, 67
English, Dr Ada, 78

Fascism in Ireland: *see* Blueshirts.
feminism, linked to labour cause, 20, and
nationalism, 80
Fianna Éireann, conspiracy allegation,93
Fianna Fáil, attitude to women in politics, 81,
and IRA, 156, republican aspirations, 157
Finlay, Fr. P., S.J., excommunication of SPI
members, 88
FitzGerald, David, 156
Fitzpatrick, Michael, 156
Flynn, Elizabeth Gurley, 23
Foley, Brigid, 76
Foran, Thomas, 82, 98–100, 108, 137, 138
Fox, Ralph, 94
Free State, 81, 93

Gallagher, Frank, 112
Gallacher, William, 128
Gilmore, George,122, 134, 147, 156
Gonne, Maud: *see* MacBride.
Griffith, Arthur, 110, 111

Hardie, J.K, 112
Harp, The, journal of ISF, Connolly as
editor of, 37, 43, move to Dublin, 44,
naming of, 48
Herve, Gustave, 65
Hobson, Bulmer, 71
Home Rule,46
Hyndman, Henry, 36, and SDF, 33

Independent Labour Party (ILP),
conference in 1908, 41, organisational
proposal, 49, merging of Belfast
branches of, 56
Independent Working Class Education
Movement, 92
Industrial Unionism, Connolly's views on,
38, 39, debate within the Labour
movement, 84, and Trade Union
Conference Commission of Inquiry in
1936, 105: *see also* syndicalism.
Industrial Workers of the World (IWW), 36,
anti-political stance, 37, 40, convention
in 1908, 37, membership, 83
International Brigade, 147
International Socialist Congress, 68
Irish Citizen, suffragette newspaper,
criticism of the *Voice of Labour,* concern
that nationalist struggle weakened
feminist movement, 80
Irish Citizen Army, ICA, 24, 54, socialist
objectives of,46, constitution of, 47,
founding of, 61, as revolutionary
vehicle, 62, 124, intervention in strike,
64, participation in Easter Rising, 73–5,
86 women in, 79, 85, links with IWWU,
81,82, and religion, 86, Chief of Staff,
87, decline of, 138–142, and Workers
Army, 146, post-Rising, 150
Irish labour movement, 70, 75, alliance with
nationalist movement, 47, and Roman
Catholic Church, 87–89, 95, 96 influence
of Connolly's writings, 100, support for
Soviet ideas, 101, and syndicalist vision
of general strike, 102, and disregard of
Connolly's ideas, post-Rising, 111,
relationship with Sinn Fein, 117, 118,
neglect of Connolly's writings, 155
Irish Labour Party (ILP), Annual
Conference 1934, and opposition to
Communism, 94, influence of Church
on, 95, amendment to Constitution, 95,
and nationalism, 112, and Republican
Congress, 121, platform and

organisation, 135, vote in Irish elections, 136, anti-militarist manifesto, 144, 145, and Connolly's political legacy, 154, and Catholic influence, 155

Irish Labour Party and Trade Union Congress (ILPTUC), and Limerick strike, 101, and commitment to One Big Union, 102, and general strikes in 1918, 102 and abstentionist policy, 113, 114, name change from ITUCLP, 115 and Sinn Fein, 115, nationalist stance in 1918, 115, move away from Connolly's teaching, 124, chairman's address, 1918 Congress, 153

Irish National Teachers Organisation, 95, 155

Irish Nurses Union, severing links with IWWU, 83

Irish Opinion, on Connolly, 111, funding from England, 112, on Irish labour, 142

Irish Opinion: Voice of Labour, official paper of ITGWU, 112 election manifesto in 1918, 113, promotion of Connolly's ideas, 114, suppression of, 116, on Connolly and Pearse, 151

Irish Red Guard, and Easter Rising, 86: *see also* Irish Citizen Army.

Irish Revolutionary Socialist Movement, 73

Irish Republic, proclamation of, Provisional Government of, 74,

Irish Republican Army (IRA), conspiracy allegation, 93 State opposition to, 93, Church opposition to, 93, 133, increasing aggressiveness, 117, and proclamation of martial law in Kilmallock, 118, manifesto, 121, advice from Roddy Connolly, 129, links with communist movement, 132, 133, membership of WRP, 132 , left-wing republicans in, 156

Irish Republican Brotherhood, 137

Irish Rosary, 92

Irish Socialist Federation (ISF), stance on women's rights,17, foundation of, 37, aims of, 43

Irish Socialist Republic (ISR), call for creation of,16,48

Irish Socialist Republican Party (1SRP) foundation and objectives of, 50, influence of, 51, membership of, 51, disintegration of,16,17, 35,51, 52, manifesto of, 34, 42, links with SLP, 34, and Irish independence, 41, international

links, 48, delegate to ISC, 68, and William O'Brien, 106, and SPI, 125

Irish Trade Union Congress (ITUC) in 1900, 67, first woman president of, 83, and laundry worker's strike, 83, and alleged support for Communism, 94

Irish Trade Union Congress and Labour Party (ITUCLP), in 1913,19, motion passed by executive advising retention of arms, 62, congress in 1916, 98, 109, 110, non-participation in Easter Rising, 73, 74, renaming, and split, 104, 105, and Dublin Trades Council, 111, and anti-conscription campaign in 1918, 113, and nationalism, 113, withdrawal of candidates from 1918 elections, 115, and SPI, 125

Irish Transport and General Workers Union (ITGWU),18,23, 63, organisation of 38, Connolly as Secretary General of, 38, and syndicalism, 40, 98, 99, 100, 106 as revolutionary vehicle, 56, 124 non-participation in Easter rising, 73, 74, 150 relationship with IWWU, 82, 83, admission of women, 82, attacks on, 88, support for Russian Revolution , 100, promotion of Soviet idea, 101, expulsion of James Larkin, 103, 104, loss of members to WUI, 104131 and Delia Larkin, 103, destruction of headquarters, 108, and IRA, 108, 146, and SPI, 126, and ICA, 138–141, leadership of, 140, internal disputes, 143, 146, 147 and Treaty, 143 and O'Brien, 154, support for Connolly, 150 post-Rising, 150

Irish Volunteers, 74, 75, 79, 86

Irish Women's Council: *see* Cumann na mBan.

Irish Women's Franchise League (IWFL), 18

Irish Women Workers Union (IWWU), 18, reorganisation after 1916, 81, relationship with ITGWU, 82,83, need for, 84, and Delia Larkin, 103

Irish Worker and James Larkin, 130

Irish Workers League (IWL) formation of, recognition of by Comintern, 130, control by James Larkin, 131

Irwin, Tom, 145

'James Connolly Unit', 147

Jaures, Jean, 68

Johnson, Thomas, 62, 92, 98, 101,
    relationship with Connolly,108,
    influence on Irish Labour, speech at
    Sligo Conference, 109, 110, 112, 114,
    120, 121, 135, 146, 151, 152, 154
Justice, on Connolly's involvement in the
    Rising, 107, 108,
Kane, Fr. Robert, SJ, 28, 29
Kearney, Peadar, 141
Kelly, Michael, 145,
Kollantai, Alexandra, 78
Kyle, Samuel, 105

Labour movement: *see* Irish labour
    movement.
Labour Party: *see* Irish Labour Party.
Labour Defence League, 132, 133
Larkin, Delia, 82, 103, 143
Larkin, James, jnr. 132, 133, 157
Larkin, James, 38, 82, 98, 99, 103, 104, 106,
    112, 130–32, 136, 139, 140, 146, 152
Lawrence, Fr., 30
Liberty Hall, headquarters of ITGWU,
    destruction of, 108, order to close,
    138,139, picketing of, 147
Limerick strike of 1919, 102
Litvinoff, Maxim,125
Lenin, Vladimir I., 30, 38, 45, 63, views on
    insurrection 65–67, 125
Leo XIII, 91
Leslie, John, 26, 49, assessment of Easter
    Rising, 107, 108,
Luxemburg, Rosa, 65
Lynch, Eamonn, 105
Lynch, Liam, 120, 129
Lyng, John, 36
Lynn Kathleen, 79, 82, 111
Lyon, J.M., funding of *Irish Opinion*, 112, 113

MacBride, Maud Gonne, 23, 87
MacBride, Sean, 156
MacDermott, Sean, 152, 153
MacDonagh, Thomas, 149
MacDonald, Ramsay, 41
McGowan, Seamus,128, 131, 147
McInerney, Father,
Macken, Peter, 108
McKenna, Rev. E, 89, 90
McLoughlin, Sean, 128, 129, 142, 157
MacManus, Arthur, description of
    Connolly, 67
MacMullen, William, 135
MacNeill, Eoin, 71

MacRory, Cardinal, 93
MacSwiney, Mary, 78, 80
Mallin, John, 87
Mallin, Joseph, 87
Mallin, Michael, 87, 108, 139, 140
Mallin, Una, 87
Malone, A.E.: *see* Byrne, L.P.
Markievicz, Constance de, 23, 76–78, 81,
    82, 86, 87, 89–91, 111, opposition to
    Treaty, 123
Marriage, Connolly's views on, 22
Marx, Karl, 26, 34, views on insurrection, 64
Marxism, and Connolly, 32, 33, 67
Matheson, J. Carstairs 19, 26, 56, 157
Millerand, Alexandre, votes against at
    International Socialist Congress, 68
Moloney, Helena 23, 76, 82–84, 85
Morning Post, 151, 152
Mullen, Michael, 103
Murray, Sean, 94, 157

National Dock Strike of 1912, and
    'strikers' police' 62
Nationalism, as component of Connolly's
    socialism, 41–48, 122, and Lenin, 45,
    and women's role, 81,
Nationalist movement, and women, 85
Norton, William, 94, 95, 104, 105
Ni Connaire, Margread, address to Irish
    Nationalist women, 79, 80

Oath of Allegiance, Connolly's views on,
    30, 119,
One Big Union concept: *see* syndicalism:
    see also Industrial Workers of the
    World, and industrial unionism
O'Brien, William, 46, 62, 82, 98, 100, 102,
    104–106, 108–110, 114,118,125, 127,
    137–140, 143, 145, 146, 151–154
O'Carroll, Richard, 108
O'Donnell, Peadar, 111, 132, 134, 135,
    140, 146, 147, 156
O'Donel, Lile, 146
O'Malley, Ernie, 119, 123, 146
O'Neill, James, 139,140,
O'Reilly, Rev. E.P., 88
O'Riordan, Michael, 135
O'Shannon, Cathal, 63, 94, 99, 100, 101,
    108, 109, 112, 118, 120, 125, 135, 137,
    140, 144, 151, 152, 156

Pacelli, Cardinal, 94
Pankhurst, Sylvia, 62

Partition, of Ireland, Connolly's opposition
 to, 45, 62
Plunkett Assembly, 110
Plunkett, Joseph, 153
'People's Army', 62
Perolz, Maire, 76
Pearse, Patrick, 71, 79, 149, 151
Pearse, Margaret 78
Pollock, George, 129, 131
Price, Michael, 121, 134, 147, 156
Preparatory Committee for the formation of
 a Workers Revolutionary Party
 (PCWRP) founding of, 132
Protestants, and socialism, 29, and
 participation in Easter Rising, 86

religion, Connolly's views on, 27, 28,
 Lenin's views on, 30
Republic (*see* Irish Republic), post-Rising,
 73 proclamation of, 77, as cause of Left
 disunity, 124
Republican Congress, hostility to ILP, 121,
 and IRA, 133, 'Athlone manifesto' 134,
 and Connolly's teachings, 134, disunity
 of, 135
Republican Congress, on importance of
 Connolly's vision of Workers Republic,
 134, demise of, 135
republicanism, 73, and Irish Labour Party,
 119, support for, 120, George Gilmore's
 views, 122: *see also* Irish Socialist
 Republic.
Revum Novarum (encyclical of Leo XIII),
 Connolly's comments, 91
revolution, 55, Marx's view, 64, Lenin's
 views, 65, 67, Connolly's views 67, 68,
 70, 71, 149, and Connoly's political
 legacy, 157
Revolutionary Workers Group (RWG),
 attack on headquarters of, 93,94,
 reconstitution from WRP, foundation of
 Communist Party, 133
Robbins, Frank, 94, 139, 140, 141
Roman Catholic Church, 25– 27, and
 socialism, 28–30, and the labour
 movement, 87–89, 91, and conversions to,
 87, Connolly's opinion of, 89, and curbing
 republican and left-wing organisations,
 93, influence on labour party, 94 influence
 on labour movement, 95
Roman Catholicism, and Connolly, 25, 28
 and Irish nationalism, 86, 87 and Easter
 Rising, 86, Connolly's opinion of, 90

Ryan, Desmond, 157
Ryan Frank, 134, 147, 156
Ryan, Nell, 76

St. Stephen's Green Command. 87
Saniel, Lucien, 54
Saor Eire, conspiracy allegations against,
 93, State opposition to, 93, Church
 opposition to, 93, 133, formation of,
 133, collapse of, 134, 135
Scottish Socialist Federation (SSF), 32, 49, 67
Scottish Socialist Labour Party (SLP): *see*
 Socialist Labour Party (Scotland).
Seanad, meeting with Dáil, 151
Second International, 32, 65, 68
sexism, in the labour movement, 83
Sheehy-Skeffington, Francis, 18, 104, 108
Sheehy-Skeffington, Hanna, 19, 23, 77, 79,
 81
Sinn Féin, 78, executive, 79, reorganisation
 meeting in 1917, 111, and *Irish
 Opinion*, 112, and 1914 election, 113,
 relationship with Labour Party, 115–17
 complaints of anti-labour tendencies,
 117, 118, and ICA, 142
Social Democratic Party, 52
Social Democratic Federation (SDF) 32,
 inaugural manifesto, 33
Social Revolution: *see* revolution.
socialism, and family life, 21, 22, and
 religion, 25, 28, 29, and protestants, 29,
 and nationalism, 41, 42, 43, 44, attitude
 of Roman Catholic Church to, 93
Socialist Labor Party (America) (SLP),17,
 links with ISRP, 34, organisation of, 52,
 Connolly's membership of, 35, 36, 53,
 54, Connolly's resignation from, 54
Socialist Labour Party (Scotland) SLP
 founding of, manifesto of, 35
Socialist League, 49
Socialist Party of America, Connolly as
 National Organiser, 37
Socialist Party of Ireland (SPI), invitation
 to Connolly to return to Ireland 38, as an
 'international party' 47, change of title,
 56, non-participation in Easter rising,
 73, excommunication of members, 88,
 after Connolly's death, 124, and ISRP,
 125, and ITUCLP, 125, reply to attack
 on leadership, 126, expulsion of
 O'Brien and O'Shannon, 127, name
 change to CPI, 127, and ICA, 142 post-
 Rising, 150

Socialist press, and women's rights 19, and ICA, 140, and Connolly's writings, 155, 156
Socialist Trade and Labour Alliance, 34, 36
Socialist revolution, violence and 60, 61
Society of Freedom: *see Cumann na Saoirse*.
'Soviet idea', establishment of Soviets in Ireland, 101
Spanish Civil War, Irish involvement, 94, 147, CPI support for, 135
Stevenson, Paddy, 142
Stuttgart Congress in 1907, debate on use of force, 65
suffragettes, and Connolly's support for, 19, and Charlotte Despard
syndicalism, and Connolly, 33, 34, 40, 54, 100 and Lenin, 38 Marxist view of, 38, and anarchism, 38., debate within the labour movement in 1937, 84, and ITGWU, 98, 102
syndicalists, anti-political stance, 37

Third International: *see Comintern*.
Tipperary Star, 137
trade unions, and capitalism, 32, and social order, 33, 35, Commission of Inquiry into Trade Union Organisation in 1936, 105, attempted restructuring, 106, and ILP, 95
Treaty, opposition to, 80, 128, and Irish Labour Party, 119, 120, debate in Dáil in 1922, 123, and ILP anti-militarist manifesto, 144
Trotsky, Leon, 125

United Irish League (UIL), and women's rights, 17
Universal suffrage: *see* women's suffrage.

violent struggle, Connolly's position, 64, and women, 85
Voice of Labour, criticism of women, 83 and IWWU convention in 1927, 83, review of *Towards the Republic*, position on religion, 88, and Connolly's writings, 99, support for 'Soviet idea', 101, on Governor-General, 119, on women's support for Labour, 120, and Connolly, 138, 142, 143, disputes at

ITGWU meeting, 143 and neutral stance on treaty, 143, on goal of workers' republic, 144, on use of weapons, 144, on workers' demonstration in Dublin, 145 and assaults by IRA on Union members, 146
Vogt, Hugo, 54

Walker, William, 47
war, Connolly's opinion of, 64
Watchword of Labour and SPI, 88, editorial on Connolly, 116, on labour and Sinn Féin, 117–118
'Wobblies': *see* Industrial Workers (IWW)
women, participation in Easter Rising, 76, 77, 85
women's movement in Ireland, 17–21
women's rights, De Leon's views on, Connolly's views on 17, 81
Women's Social and Political Union, 18
Women's suffrage, 77, Connolly's support of, 16, 18, and militancy, 17–19, 21, 24
Workers Bulletin, issued by Limerick proletariat, 101
Workers Communist Party, 126
Workers Party of Ireland (WPI), formation of, rejection of by Comintern, 131
Workers Army, 144
Workers' Republic, and Catholic teaching, 88, and Catholic Church opposition to, 95, organised labour, commitment to, 119, and Markievicz, 120, Irish republican commitment to, 124, resolution regarding at Republican Congress in 1934, 134
Workers Republic, subscriptions to, 52, accepting British money, 112, cessation of publication, 129
Workers Revolutionary Party (WRP), membership, links with IRA, 132, reconstitution as RWP, 133
Workers Union of Ireland (WUI), foundation of, 104, and Larkin, 132
working class, and socialist revolution, 21, 45, and class war, 35, Church's concern over Connolly's influence on, Connolly's view of strength of, 69, and support for nationalist movement, 117
World War I, Connolly's opposition to, 63, Lenin's opposition to, 63, 65, 66